# THE BIG BOOK OF
# Low···CARB

## 250 Simple, Delicious, Nutritious Recipes

BY KITTY BROIHIER, MS, RD, AND KIMBERLY MAYONE

CHRONICLE BOOKS
SAN FRANCISCO

Library of Congress Cataloging-in-Publication Data available.

ISBN 0-8118-4541-9

Manufactured in Canada.

Designed by John Givens
Typesetting by John Givens
Prop styling by Robin Turk
Food styling by Basil Fredman

Distributed in Canada by Raincoast Books
9050 Shaughnessy Street
Vancouver, British Columbia V6P 6E5

10 9 8 7 6 5 4 3 2 1

Chronicle Books LLC
85 Second Street
San Francisco, California 94105

www.chroniclebooks.com

THE BIG BOOK OF
# Low···CARB

For my siblings, Jeff, Mary, Michelle, Elisa,
Mimi, and Christiane. And in special memory
of our brother Jared, who loved to cook, eat,
and read good writing about both.
—K.B.

To my terrific children, Sophia and Harrison
Mayone, with love.
—K.M.

**ACKNOWLEDGMENTS**

This, our biggest cookbook yet, was a daunting but enormously pleasurable undertaking for me. This is due, in great part, to the assistance of the following people:

- Our top-notch agent, Lisa Ekus, who supports all our efforts with professionalism, enthusiasm, and unfailing good humor.

- Our editor, Bill LeBlond, who took a chance on us and made it all easy; we're thrilled to be Chronicle authors! Thanks also to Amy Treadwell and our entire Chronicle team for their hard work on this project.

- My neighbors, friends, siblings, and parents, who nurtured me in so many ways during the months of writing.

- Our many recipe testers, who provided valuable assistance and constructive comments.

- My children, Jack and Amelia Scofield, who were more understanding and self-sufficient than I ever thought they could be. I owe you both, big-time.

- And finally, my husband, Daniel Scofield, who once again, without complaint, shouldered more than his fair share of the household and child-care burden during the months of this book's gestation. Thank you for the gift of allowing me to pursue this passion unfettered. I owe you big-time, too.

— KITTY BROIHIER

When you write a cookbook, there are so many people who support you through the process—culinary associates who offer their expertise, neighbors who are willing to taste-test, and friends who whisk you off to dinner because they know you need a break from cooking. Thanks to all of you who did these things for me, and special thanks to:

- My incredible husband, Mark Mayone, for doing the dishes, entertaining the children while I worked, and for loving me through the ups and downs of writing a cookbook. You are simply the best. Also, thanks to my ever-patient little sous chefs, Sophia and Harrison Mayone. You fill my life—and my kitchen—with joy.

- My parents, Harry and Patricia Sundik, for their constant love and support. Thanks to my sister, Alice Mahoney, for listening, and to my brother, Greg Sundik, for the caffeine hits when I was working late, and for just being "Uncle Greggy."

- My circle of friends, who keep me balanced and smiling: Dyan Albano, Meg Austin, Mary-Jo Chapman, Lisa-Jo Cohen, Julie Drake, Pamela Fischer, Kellie Ford, Anne Heisler, Jen Hobbs, Barr Hogen, Karen Lucas, Sean Madison, and Lise Stern.

- My strong, spirited foodie friend, Barbara Gulino—you inspire me.

- My skilled colleagues and captive consultants at Southern Maine Community College: Wilfred Beriau, Paul Charpentier, Maurice Leavitt, David Libby, Moira Rescati, and Laura Stegner.

- Our wonderful editor at Chronicle, Bill LeBlond, for giving us the opportunity to work on this Big Book.

- Our amazing agent, Lisa Ekus, for all she does to support the Kitty/Kim team.

— **KIMBERLY MAYONE**

# CONTENTS

# QUICK REFERENCE RECIPE GUIDE

11

## LOW-CARB EATING IS NOT A NEW IDEA.

Indeed, some trace it all the way back to our "cave man" ancestors, and have fashioned low-carb food plans around the likely diet of those times. The modern low-carb diet movement is typically credited to the late Robert C. Atkins, M.D., who published his first low-carb weight-loss book, *Diet Revolution,* in 1972. He was not the only one touting a lower-carb lifestyle, but he did publish the first widely read book on the subject. Today there are numerous authors (some of them physicians or allied health professionals) who recommend a restricted carbohydrate program, and myriad variations on the low-carb diet theme.

This book is not a low-carb diet book. Rather, it is a book that's chock-full of recipes to help you cook delicious foods suitable for a reduced-carbohydrate eating plan. Some of our recipes are higher in carbs (yet still very much in the low-carb realm), while others are extremely low-carb. You choose those that mesh the best with your eating plan, whether it be a strict regimen or a more lenient, "healthy-carbs-only" approach. We do not endorse one low-carb plan over another, nor have we tried to make all of the recipes fit a certain plan. What we've strived to do is provide low-carbers of all types with a large selection of interesting, satisfying recipes.

Whether you're a low-carb "newbie" or an old pro, some fresh ideas in the kitchen are always welcome. After all, one can only live on mozzarella sticks, pickles, and salami slices for so long! This book contains a wide variety of recipes, from meat, fish, and poultry entrées to up-to-date vegetarian fare. Whatever the time of day, we've got something to feed you—breakfast foods, snacks, beverages, and plenty of low-carb desserts. And, because eating low-carb doesn't mean having to eat in isolation, we've given you plenty of options for entertaining. You'll find recipes to help you host a brunch buffet, have a cookout, serve a fancy sit-down dinner, or bring a potluck dish to the neighborhood party.

Most of our recipes are easy; a few are more challenging. Some require specialized equipment (an ice-cream maker, for example), but most do not. Whatever your culinary skill, we know that extra information is always welcome. So to help you along the way, we've provided lots of tips and suggestions for everything from where to shop for ingredients to techniques for prepping ingredients to how to combine dishes to make a menu.

Eating low carb need never be boring, so if you find yourself in a low-carb rut, crack open this book, shake out your apron, and sharpen your knives. We're sure that you'll find enough variety in this book to keep you noshing happily on your low-carb program for many months (or years) to come.

# BASICS

## HINTS, HELP, AND TECHNIQUES FOR LOW-CARB COOKING

# HINTS
This section presents a collection of tips that we've found to be helpful for general cooking. We've referred to many of them in various places throughout the book, so you may find yourself turning back to these pages frequently. To make it easy to find the specific hint you're looking for, we've given each one a simple and obvious title.

## BREAD CRUMBS

Having Low-Carb Buttered Bread Crumbs (page 294) on hand is very convenient. The best time to make the crumbs is when you have some low-carb bread that's getting a bit stale anyway. Store the finished Low-Carb Buttered Bread Crumbs in a zip-top freezer bag, and keep them in the freezer—they'll stay fresh-tasting much longer that way.

## COLD BUTTER

A few recipes in this book call for cold, diced butter. An easy way to ensure that you have cold butter handy is to always keep one stick of butter in the freezer. When needed, you can coarsely grate the butter on a hand-held grater, using the markings on the butter wrapper as a guide. Or, simply place a stick of butter in the freezer for 4 minutes. Remove the butter and dice the amount you need using a small, sharp knife.

## COOKING TIMES: YOURS VS. OURS

In general, we've offered a range of cooking times in these recipes because we realize that there are a few factors that impact actual cooking time. For example, the type of range you're using (see below), the temperature of the ingredients, and the type and quality of cookware used all can increase or decrease actual cooking time. The best bet is to check the food at the shortest cooking time given—you can always cook it a little longer if need be.

## COOKING TIMES: GAS VS. ELECTRIC RANGES

If you're cooking with an electric range, you may need to increase the cooking times slightly, as the recipes in this book were developed using gas ranges. Chefs tend to prefer gas stoves because it's easier to see the level of heat the food is receiving, and therefore it's easier to control the heat. However, bakers prefer electric ovens because they tend to maintain a more even heat. Regardless, all of the recipes in this book can be prepared in just about any kitchen, and were tested not only in our homes (which contain standard equipment), but also in average home kitchens around the country.

## GARLIC

Don't be afraid to buy bottled garlic—it's a great time-saver. We taste-tested dishes made with fresh garlic against those prepared with bottled garlic, and in most cases only a savvy few tasters could discern the difference. Garlic is an important flavor enhancer, yet it can be a pain to peel. Definitely keep a jar of prepeeled whole garlic cloves or bottled minced garlic in your refrigerator.

## GARNISHES

You may wonder why we've included so many optional garnishes. The simple answer is that we like the visual and/or taste enhancement they provide. For entertaining, we consider them a "must." For a weeknight family dinner, we know that most people don't have the time or inclination to elaborately garnish each food portion, so it's fine to skip them if you like.

## GRILLS: CHARCOAL VS. GAS

There are probably a million different opinions about which type of grill is best, and both gas and charcoal have their pros and cons. Gas grills are convenient, quick to start, and offer a great variety of stable cooking temperatures. On the other hand, they don't contribute as much flavor to the foods cooked on them, and if you run out of propane you're just out of luck. Charcoal grills offer better flavor (you can add certain varieties of wood chips to the charcoal for even more flavor), but it is harder to control temperature with them. It can also take quite a while for charcoal to get to the right cooking temperature. You decide what's best for you, and what is convenient for your cooking needs. Since some people like to grill year-round (even in places where it gets very cold, like Maine), a grill pan or countertop electric grill may be a good investment. With the latter two options you won't get real cookout flavor, but you will get the grill marks, minus the frostbite.

## HEATING OIL AND BUTTER

Tossing ingredients into a pan with oil or butter that's not hot enough can start a dish out incorrectly because the food will absorb the fat, rather than cook in it. We like to teach home cooks to place one small piece of an ingredient (a small slice of onion, for example) into the pan with the oil. When it starts to seriously sizzle, the oil is hot and ready for the other starting ingredients. With butter, look for it to become foamy but not browned before adding your tiny "tester" ingredient.

## INGREDIENT TEMPERATURES: WHY THEY MATTER, WHEN THEY MATTER

In general, aside from food safety reasons, the temperature of ingredients only impacts the length of cooking time. Food cooked directly from the refrigerator (or freezer, for that matter) will take longer to cook. In fact, it's a great professional cook's trick to "take the chill" out of ingredients before they hit a hot pan or oven by taking all ingredients out of the refrigerator and letting them sit on the counter before starting to cook. A few minutes at room temperature reduces the cooking time slightly, and reduces the chance of burning the surface of foods while trying to get the center cooked. Having everything ready to go and visible also reduces the chance that you'll forget to include an ingredient.

For baked goods, having ingredients at the proper temperature impacts more than just cooking time. For example, egg whites that are cold (direct from the refrigerator) won't whip up as high as those at room temperature, and cream cheese that's cold won't blend as easily. Sometimes, such as with diced, cold butter, it's important that the ingredient be very cold to achieve the proper consistency or "crumbled" mixture that's desired.

## INGREDIENT TEMPERATURES: FOOD SAFETY MATTERS

Bringing a refrigerated ingredient to room temperature usually only takes 30 minutes to 1 hour on the countertop. Do not leave refrigerated ingredients at room temperature longer than $1\frac{1}{2}$ hours before cooking, as bacteria can multiply quickly in warm food. For the same reason, do not thaw frozen meat at room temperature. Meat should be thawed in the refrigerator. If you plan ahead a little, you can usually put it in the refrigerator the night before you need it and it will be thawed the next evening. If not, the microwave (set on low or defrost) can help things along, if necessary. Finally, always refrigerate leftover cooked food immediately after the meal is finished.

## MEATY MATTERS

**Chicken Breasts:** What most of us refer to as a skinless, boneless chicken breast is actually a breast half. To avoid confusion, we frequently call for a total weight of chicken breast meat, for example, "2 pounds skinless, boneless chicken breast." This also solves the problem of the widely varying weights of commercially available chicken breast halves (we found one half-breast that weighed a whole pound). As a general rule, 4 medium skinless, boneless chicken breast halves weigh a total of about 2 pounds. You may need to trim some excess fat before cooking, but there's no need to consider this "lost weight" when figuring how much chicken to purchase— the recipes will work fine.

**Pork:** In most recipes, pork sirloin cutlets and center-cut, boneless pork loin chops can be interchanged, especially if the pork is cut up prior to cooking. We like to buy meat on sale, and therefore have substituted one for the other on numerous occasions with good success.

## NET CARBS: WHAT ARE THEY?

In this book we use the term "net carbs" when giving the carbohydrate information. You may be familiar with this term, as many cookbooks and food manufacturers use it as well. Others use "impact carbs," "true carbs," or "effective carbs." These are all the same thing. Net carbs are the result of subtracting the grams of fiber and sugar alcohols from the total carbohydrate grams per recipe. Most of our recipes don't have a lot of sugar alcohols, except for some of the desserts, so in the majority of cases we only had to subtract the fiber from the total carbohydrates to get the net carb value.

## NUTRITIONAL CONTENT: HOW IT'S FIGURED

When analyzing the nutritional content of each recipe in this book, there were a few ways that we standardized the process. These include: using generic ingredient computer values as opposed to branded ingredients, when no brand is specified in the recipe (such as "low-fat yogurt" instead of a particular brand of yogurt); using values for cooked meats (taking into account product shrinkage and cooking losses) instead of using raw meat weights; using drained weights on canned ingredients (such as beans and olives), unless specified otherwise in the recipe; and using the weight of an ingredient over the size as often as possible (such as 8 ounces of green pepper, instead of 1 medium green pepper). Because of this, you can feel confident that if you follow the recipe carefully, your finished product will be very close in nutrient content to our specified analysis.

## NUTRITIONAL CONTENT:
## WHY IT'S ONLY APPROXIMATE

The nutritional contents cited for the recipes (most often for one serving of the dish), specifying calories, protein, net carbs, fat, cholesterol, and sodium, are approximate. The reason that we use "approximate" here is that, although we've used a well-regarded nutritional analysis computer program (Food Processor, by Esha Research), no nutritional analysis is perfect. There are a number of reasons why our best efforts still represent only an estimate of the nutritional content of the actual recipe that you make at home, including human error in measurement of ingredients, variances in the trimming of fat from meat, variations between brands of prepared foods or mixes, differences in the amount of natural fats in meats and poultry, the length of time food is cooked (well-done meat versus rare meat will differ nutritionally), and even significant differences between multiple computer nutritional values for the same food. Therefore, although we've made every effort to standardize our analysis technique in order to yield the most accurate results, the nutritional content information is still just an approximation. For most people's purposes, this should be sufficient for adhering to a low-carb diet plan.

## RESTING FOODS

There are many recipes in this book where we recommend letting foods rest before serving them. The reason for this is very simple, but important. By letting foods rest before cutting or serving, you allow the ingredients to relax. A casserole, for instance, can set a bit and cool slightly during a brief resting period, while in meat, much of the natural juices can be absorbed back into the muscles of the meat. If you slice a steak right off the grill without letting it rest first, the juices will run right out of the meat and over your plate. If you let the steak rest, more juices will stay in the meat, making for a very juicy steak.

## SALAD GREENS

We like the sealed bags of prewashed and sorted salad greens available in well-stocked supermarkets because they're convenient, provide a variety of lettuces in one package, and generally are good quality (be sure to check the "best if used by" dates on the packages before purchasing them). But if you don't like salad-in-a-bag, or don't feel like paying those kind of prices for lettuce, make your own salad mixtures by washing and tearing heads of lettuce, then storing them in large zip-top bags with a few holes punched in them. Keep the bags in your veggie drawer in the refrigerator, and you have instant greens when you want them. You can do the same thing with cut-up vegetables such as carrots, celery, and radishes so you can throw together a salad in an instant.

## SEASONING ADVICE

Go through your spice cabinet or rack at least once a year. This is crucial, as some spices lose their flavor and get stale rather quickly. Since spices are expensive, it makes the most sense to buy them in small containers, so you don't end up wasting it all when you toss out any old ones. We have found the biggest spice bargains to be found in the bulk spice section of natural-food stores and some well-stocked supermarkets. We're also huge fans of Penzey's Spices (www.penzeys.com), where you can find practically any spice you'd ever need, and they're available in small, no-frills containers.

## SERVING SIZES

We've made every attempt to make the portions in this book reasonable for low-carb dieters. In some cases, this means that they are quite large, as we've found that in order to feel full, low-carbers sometimes need more food (since there's no bread or starch around to take up tummy space). Nevertheless, it makes sense to keep portion sizes in mind, as eating too much food (and getting too many calories) will lead to weight gain. If you follow the recommended number of servings for each recipe, your portions will be reasonable and satisfying. Because high-protein foods are filling, you may even find that you'll get full on portions that you initially thought were too small! Our recipes list the nutritional content for one serving of the dish, in most cases (exceptions will be noted). If you eat more than one serving of a recipe, you'll obviously need to multiply the nutritional content of that recipe accordingly to reflect your actual consumed portion.

## SWEET INGREDIENTS: WHEN AND WHY WE SOMETIMES USE THEM

In some cases, you'll note that our recipes include some ingredients that are typically forbidden on low-carb diets, such as all-purpose flour, real maple syrup, and even sugar. These are not typographical errors! For example, in many desserts you'll find that we've used a combination of Splenda Granular (our sweetener of choice) along with a small amount of real sugar. We find that this combination often improves the final flavor dramatically, while making little or no difference in the carb content per serving. Overall, this technique gives us the taste of real sugar, as opposed to an artificial-sweetener taste. In baked goods, a little all-purpose flour accomplishes the same thing with regard to product texture and overall acceptability. We keep these ingredients to a minimum to preserve the low-carb nature of the recipes, of course. You may prefer to eliminate these ingredients completely, but be forewarned that the resulting product could suffer as a result.

# HELP This section contains useful charts, lists, and general resource information.

## MEET DONENESS

| TYPE OF MEAT | TEMPERATURE |
| --- | --- |
| Ground beef, pork, lamb | 160°F |
| Ground poultry | 165°F |
| Chicken/turkey | |
| Whole | 180°F |
| Wings/thighs | 180°F |
| Breasts | 170°F |
| Roasts* | |
| Beef, veal, lamb | |
| Medium-rare | 150° to 155°F |
| Medium | 160°F |
| Medium-well | 165°F |
| Well | 170°F |
| Pork (including chops) | 160°F |
| Ham | |
| Packaged as "fully cooked" | 140°F |
| Purchased as "fresh" or | |
| "cook before eating" | 160°F |

\* DO NOT SERVE ANY ROLLED, TENDERIZED, OR SCORED LARGE CUTS OF BEEF, VEAL, OR LAMB BELOW 160°F. BEEF ROASTS AND STEAKS ARE CONSIDERED SAFE IF COOKED TO 145°F, AS LONG AS THE SURFACE HASN'T BEEN SCORED OR PUNCTURED. THE PROCESS OF CUTTING OR PUNCTURING MEATS BEFORE COOKING MAY FORCE ANY SURFACE BACTERIA INTO THE CENTER. BE AWARE THAT THE TEMPERATURE OF A ROAST WILL RISE SLIGHTLY DURING RESTING. IT'S IMPORTANT TO USE AN INSTANT-READ THERMOMETER TO TEST THE INTERNAL TEMPERATURE OF THE ROAST BEFORE SERVING.

## THERMOMETER TIPS

– An instant-read thermometer is recommended for testing the doneness of meat and poultry. This type of thermometer is not designed to stay in food during cooking (unlike an ovenproof, dial meat thermometer). To use an instant-read thermometer, place the tip of the probe in the center of the thickest part of the food. It takes about 10 seconds for an accurate temperature reading.

– To prevent overcooking, begin checking the temperature of meats toward the end of cooking, but before you expect the dish to be done.

– To clean your thermometer, wash it in hot, soapy water and rinse in hot water. Clean it before and after use.

**Measurement Equivalents**

| | | |
|---:|:---:|:---|
| Dash/pinch | = | less than $\frac{1}{8}$ teaspoon |
| 3 teaspoons | = | 1 tablespoon |
| 4 tablespoons | = | $\frac{1}{4}$ cup |
| 16 tablespoons | = | 1 cup |
| 2 cups | = | 1 pint |
| 2 pints | = | 1 quart |
| 4 quarts | = | 1 gallon |
| | | |
| 1 fluid ounce | = | 2 tablespoons |
| 8 fluid ounces | = | 1 cup |
| | | |
| 16 ounces | = | 1 pound |

## BASIC COOKING EQUIPMENT

Small, medium, large skillet or sauté pans

Cast-iron skillet

Small, medium, large saucepans with lids

Stockpot with lid

8-by-8-inch baking pan

9-by-9-inch baking pan

1$\frac{1}{2}$-quart casserole dish or baking dish

2-quart casserole dish or baking dish

13-by-9-inch baking dish

9- or 10-inch pie plate

8- and 9-inch springform pans

Baking sheets

Blender or immersion blender

Colander

Grater (one that grates both coarse and fine is best)

Ladles (one large, one small)

Measuring cups (set of dry-measure cups; 8-ounce liquid cup, 32-ounce liquid cup)

Measuring spoons

Oven mitts

Plastic storage containers of various sizes (for leftovers and prepped ingredients)

Plastic wrap

Plastic zip-top bags (1-quart size and 1-gallon size)

Rolling pin

Rubber spatulas

Fine-mesh sieve

Sharp knives (medium chef's knife, long serrated knife, and small paring knife are the essentials)

Tongs (spring-action ones are best)

Vegetable peeler

Whisk

Wooden spoons

Zester (if you don't have a fine grater)

## EXTRA EQUIPMENT THAT'S NICE TO HAVE

Food processor

Ice-cream maker (we like Cuisinart's)

Meat mallet

Small, electric food chopper

Wok

## STOCKING THE LOW-CARB KITCHEN

### Pantry items

Anchovy paste or canned anchovies

Bacon (precooked real bacon strips or bits)

Bouillon cubes or paste (we like Better Than Bouillon)

Capers

Canned broth (chicken, beef, vegetable)

Canned green chiles

Canned tomato products (crushed tomatoes, tomato paste, diced tomatoes, diced petite tomatoes)

Canned soybeans (white and black)

Cooking spray

Low-carb BBQ sauce

Low-carb ketchup

Low-carb peanut butter

Low-carb, sugar-free preserves

Low-carb convenience mixes (brownie mix, muffin mix)

Minced garlic (bottled/prepared)

Mustard: brown, Dijon, yellow

Oils: canola, olive, extra-virgin olive, vegetable, peanut

Olives: black, Kalamata, and pimiento-stuffed

Roasted red peppers (bottled/prepared)

Salad dressings: bottled vinaigrette, Good Seasons dressing mix packets

Seasonings: adobo, dried minced onions, chili powder, crushed red pepper flakes, ground black pepper, kosher salt, dried oregano, dried thyme, dried rosemary, ground cayenne, ground cinnamon, ground nutmeg, ground ginger, ground paprika, dry mustard, Chinese five-spice powder

Tabasco sauce

Vinegars: balsamic, cider, white, red wine, rice, sherry

### Refrigerated Items

Butter

Cheeses: shredded Asiago, Cheddar, Monterey Jack, mozzarella; grated and/or shredded Parmesan; cream cheese; Boursin cheese

Cream: light, heavy, half-and-half

Eggs

Low-carb milk

### Produce

- Berries
- Fresh herbs
- Lemons
- Limes
- Mushrooms
- Onions
- Salad-in-a-bag
- Variety of vegetables (also frozen, bagged vegetables)

### Meats

Purchase meat on sale whenever possible, then use it immediately or freeze it for later use. Look for lean ground beef (90 percent lean if possible), steaks, roasts, poultry (whole and pieces), and pork chops and cutlets.

### Miscellaneous

- Low-carb tortillas
- Low-carb bread, buns, and rolls
- Low-carb tortilla chips
- Low-carb candies
- Red and white wines

## RESOURCES

Given the rate at which new low-carb foods are being introduced, we couldn't even begin to provide you with a comprehensive list of low-carb foods or food manufacturers. A quick search for low-carb foods on the Internet will yield hundreds of options! However, we have listed here certain manufacturers of products that we've recommended throughout this book, along with their contact information. If you're lucky enough to live in an area that has a low-carb store that specializes in selling products suited to low-carb diets, you might find these ingredients there, or try your local health-food store. If not, check the manufacturers' Web sites. Also, as low-carb has become a mainstream food trend, regular grocery stores now carry a wide variety of low-carb products that are produced by large, well-known food companies. Finding low-carb ingredients and foods has never been easier!

Arrowhead Mills, Inc.
The Hain Celestial Group
734 Franklin Avenue, Suite 444
Garden City, NY 11530
(800) 434-4246
www.arrowheadmills.com
**Various flours and other baking ingredients**

Atkins Nutritionals, Inc.
2002 Orville Dr. North, Suite A
Ronkonkoma, NY 11779
(800) 2-ATKINS
www.atkins.com
**Various mixes and prepared foods**

Bernard Food Industries, Inc.
1125 Hartrey Avenue
Evanston, IL 60204
(800) 323-3663
**Sweet-N-Low brand cake mixes and frosting mixes**

Bob's Red Mill Natural Foods
5209 SE International Way
Milwaukie, OR 97222
(800) 349-2173
www.bobsredmill.com
**Almond meal and whole-grain products**

CarboLITE Foods, Inc.
1325 Newton Avenue
Evansville, IN 47715
(812) 485-0002
www.carbolitedirect.com
**Various shakes, bars, and candies**

CarbSense
1100 East Marina Way, Suite 223
Hood River, OR 97031
(541) 387-3330
www.carbsense.com
**Various snacks and mixes**

Expert Foods, Inc.
P.O. Box 1855
Ellicott City, MD 21041
(888) 621-9059
www.expertfoods.com
**Various cooking and baking ingredients**

Keto Foods & Snacks, Inc.
56 Park Road
Tinton Falls, NJ 07724
(800) 542-3230
www.ketofoods.com
**Various pasta, bars, and prepared foods**

La Tortilla Factory
3635 Standish Avenue
Santa Rosa, CA 95407
(800) 446-1516
www.latortillafactory.com
**Low-carb tortillas in various flavors**

O' So Lo Foods, Inc
790 Jacksonville Road
Warminster, PA 18974
(877) 676-5636
www.osolo.com
**Low-carb rolls, breads, muffins, and snack foods**

Russell Stover
(800) 477-8683
www.russellstover.com
**Low-carb and sugar-free candies**

# TECHNIQUES
If you need to brush up on some of your basic cooking techniques, this is the place to start. We've only included methods that we relied on frequently when developing this book. Also included are some quick ideas for making the cooking process easier on the cook—tips that will help you be more organized and efficient, and get more pleasure out of the process.

## BLANCHING AND SHOCKING VEGETABLES

Basically, blanching is just boiling food very briefly, and "shocking" is plunging it into very cold water to stop the cooking process. Blanching precooks vegetables slightly (they should not be completely tender after blanching), and for certain vegetables also takes away a bit of bitterness. These techniques are often a preparation step for stir-fry dishes or other recipes where you want the final cooking to go quickly. To blanch, fill a stockpot halfway with water and bring it to a boil over high heat. While waiting for the water to boil, fill a large bowl halfway with cold water and add several ice cubes to the water. Set the bowl near the sink so it will be ready for shocking. When the water on the stove is boiling, add the vegetables and stir them for about 1 minute, or until their color becomes bright (peas will turn bright green, for example) but the vegetables are still crunchy. Immediately drain the vegetables in a colander, then quickly plunge them into the bowl of ice water. Let the veggies float in the ice water for about 5 minutes, or until they've cooled completely, then drain before using them in a recipe.

## PARBOILING SAUSAGES

Parboiling is a method of precooking; in this case, it reduces the amount of fat in the sausages (some of the fat is released into the water), and it also makes them easier to slice. To parboil, simply put the sausages in a pot and add enough water to cover. Bring the water to a simmer and cook the sausages until they're only slightly pink in the center, 7 to 10 minutes.

## PRECOOKING POULTRY MEAT

Some recipes in this book call for cooked chicken or turkey meat. If you have no leftover poultry, there's no need to worry, as it's easy to quickly cook some up (stocking up when it's on sale is a good idea). Keep in mind these yields:

1½ pounds uncooked skinless, boneless chicken or turkey breast meat (excess fat trimmed) = 4 cups cubed or chopped cooked meat

2 pounds uncooked skinless, boneless chicken or turkey breast meat (excess fat trimmed) = 5 cups cubed or chopped cooked meat

Following are the methods we use to precook poultry meat. Choose your favorite:

– Rub split chicken breasts (skin on and bone-in) with olive oil and sprinkle with kosher salt and ground black pepper. Bake at 375°F for 45 minutes, or until cooked through. Let the breasts cool, pull off the skin and discard it, then pull the meat off the bones.

– Cut skinless, boneless chicken breast meat into bite-sized cubes. Coat a skillet or sauté pan with cooking spray. Warm the pan over medium heat; when hot, add the chicken cubes and sprinkle with kosher salt and ground black pepper. Cook, stirring, for 7 to 8 minutes, or until the chicken is opaque throughout and slightly browned on the outside.

– Poach skinless, boneless chicken breasts in the microwave. Place cubed raw chicken in a 2-quart microwavable casserole dish; sprinkle with kosher salt and ground black pepper. Add 1 cup water. Microwave on medium power for 5 minutes, then stir the chicken and cook for up to another 5 minutes, or until the chicken is opaque throughout. Drain the chicken pieces in a colander and let cool.

## TOASTING NUTS

Nuts are easily toasted in the oven at 350°F. Place them in the center of the oven on a rimmed baking pan and bake for about 5 minutes. Watch them carefully—do not walk away, as they can burn quickly. Remove from the oven and let cool. You can also toast nuts in a dry skillet over medium-low heat, but stir them constantly with a wooden spoon, and again, watch carefully to prevent burning.

## ZESTING CITRUS FRUIT

The zest of a lemon, lime, or orange is the thin, colored outer layer. Using citrus zest is a great way to add citrus flavor to a dish, since the flavorful oils are located in this layer—without adding carbs or calories. Citrus zest also makes a nice garnish. To zest fruit, you can use the fine holes of a handheld grater, or invest in a microplane grater, which is a long, rectangular metal grater specifically designed for zesting. When using a grater, be sure to grate just the colored outer layer of the skin—the white layer beneath, called the pith, is bitter. If you don't have an appropriate grater, a very sharp paring knife can be used to cut off the outer layer of skin; then finely mince the peel.

## EASY ON THE COOK!

Here are some ideas that will help make your cooking experience more enjoyable, quicker, easier, and more efficient. Enjoy!

- Before beginning to cook, set out all the ingredients to make sure you have everything you need. Measure out all the seasonings you'll need for the recipe; it's okay to mix them if they're to be added at the same time.

- If you like to measure as you go, place all the seasoning jars and bottles on the right side of your bowl or skillet; then as you add them to the dish, move the jars to the left side. No more wondering if you remembered to add the salt!

- Keep a small cutting board for meats, poultry, and seafood preparation. Using it only for the raw protein items means you won't have to wash and sanitize your entire work area or large cutting surface when you switch ingredients or finish the prep—you'll only have to clean that board.

- Marinate and rub often! These two easy do-ahead techniques not only deliver flavor, they make it easier to throw together a quick meal.

- Many recipes in this book can be made a day ahead of time, or at least partially prepared ahead of time. This saves time on the day of cooking—no more rushing around after work trying to get a meal on the table while everyone stands around complaining that they're hungry! Plus, by breaking down the cooking over two days, you'll probably enjoy the process more, since it will be more leisurely.

- Kim's favorite time to cook is *after* dinner! No one is hungry, no one is rushed, and she can put on some music and enjoy the task. She's also that much more ahead of the game the next day. Many soups, stews, homemade salad dressings, and even some salads, such as Muffuletta Salad (page 102), taste better the next day, anyway!

- Not feeding a family? When you prepare a dish, save half of it for the freezer or for "planned-overs" (leftovers that you planned on). Two meals for the time investment of one is a great thing. Plus, there's nothing more fun than making your co-workers jealous when they smell your divine leftovers lunch!

- Don't feel tied to serving a dish either hot or cold—room temperature food is wonderful in many cases (and trendy, to boot!). Side dishes, especially, often taste better at room temperature than they do hot (our Green Beans with Almonds, Onions, and Bacon, page 278, is an example). Additionally, some meal salads, like the Italian Sandwich Salad (page 101), are also more flavorful when served at room temperature rather than right from the refrigerator. The beauty of serving room-temp food is that it takes some of the pressure off the cook—not everything needs to be done at exactly the same time. You can make some dishes earlier in the day, refrigerate them, then just let them come to room temperature before serving.

- If you only need a teaspoon or tablespoon of fresh lemon or lime juice, but don't want to waste the rest of the fruit every time, squeeze out all the juice from a whole lemon or lime, then freeze it in ice-cube trays (2-tablespoon-sized cubes are useful). When frozen, just pop the cubes out and store them in a small freezer bag (don't forget to label it!). Thaw the juice cube in a bowl on the counter, or place a cube in a plastic bag and run warm water over it to melt the juice.

- Sharp knives make for easy chopping and slicing, and safer preparation overall. If you don't own a knife sharpener and are not proficient at sharpening knives with a steel, then by all means pay a professional to do it for you. It doesn't cost much, and it will make your cooking life much more enjoyable! Check at gourmet stores and knife stores for sharpening services.

# 1

## BREAKFAST AND BRUNCH

# FOR MANY LOW-CARBERS, THE FIRST MEAL OF THE DAY IS A CHALLENGING ONE.

You might think it would be easy to start each day with high-protein eggs and perhaps some bacon, ham, or sausage on the side—and you'd be right. But after a while, even this easy low-carb fare gets mighty dull. Commercial protein bars are an alternative, but they're pricey and not always satisfying (ditto for the low-carb shakes).

If you've been lusting after the pancakes, French toast, muffins, and other traditionally high-carb foods that your breakfast companions are indulging in, take heart! This chapter should quench your cravings. PB&J Breakfast Bars or the Nuts and Seeds Breakfast Cookies will get you out the door quickly on busy weekday mornings. When you've got a little more time, try Banana French Toast, Blueberry Mini-Muffins, or the frittata or quiche recipes.

Many of this chapter's recipes, such as Berry Breakfast Strata (a sweet casserole-type dish layered with mixed berries, low-carb bread, and cream cheese), Walnut-stuffed Baked Apples, or Raisin Bread Pudding, are suitable for brunch guests, should some early-day entertaining be on your agenda.

# HAM AND CHEDDAR FRITTATA

Frittatas are an Italian invention. They're a lot like omelets in that they can be prepared in an unlimited number of ways, using all manner of ingredients. Yet, they're much easier to prepare than omelets—there's no flipping required! This version relies on those tried-and-true omelet staples—ham and Cheddar—for a classic taste that will appeal to children as well as adults. After you get comfortable with making frittatas, we're sure you'll come up with some inventive flavor combinations of your own.

10 eggs

$1/2$ teaspoon kosher salt

$1/2$ teaspoon ground black pepper

$1/4$ teaspoon Tabasco sauce

$1 1/2$ cups (6 ounces) shredded mild Cheddar cheese, divided

8 ounces good-quality cooked ham, coarsely chopped (about 1 cup)

1 tablespoon butter (2 tablespoons if pan is not nonstick)

Preheat the oven to 400°F. In a medium mixing bowl, whisk together the eggs, salt, pepper, and Tabasco. Add 1 cup of the cheese and stir to combine.

In a microwavable bowl, microwave the ham on medium power for 45 seconds; drain off any water.

In a medium ovenproof skillet or sauté pan over medium heat, melt the butter. Tilt the skillet to swirl the butter and coat the entire inside surface. Pour in the egg mixture and reduce the heat to medium-low. Using a spatula, push the cooked edges of the eggs into the center of the pan and tilt the pan so the uncooked egg runs to the edge. Cook the eggs 5 to 8 minutes, until the mixture is beginning to set but is still quite loose. Sprinkle the ham and remaining $1/2$ cup cheese over the eggs.

Bake for 10 to 15 minutes, until the center of the frittata is set. Let cool for 5 minutes before serving.

Each serving contains approximately:
CAL: 315 PRO: 27g NET CARB: 1.5g FAT: 22g CHOL: 411mg SOD: 843mg

SERVES 6

# SHRIMP AND HAVARTI FRITTATA

This isn't your typical "leftovers" frittata. With quality ingredients like shrimp, fresh chives, and Havarti, this dish is suitable for company. We recommend buying raw shrimp (frozen is fine) and cooking them at home before beginning the frittata. Purchasing precooked shrimp that has been frozen afterward is not recommended, as it leads to a watery product (and a waste of expensive ingredients). If you *must* buy precooked shrimp, be sure to heat them in the microwave for 45 to 60 seconds on medium power to release their water before adding them to the frittata.

10 eggs

1/2 teaspoon kosher salt

1/2 teaspoon ground black pepper

1/4 teaspoon Tabasco sauce

3 tablespoons minced fresh chives

1 1/2 cups (6 ounces) shredded Havarti cheese, divided

12 ounces cooked, peeled medium shrimp (31 to 35 per pound), divided

1 tablespoon butter (2 tablespoons if pan is not nonstick)

Preheat the oven to 400°F. In a medium mixing bowl, whisk together the eggs salt, pepper, Tabasco, and chives. With a wooden spoon, stir in 3/4 cup of the cheese and half of the shrimp.

In a medium ovenproof skillet or sauté pan over medium heat, melt the butter. Tilt the skillet to swirl the butter and coat the entire inside surface. Pour in the egg mixture and reduce the heat to medium-low. Using a spatula, push the cooked edges of the eggs into the center of the pan and tilt the pan so the uncooked egg runs to the edge. The chives will tend to float to the top of the egg mixture; just keep stirring them in while the eggs cook. Cook the eggs 5 to 8 minutes, until the mixture begins to set but is still quite loose. Sprinkle the remaining shrimp and cheese over the eggs.

Bake for 10 to 15 minutes, until the center of the frittata is set and the shrimp are cooked through. Let cool for 5 minutes before serving.

Each serving contains approximately:
CAL: 338 PRO: 30g NET CARB: 2g FAT: 23g CHOL: 507mg SOD: 497mg

SERVES 6

# CORNED BEEF HASH FRITTATA

This frittata was inspired by Kitty's husband, Dan, who loves corned beef hash in any form. You'll notice that the number of eggs and the inclusion of additional egg whites makes this recipe a bit different from our other frittatas, but it's necessary to give the right texture to the finished product. Enjoy it at breakfast with berries, or with a salad at lunch or dinner. (Leftover hash keeps well in the refrigerator for a few days.)

1 cup canned corned beef hash

4 eggs

4 egg whites

2 scallions, chopped

$1/4$ teaspoon ground black pepper

Cooking spray

Preheat the oven to 400°F. In a small, nonstick skillet over medium heat, cook the hash for 4 minutes without stirring, or until lightly browned and crispy on the bottom. Using a spatula, flip the hash and cook for another 4 minutes. Remove from the heat and set aside.

In a medium mixing bowl, whisk together the whole eggs, egg whites, scallions, and pepper. Add the hash and stir together with a wooden spoon; set aside.

Heat a medium ovenproof skillet or sauté pan over medium heat until hot. Coat the skillet heavily with cooking spray. Add the egg-hash mixture and reduce the heat to medium-low. Using a spatula, push the cooked edges of the eggs into the center of the pan and tilt the pan so the uncooked egg runs to the edge. Continue to cook for 5 minutes, until the mixture begins to set but is still quite loose.

Bake for 10 to 15 minutes, or until the center of the frittata is set and the top is lightly browned. Let cool for 5 minutes before serving.

Each serving contains approximately:
CAL: 193 PRO: 15g NET CARB: 7g FAT: 11g CHOL: 231mg SOD: 416mg

SERVES 4

# LOW-CARB
# QUICHE CRUST

OK, it's not the kind of piecrust Grandma used to make, but it's got more protein and fewer carbs than hers did! It comes together and rolls out just like a regular homemade crust, and bakes up flaky and tender, too.

1/2 cup wheat gluten, plus extra for dusting

1/2 cup whole-wheat pastry flour

1/4 cup almond meal or finely ground almonds

1/4 teaspoon kosher salt

1 egg yolk, lightly beaten

3 tablespoons vegetable shortening

3 to 4 tablespoons cold water

Cooking spray

In a small mixing bowl, stir together the wheat gluten, pastry flour, almond meal, and salt. Using a fork, stir in the egg yolk. Add the shortening and, using the fork, work it into the dry ingredients until the mixture forms coarse crumbs.

Using the fork, stir in the water, 1 tablespoon at a time, using only as much water as needed to get the mixture to form a ball. Let the dough ball rest for 2 minutes while you prepare the work surface for rolling.

Dust a clean work surface and rolling pin with wheat gluten. Transfer the dough ball to the work surface and dust it lightly with wheat gluten. With clean hands, press the dough ball into a disk. Roll out the dough with the rolling pin until you have a disk roughly 1/2 inches larger all around than the pie plate.

Coat a 9-inch pie plate with cooking spray. Using a spatula, carefully fold the crust in half and gently ease it into the prepared pie plate. Crimp the edge as desired.

Each serving (one-sixth of the crust) contains approximately:
CAL: 168 PRO: 7g NET CARB: 11.5g FAT: 10g CHOL: 36mg SOD: 90mg

MAKES ONE
9-INCH CRUST

# BACON AND SCALLION QUICHE

When you're in the mood for your eggs in an honest-to-goodness crust, try this quiche. Savory bacon and scallions flavor the filling, but you can easily devise different fillings (see our suggestions below). The crust is rolled out just like a regular piecrust, then glazed with egg white and prebaked for a few minutes to help prevent it from getting soggy. Quiche is also great for a simple dinner.

1 egg, separated

One 9-inch Low-Carb Quiche Crust, unbaked (page 41)

### FILLING

1 tablespoon butter

5 scallions, chopped

5 eggs

$1^1/_2$ cups light cream

$^1/_2$ teaspoon kosher salt

$^1/_2$ teaspoon ground black pepper

3 slices bacon, cooked crisp and coarsely chopped (about $^1/_2$ cup)

1 tablespoon grated Parmesan cheese

Each serving contains approximately:
CAL: 397 PRO: 17g NET CARB: 14g FAT: 30g CHOL: 297mg SOD: 293mg

SERVES 6

Preheat the oven to 425°F. In a small bowl, lightly beat the egg white with a fork (reserve the yolk to add to the filling mixture). Using a pastry brush, coat the inside of the crust with a little of the egg white; discard the excess. Bake for 3 to 5 minutes, until the surface is dry but the edges of the crust are not at all browned. Remove from the oven, leaving the oven on, and let cool while preparing the filling.

**To make the filling:** In a small skillet or sauté pan over medium heat, melt the butter. Add the scallions and cook, stirring, for 2 minutes, or until the scallions begin to soften. Remove from the heat and set aside.

In a medium mixing bowl, whisk together the eggs, the reserved egg yolk, the cream, salt, and pepper until combined. Spread the scallions over the bottom of the crust. Pour the egg mixture over the scallions (some scallions will rise to the top). Sprinkle the filling with the bacon pieces. Bake for 10 minutes; turn the heat down to 325°F and bake for another 35 minutes, or until the quiche is set and nicely browned. Remove from the oven and sprinkle with the Parmesan. Let cool for at least 10 minutes before serving.

## Variations
In place of bacon and scallions, try the following combinations for quiche:

- SLICED, SAUTÉED MUSHROOMS, ROASTED RED PEPPERS, AND PROVOLONE

- CHOPPED, BLANCHED BROCCOLI AND CHEDDAR CHEESE

- CHOPPED ARTICHOKE HEARTS, PROSCIUTTO, AND PARMESAN

- CHOPPED BASIL, SUN-DRIED TOMATOES, AND SHREDDED MOZZARELLA

- SLICED, SAUTÉED LEEKS AND WILD MUSHROOMS

- CUBED, COOKED HAM AND SPRING PEAS

- CUBED, COOKED TURKEY, JACK CHEESE, AND CHILI POWDER

- COOKED, DRAINED SPINACH, SHRIMP OR CRAB, AND ASIAGO CHEESE

- CHOPPED, SAUTÉED KIELBASA AND GREEN PEPPERS

# RICOTTA PANCAKES

These cheese-based pancakes are a surprisingly satisfying alternative to regular, carb-heavy pancakes. Try serving them with Wild Blueberry Sauce (page 315), Sweet Vanilla-Cinnamon Butter (page 313), or your favorite sugar-free maple syrup.

$1/4$ cup light cream

$2/3$ cup ricotta cheese

2 eggs, separated

2 tablespoons flour

3 tablespoons whole-wheat flour

1 tablespoon toasted wheat germ

1 teaspoon sugar

1 teaspoon Splenda Granular sweetener

$1/4$ teaspoon baking powder

Pinch of kosher salt

$1/4$ teaspoon vanilla extract

Cooking spray

In a blender or food processor, combine all of the ingredients except the egg whites and cooking spray. Process until smooth and creamy. Transfer the batter to a medium mixing bowl.

In a small mixing bowl, using an electric mixer on high speed, beat the egg whites until stiff peaks form. Using a rubber spatula, gently stir the beaten egg whites into the batter.

Heat a griddle or medium skillet over medium heat; when hot, coat the griddle with cooking spray. Drop $1/4$ cup of batter onto the warm griddle and cook for 2 minutes, or until bubbles form on the pancake surface, then flip with a spatula and cook for another $1\frac{1}{2}$ minutes, or until the bottom is golden brown. Repeat with the remaining batter, using more cooking spray as needed. If you'd like to serve the pancakes all at one time, transfer each batch of cooked pancakes to an ovenproof platter, cover the platter with aluminum foil, and keep it in a warm (200°F) oven until all the pancakes are cooked.

Each pancake contains approximately:
CAL: 66 PRO: 4g NET CARB: 4g FAT: 4g CHOL: 49mg SOD: 43mg

MAKES ABOUT
11 PANCAKES

# BANANA FRENCH TOAST

Miss bananas? We do, too. This recipe is a tasty way to spread out a little bit of banana so you still get great flavor, but fewer carbs. Try this toast topped with sugar-free maple syrup or your favorite Jam Butter (page 311).

$1/_2$ medium ripe banana, mashed (about $1/_4$ cup)

2 tablespoons light cream

2 eggs, lightly beaten

$1/_4$ teaspoon vanilla extract

4 slices low-carb white bread, crusts trimmed

Cooking spray

$1/_8$ teaspoon ground nutmeg for garnish (optional)

3 tablespoons toasted pecans for garnish (optional)

In a shallow dish or bowl, using a fork, stir together the banana, cream, eggs, and vanilla until well mixed; set aside.

Heat a griddle or medium skillet over medium heat until hot. While waiting for the griddle to heat, briefly soak the bread slices in the egg mixture, flipping to coat both sides.

Coat the griddle with cooking spray and transfer the soaked bread slices to the hot griddle. Cook for about 2 minutes, or until golden brown on the bottom, then flip with a spatula and cook for another 2 minutes, until the bottom is lightly browned. Transfer the toast to individual plates and sprinkle with nutmeg and pecans, if desired.

Each serving contains approximately:
CAL: 236 PRO: 16g NET CARB: 11g FAT: 12g CHOL: 230mg SOD: 223mg

SERVES 2

# FRENCH TOAST "WAFFLES"

This is a novel way to make two quick, tasty "waffles"—without stirring up any batter at all. Although it's a single-serve recipe, you can easily multiply the ingredients to serve a family.

1 **egg**

1 **tablespoon light cream**

1 **tablespoon Splenda Granular sweetener**

1/8 **teaspoon vanilla extract**

2 **slices low-carb white bread, crusts trimmed**

**Cooking spray**

**Sugar-free maple syrup for serving (optional)**

Preheat a Belgian waffle iron. In a shallow dish or bowl, using a fork, whisk together the egg, cream, Splenda, and vanilla until blended.

Briefly soak the bread slices in the egg mixture, flipping to coat both sides. When the iron is ready, coat it lightly with cooking spray.

Transfer the soaked bread slices to the hot waffle iron, then press down firmly to close the iron. Cook the "waffles" for 2 to 3 minutes, until lightly browned and cooked through. Serve immediately, with syrup, if desired.

Each serving contains approximately:
CAL: 209 PRO: 16g NET CARB: 5g FAT: 12g CHOL: 230mg SOD: 222mg

SERVES 1

# FRENCH TOAST STUFFED WITH ORANGE-CURRANT CREAM CHEESE

This dish was inspired by Kitty's desire for a special, low-carb French toast recipe suitable for serving on Christmas morning. Fresh oranges are plentiful during the winter months—even in Maine—so they provide the major flavor in the filling. If you don't have currants on hand, use chopped raisins.

**CHEESE FILLING**

- 4 ounces cream cheese, softened
- 2 teaspoons currants
- 2 tablespoons Splenda Granular sweetener
- 2 teaspoons fresh orange juice
- $1/2$ teaspoon orange zest (see page 33)
- $1/8$ teaspoon ground cinnamon

- 4 eggs
- $1/2$ cup light cream
- 4 teaspoons Splenda Granular sweetener
- $1/4$ teaspoon ground cinnamon
- 8 slices low-carb white bread, crusts trimmed

Cooking spray

Sugar-free maple syrup for serving (optional)

To make the filling: In a small mixing bowl, stir together all the ingredients with a wooden spoon until blended; set aside.

In a shallow dish or bowl, whisk together the eggs, cream, Splenda, and cinnamon until blended; set aside. Heat a griddle or medium skillet over medium heat.

While waiting for the griddle to heat, assemble the toast: Spread 4 of the bread slices each with one-quarter of the cream cheese mixture on one side only; do not spread it all the way to the edges or it will leak out during cooking. Top each slice with another slice of bread and gently press together, making four stuffed "sandwiches." Dip each "sandwich" into the egg mixture briefly, flipping to coat both sides.

Coat the hot griddle with cooking spray. Transfer the stuffed "sandwiches" to the hot griddle and cook for about 3 minutes, or until nicely browned on the bottoms; flip with a spatula and cook for another 2 minutes, or until the bottoms are lightly browned. Transfer each stuffed toast to a plate and cut in half on the diagonal using a long, sharp knife. Serve immediately, with syrup, if desired.

Each serving contains approximately:
CAL: 328 PRO: 18g NET CARB: 8g
FAT: 23g CHOL: 264mg SOD: 314mg

SERVES 4

# BERRY BREAKFAST STRATA

A strata is a casserolelike dish that typically includes layers of bread and cheese topped with an egg-and-cream mixture. Quite frequently, baked stratas feature savory ingredients such as ham and vegetables, but this one is filled with vanilla-accented cream cheese and a beautiful mixed berry sauce. It's unusual, yet just as much a "comfort food" as any other strata you may run across.

**BERRY SAUCE**

One **12-ounce package frozen mixed berries (no need to thaw)**

$1/4$ cup **sugar-free strawberry preserves (such as Smucker's Light)**

$1/2$ cup **Splenda Granular sweetener**

$1/4$ cup **cold water**

1 tablespoon **lemon juice**

2 teaspoons **low-carb thickener (such as Expert Foods' ThickenThin not/Starch)**

**Cooking spray**

One **8-ounce package cream cheese, softened**

1 teaspoon **vanilla extract**

8 slices **low-carb white bread, crusts trimmed**

4 **eggs**

$1/3$ cup **light cream**

**To make the sauce:** In a medium saucepan over medium-low heat, stir together the berries and the preserves; let cook for 2 minutes without stirring. While the berries are cooking, stir together the remaining sauce ingredients in a 1-cup liquid measuring cup or a small bowl, mixing until no lumps remain. Pour the mixture into the saucepan with the berries and raise the heat to medium. Cook the sauce, stirring, for 5 minutes, or until slightly thickened. Remove from the heat and set aside. (The sauce can be made 1 day ahead and refrigerated until needed.)

Preheat the oven to 350°F. Coat a 9-by-9-inch baking dish with cooking spray; set aside. In a small mixing bowl, using an electric mixer, beat together the cream cheese and vanilla on medium speed until well combined and smooth. Using a butter knife or small rubber spatula, spread 4 of the bread slices on one side with the cream cheese mixture, using up all the cream cheese. Using a sharp knife, slice all of the bread slices (including those with the cream cheese on them) in half diagonally, making triangles.

In a shallow dish or bowl, whisk together the eggs and cream. Dip the 8 bread triangles with cream cheese into the egg mixture, soaking only the sides without the cheese. Lay the triangles, cheese side up, in the bottom of the prepared baking dish, arranging them to fit the dish. Spoon $1/3$ of the berry sauce over the cream cheese (it won't completely cover the bread layer).

Dip the remaining bread triangles into the egg mixture, soaking both sides. Place them on top of the berry sauce, arranging to fit the dish. Pour the remaining egg mixture over the top of the strata; cover with aluminum foil and bake for 30 minutes, or until set and cooked through.

Remove from the oven, leaving the oven on. Remove the foil and pour the remaining berry sauce over the top, making sure that all exposed bread pieces are covered with sauce. Return the strata to the oven, uncovered, and bake an additional 10 minutes, until the sauce is heated through. Let cool 10 to 15 minutes before serving.

**Each serving contains approximately:**
CAL: 301 PRO: 13g NET CARB: 13g FAT: 21g CHOL: 192mg SOD: 264mg

SERVES 6

# RAISIN BREAD PUDDING

This easy pudding is all the things bread pudding should be—warm, comforting, and full of cinnamon and raisins. It would make a nice addition to a brunch menu that features ham. If you have any leftovers, you can easily reheat them in the microwave or a warm (300°F) oven.

Cooking spray

- 6 slices "light" raisin bread, crusts trimmed
- 6 slices low-carb white bread, crusts trimmed
- 1 1/2 cups light cream
- 1 cup low-carb whole milk
- 2 eggs
- 2 teaspoons vanilla extract
- 1/2 cup Splenda Granular sweetener
- 2 teaspoons ground cinnamon

Real Whipped Cream (page 332) for garnish (optional)

Coat a 9-by-9-inch baking dish with cooking spray; set aside. Cut the bread into 1-inch cubes; set aside.

Preheat the oven to 325°F. In a medium mixing bowl, combine the cream, milk, eggs, vanilla, Splenda, and cinnamon and whisk until well blended. Add bread cubes to the cream mixture and stir with a wooden spoon until all the bread cubes are well coated. Let the bread soak in the bowl for 15 minutes, pressing down occasionally with the spoon or a clean hand to ensure that all the bread is soaked.

Stir the bread one more time, then transfer the mixture to the prepared baking dish. Bake 55 minutes to 1 hour, until the pudding is nicely browned on top and does not jiggle when the pan is gently shaken. Let cool at least 15 minutes before serving. Top each portion with the whipped cream, if desired.

Each serving contains approximately:
CAL: 217 PRO: 13g NET CARB: 10g FAT: 12g CHOL: 78mg SOD: 248mg

SERVES 9

# WALNUT-STUFFED BAKED APPLES

Low-carb eaters: Do not let apples scare you away! Although they are higher in carbs then some fruits, they're also full of fiber. What's more, you can't beat the sweet flavor and satisfying crunch of an in-season apple. Here we've stuffed apple halves with a rich filling of walnuts, oatmeal, and cinnamon. If you are going to enjoy fruit and stay low-carb, morning may be the best time of day for you to indulge.

**STUFFING**

$1^1/_4$ cup walnuts, finely chopped

$^1/_2$ cup Splenda Granular sweetener

$^1/_3$ cup sugar-free maple syrup

$^1/_3$ cup old-fashioned rolled oats

$^1/_4$ cup butter, melted

2 teaspoons ground cinnamon

1 teaspoon vanilla extract

**Pinch of kosher salt**

3 medium red cooking apples such as Empire, Gala, or Cortland, washed and wiped dry

**Real Whipped Cream (page 332) for garnish (optional)**

Preheat the oven to 350°F.

**To make the stuffing:** Stir together all the stuffing ingredients in a medium mixing bowl; set aside.

Using a paring knife, cut each apple in half horizontally (this will enable the apples to sit upright in the pan). Using a melon baller or teaspoon, remove the seeds, as well as about three additional balls of apple pulp from each apple half to create cavities for the filling. (Use the apple balls as a snack for kids, or save them for a salad, if you like.) Place the apple halves, hollowed side up, in a 9-by-9-inch baking dish. Using a teaspoon, divide the stuffing between the apples, placing it in the cavities of the apples.

Bake for 30 minutes, then test for doneness by piercing the fruit with the tip of a sharp knife. If the apples don't pierce easily, bake an additional 15 minutes, then retest. When done, remove the apples from the oven and let rest 5 to 10 minutes before serving. Garnish with Real Whipped Cream, if desired.

**Note**

To save time in the morning, make these the night before, then refrigerate them, loosely covered with plastic wrap. Warm briefly in the microwave for a delicious hot breakfast treat.

Each serving contains approximately:
CAL: 283 PRO: 4g NET CARB: 14g FAT: 24g CHOL: 21mg SOD: 113mg

SERVES 6

# BLUEBERRY MINI-MUFFINS

The secret to low-carb baking is using a mixture of flourlike products such as Atkins Bake Mix, whole-wheat pastry flour, wheat gluten, and ground almonds. We like the results best when we use a small amount of regular all-purpose flour in the mix, too. Try these mini-muffins alongside a plate of eggs, or eat them split and spread with Lemon Curd (page 314) for a quick breakfast. This recipe yields 24 muffins, so freeze a few for whenever a muffin mood strikes you.

Cooking spray

$1/3$ cup low-carb 2% milk

$1/4$ cup plus 1 tablespoon light cream

1 egg

$1/2$ teaspoon vanilla extract

$2/3$ cup Splenda Granular sweetener

$1/3$ cup whole-wheat pastry flour

$1/3$ cup Atkins Bake Mix

$1/4$ cup wheat gluten

2 tablespoons all-purpose flour

2 tablespoons almond meal or finely ground almonds

$2^{1}/_2$ teaspoons baking powder

$1/4$ teaspoon ground cinnamon

5 tablespoons cold margarine or butter, diced (see page 19)

1 cup fresh or frozen blueberries (if frozen, do not thaw)

Preheat the oven to 425°F. Coat the cups of a 12-cup mini-muffin tin with cooking spray; set aside.

In a 1-cup liquid measuring cup, using a fork, stir together the milk, cream, egg, and vanilla until blended; set aside. In a small mixing bowl, stir together the Splenda, whole-wheat flour, Bake Mix, wheat gluten, all-purpose flour, almond meal, baking powder, and cinnamon until mixed. Using a pastry blender or fork, work in the margarine until the mixture resembles coarse crumbs. Pour the liquid ingredients into the dry ingredients all at once and stir with a wooden spoon until just mixed; the batter will be lumpy. Gently stir in the blueberries.

Using a tablespoon measure, drop the batter into the muffin cups, using half the batter to fill 12 mini-muffin cups. Bake for 15 to 18 minutes, or until nicely browned. Let the muffins cool in the pan for 5 minutes, then invert the pan to release the muffins onto a wire rack. Let the muffins cool for at least 5 minutes before serving (if freezing, let them cool completely). Coat the muffin tin with cooking spray again and repeat with the remaining batter to make a total of 24 muffins.

Each 2-muffin serving contains approximately:
CAL: 114 PRO: 5g NET CARB: 6g FAT: 7g
CHOL: 23mg SOD: 213mg

MAKES 24 MUFFINS;
SERVES 12

# QUICK PUMPKIN-CORN MUFFINS

There's no need to miss out on your morning muffin anymore! Full of great pumpkin flavor and pumpkin-pie spices, these muffins make an easy breakfast any day of the week. Keep them in the freezer, sealed in a gallon-size, zip-top freezer bag; then in the morning all you'll need to do is grab one, pop it in the microwave, and you're good to go. Try spreading your muffin with Sweet Vanilla-Cinnamon Butter (page 313) or Maple Butter (page 312).

Cooking spray

One 8 1/2-ounce package Atkins Quick Quisine Corn Muffin Mix

1 cup canned pumpkin (not pumpkin pie filling)

1/4 cup vegetable oil

1/3 cup water

1/4 cup heavy cream

2 eggs

1 1/4 teaspoons ground cinnamon

1/2 teaspoon ground ginger

1/4 teaspoon ground cloves

Preheat the oven to 425°F. Coat the cups of a 12-cup muffin tin with cooking spray; set aside.

In a mixing bowl, stir together the Muffin Mix, pumpkin, oil, water, cream, eggs, cinnamon, ginger, and cloves until combined. Do not overmix; the batter will be slightly lumpy. Spoon the batter into prepared muffin cups, dividing it equally; the cups should be full.

Bake for 20 minutes, or until golden brown. Let cool for 5 minutes, then invert the pan to release the muffins onto a wire rack. Let cool for at least 10 minutes before serving (if freezing, let them cool completely).

Each serving contains approximately:
CAL: 142 PRO: 9g NET CARB: 8g FAT: 7g CHOL: 42mg SOD: 188mg

SERVES 12

# PB&J BREAKFAST BARS

Packed with peanuts and wholesome peanut butter, these bars can stand in for your morning protein bar or make a filling snack. Choose your favorite sugar-free preserves—raspberry or strawberry give a classic PB&J flavor, while apricot or even orange marmalade make for a more unusual bar.

**CRUST**

- 3/4 cup low-carb peanut butter
- 3/4 cup cocktail peanuts, finely chopped
- 1/2 cup Atkins Bake Mix
- 2 tablespoons SugarTwin brown-sugar substitute
- 1/2 teaspoon baking powder
- 1/4 teaspoon ground cinnamon

**FILLING**

- 1 cup sugar-free preserves
- 1/4 teaspoon vanilla extract

**TOPPING**

- 3 tablespoons cold butter, diced (see page 19)
- 2 tablespoons whole-wheat flour
- 2 tablespoons cocktail peanuts, coarsely chopped
- 2 tablespoons quick or old-fashioned rolled oats
- 2 tablespoons SugarTwin brown-sugar substitute
- 2 teaspoons sugar
- 1/8 teaspoon ground cinnamon

Preheat the oven to 350°F. Coat an 8-by-8-inch baking pan with cooking spray; set aside.

**To make the crust:** In a small mixing bowl, stir together the crust ingredients until combined. Spoon the mixture into the prepared pan. Using clean fingers dipped in cold water, press the mixture into the bottom of the pan, forming an even crust layer. Bake for 10 to 12 minutes, until set. Let cool for 15 minutes, leaving the oven on.

**To make the filling:** In a small bowl, stir together the preserves and vanilla until mixed. Using a rubber spatula, spread the preserves mixture over the cooled crust.

**To make the topping:** In a small mixing bowl, using a fork, mash together the cold butter and the remaining topping ingredients until coarse crumbs form. Sprinkle the crumb mixture over the preserves.

Bake for 15 minutes, until the preserves are bubbling and the crumb topping is lightly browned. Let cool completely before cutting into the 12 bars.

Each serving contains approximately:
CAL: 225 PRO: 10g NET CARB: 12g FAT: 16g CHOL: 8mg SOD: 209mg

SERVES 12

# NUTS AND SEEDS BREAKFAST COOKIES

If you're tired of store-bought low-carb bars, these wholesome cookies are for you! A peanut butter dough is combined with toasted nuts, sunflower and pumpkin seeds, and coconut. They're crunchy, satisfying, and not too sweet.

2 cups old-fashioned rolled oats

$1/2$ cup sunflower seeds

$1/2$ cup pumpkin seeds

$1/2$ cup unsweetened shredded coconut

$1/2$ cup chopped hazelnuts

$1/2$ cup chopped almonds

### PEANUT-BUTTER DOUGH

1 cup (2 sticks) butter, softened

$1/2$ cup low-carb peanut butter

2 eggs, at room temperature

$1^1/4$ cups Splenda Granular sweetener

2 tablespoons whole-wheat pastry flour

2 tablespoons dark brown sugar

1 teaspoon baking soda

1 teaspoon vanilla extract

$1/4$ teaspoon almond extract

$1/4$ teaspoon kosher salt

Preheat the oven to 300°F. In a medium mixing bowl, stir together the oats, sunflower and pumpkin seeds, coconut, hazelnuts, and almonds. Spread the mixture on a baking sheet; bake for 15 minutes, or until toasted. Set aside and let cool.

**Meanwhile, prepare the dough:** In a large mixing bowl, using an electric mixer on medium speed, beat together the butter and peanut butter until fluffy; add the eggs and mix again to blend. Scrape down the sides of the bowl, then add the Splenda, flour, brown sugar, baking soda, vanilla and almond extracts, salt, and nuts-and-seeds mixture. Mix on low speed until the dough is well combined. Cover with plastic wrap and refrigerate for at least 1 hour or for up to 24 hours.

Preheat the oven to 350°F. Form the dough into 20 golf ball–sized balls. Flatten the balls slightly in your palm to make round cookies about 1/2 inch thick. Place the cookies on an ungreased cookie sheet and bake for 15 minutes. Let cool completely before removing from the cookie sheets. Wrap each cookie in plastic wrap, if desired, so they're ready to grab and go in the morning.

Each cookie contains approximately:
CAL: 244 PRO: 6g NET CARB: 8g FAT: 20g CHOL: 46mg SOD: 171mg

MAKES 20 COOKIES

# 2

## APPETIZERS AND SNACKS

# YOU'VE PROBABLY REALIZED THAT A LACK OF LOW-CARB SNACKS CAN PROVE TO BE THE DOWNFALL OF YOUR DIET.

Without them, you're much more likely to succumb to a "carby" craving. The same goes for us, so this chapter features a wide variety of tasty tidbits—packed with intense flavors, textures, colors, and aromas—that can start off any meal (or tide you over to the next one).

With the exception of the Sweet Pecans, these morsels are savory, salty, or spicy. The intensity of our appetizers and snacks make big taste impressions—without damaging your carb budget.

If a quick dip is all you need to round out your appetizer tray, our unusual Sesame Dip, Lemon-Caper Crudité Dip, or Creamy Avocado Dip all suffice nicely. (Once you've tried a flavorful, homemade dip, you may never go back to plain, purchased ranch dip again!) If a more elaborate starter is needed for your dinner party, we've provided two ways to prepare fresh mussels—in a creamy tomato sauce, or the more classic lemon and parsley treatment. A beautiful bowl filled with Entertaining Almonds is great with cocktails, or presented as a hostess gift.

Finally, don't limit yourself to enjoying these recipes only as appetizers or snacks; in many cases they could actually be a meal, especially when smartly supplemented with vegetables or salad greens.

# PEANUT BUTTER ENERGY SNAX

Peanut butter, soy protein powder, and unsweetened coconut combine to make these tasty miniature snacks. They're great for breakfast, or any time of day you need a pick-me-up. This is a fun and easy recipe for little helping hands to do, so if you've got kids, enlist their assistance.

$1/3$ cup unsweetened shredded coconut

1 cup low-carb peanut butter

$1/2$ cup Splenda Granular sweetener

$1/2$ cup plain, unsweetened soy protein powder

$1^1/2$ teaspoons vanilla extract

Pinch of salt

Place the coconut in a plate or shallow bowl.

In a medium mixing bowl, using a rubber spatula, stir together the peanut butter, Splenda, soy powder, vanilla, and salt. Using clean hands, shape the mixture into 14 balls. Roll each ball in the coconut. Place the finished balls in a sealed plastic container and refrigerate for up to 5 days.

Each snack contains approximately:
CAL: 133 PRO: 7g NET CARB: 2g FAT: 11g CHOL: 0mg SOD: 140mg

MAKES 14 SNAX

# ALMOND-STUFFED OLIVES

These savory tidbits make a tasty snack, or can help round out an hors d'oeuvres platter for guests. Toasting the almonds really augments their nutty flavor and is highly recommended. However, if you're pressed for time, you can skip that step and use raw almonds.

1½ cups raw whole almonds

1 tablespoon olive oil

One 10-ounce jar small pimiento-stuffed (Manzanilla) olives (about 100 olives)

In a heavy skillet or sauté pan over low heat, stir together the almonds and olive oil. Cook for about 8 to 10 minutes, stirring frequently, until the nuts are toasted and fragrant. Remove from the heat and let the nuts cool.

Pour the olives and their juice into a small bowl. To stuff the olives, hold an olive in one hand and a toasted almond in the other. Push the pointy end of the almond into the closed side of the olive (the side where no pimiento is visible). The almond will push some of the pimiento out of the olive, so assemble them over a bowl or the sink.

Place the stuffed olives back into the original olive jar and repeat until all olives are stuffed. Pour the olive juice back into the jar, close the jar, and refrigerate the stuffed olives for up to 10 days.

Each serving (about 5 olives) contains approximately:
CAL: 88 PRO: 2g NET CARB: 2g FAT: 8g CHOL: 0mg SOD: 341mg

SERVES 20

# SESAME DIP

If you're growing weary of ranch dip, consider this unusual option. Accented with a little honey, its flavor profile is at once slightly sweet and salty, with a bit of spiciness, too. Its versatility won us over—try it as a spread for a vegetable wrap, with crudités, or as a sauce for grilled chicken.

3/4 cup nonfat plain yogurt

1/3 cup tahini

1 tablespoon honey

1 tablespoon Splenda Granular sweetener

1 tablespoon soy sauce

1/4 teaspoon toasted sesame oil

1/2 teaspoon Tabasco sauce

In a small mixing bowl, whisk together all the ingredients until well blended. Refrigerate the dip for at least 4 hours, or preferably overnight, before serving.

Note

Tahini is a thick, pastelike spread made from finely crushed sesame seeds. Sold in supermarkets in the ethnic-foods section, it often comes in rather large cans or jars. Not to worry; it keeps well when refrigerated.

Each 2-tablespoon serving contains approximately:
CAL: 62 PRO: 2g NET CARB: 4g FAT: 4g CHOL: 0mg SOD: 119mg

MAKES ABOUT 1 1/4 CUPS;
SERVES 10

# CREAMY **AVOCADO DIP** Different from a guacamole, this creamy dip contains sour cream and yogurt, which gives it a lighter texture and a bright flavor. It pairs fantastically with crudités or low-carb tortilla chips.

- 2 ripe Haas avocados
- $1/2$ cup sour cream
- $1/2$ cup nonfat plain yogurt
- $1/4$ medium red onion, finely chopped (about $1/2$ cup)
- 1 tablespoon fresh lime juice
- 1 teaspoon Tabasco sauce
- 1 clove garlic, minced (about $1/2$ teaspoon)
- $1/4$ teaspoon ground black pepper
- $1/4$ teaspoon kosher salt

Using a sharp knife, carefully slice the avocados in half, around the pits. Remove the pits and cut each avocado in half again, making quarters. Remove the avocado skins from the quarters and, using the back of a fork, mash the avocado pulp in a small bowl.

Using a wooden spoon, mix the rest of the ingredients into the avocado until blended. If not serving immediately, cover the top of the dip with plastic wrap, pressing it directly onto the top of the dip to prevent it from browning.

Note

Supermarket avocados are often not ripe when you purchase them. To hasten ripening at home, place the avacados in a brown bag, roll down the top of the bag to close, then leave the bag on a countertop. Check their progress every day. A ripe avocado will yield to gentle pressure with a thumb.

Each 2-tablespoon serving contains approximately:
CAL: 50 PRO: 1g NET CARB: 1.5g FAT: 4g CHOL: 3mg SOD: 17mg

MAKES ABOUT $1^{1}/_{4}$ CUPS;
SERVES 20

# LEMON-CAPER CRUDITÉ DIP

This creamy dip, accented with lemons and capers, is a tangy match for raw vegetables, especially celery and cucumber slices. Both of us adore lemons and capers, and they're handy ingredients to have around when cooking low-carb, as they contribute lots of flavor for next to no carbs. If you like this dip, you'll no doubt like our Lemon Chicken Salad (page 128) as well, since it utilizes this dip as a dressing.

1/2 cup mayonnaise

1/2 cup sour cream

1 tablespoon lemon zest (see page 33)

1 tablespoon drained capers, crushed and finely chopped

1 teaspoon fresh lemon juice

1/4 teaspoon minced anchovy or anchovy paste

1/4 teaspoon Tabasco sauce

Pinch of ground black pepper

In a small bowl, whisk together all the ingredients until well blended. Refrigerate the dip for at least 4 hours, or preferably overnight, before serving.

Note

Capers can be easily crushed by pressing them firmly with the side of a French knife.

Each 2-tablespoon serving contains approximately:
CAL: 104 PRO: 1g NET CARB: 1g FAT: 11g CHOL: 12mg SOD: 105mg

MAKES ABOUT 1 1/4 CUPS;
SERVES 10

# ROASTED RED PEPPER AND WHITE BEAN SPREAD

A jar of roasted red peppers is a staple in both of our kitchens. Not only are they much more convenient than roasting peppers individually as needed, but their flavor is fabulous, providing plenty of punch for very few carbs. This spread marries roasted red peppers with mild, white beans, which also provide some texture and balance. Try it in sandwiches, wraps, or as a dip for crudités.

One 15$^1$/$_2$-ounce can white beans, rinsed and drained

$^3$/$_4$ cup purchased roasted red peppers, drained and patted dry

2 tablespoons olive oil

1 tablespoon minced shallot

1 tablespoon minced fresh thyme

$^1$/$_2$ teaspoon Tabasco sauce

$^1$/$_2$ teaspoon sherry vinegar

$^1$/$_4$ teaspoon ground black pepper

$^1$/$_4$ teaspoon kosher salt

Combine all the ingredients in a blender and process for 1 to 2 minutes, until smooth. Refrigerate the spread overnight before serving.

Each 2-tablespoon serving contains approximately:
CAL: 42 PRO: 2g NET CARB: 4g FAT: 2g CHOL: 0mg SOD: 10mg

MAKES ABOUT 2 CUPS;
SERVES 16

# ANTIPASTO ROLL-UPS

Roasted red peppers, salami, basil, and extra-virgin olive oil combine to make an eye-catching appetizer with lively flavors. These roll-ups are a nice addition to an antipasto platter, a composed salad, or to round out a buffet table.

One 12-ounce jar prepared roasted red peppers, drained and patted dry (there will be leftover peppers)

12 thin slices provolone cheese (about 1/3 pound)

12 thin slices hard salami (about 1/4 pound)

36 toothpicks

3 tablespoons extra-virgin olive oil

1/2 teaspoon ground black pepper

1 tablespoon chopped fresh basil

Cut the red peppers lengthwise into 1-inch strips (some pieces of pepper may not need to be cut).

To assemble the roll-ups, work in assembly-line fashion: First, lay the provolone slices down on a clean work surface. Top each cheese slice with a slice of salami. Lay a red pepper strip across the bottom of each salami circle. (Return any unused red peppers to their original jar and refrigerate.)

Tightly roll up each stack starting at the bottom, so that the red pepper is on the inside. Place a toothpick in the center of each roll-up, and two more toothpicks at either end. Using a sharp knife, slice between the toothpicks, creating three short rolls.

Place the rolls on a platter. (If not serving them immediately, cover them lightly with plastic wrap and refrigerate until ready to serve.) To garnish, drizzle the olive oil over the roll-ups, then sprinkle with the pepper and chopped basil and serve.

Each serving (4 pieces) contains approximately:
CAL: 152 PRO: 7g NET CARB: 2g FAT: 13g CHOL: 20mg SOD: 509mg

SERVES 9

# SMOKED SALMON ROLL-UPS

The classic combination of smoked salmon, cream cheese, and red onions appears here in a tidy little roll-up—a presentation that stretches the pricey smoked salmon. Not only are these perfect for social nibbling, any leftovers are great alongside a lunch salad.

**4 ounces good-quality sliced smoked salmon (about 5 or 6 slices)**

**4 ounces cream cheese, softened**

**1/8 medium red onion, finely chopped (about 1/4 cup)**

**Pinch of ground black pepper**

Separate the salmon slices and lay them all on a clean work surface. In a small bowl, using a spoon, stir together the cream cheese, onion, and pepper until blended.

Spoon a scant tablespoon of the cream cheese mixture onto each salmon slice, placing it toward the short ends of the salmon slices. Using your fingers, roll each portion of cheese into a log shape, then roll each salmon slice around the cheese "log."

Using a sharp knife dipped in hot water and wiped with a clean cloth, cut each salmon roll into 3 or 4 pieces, for a total of 16 pieces. (You'll need to dip the knife in the water often in order to make really clean slices.) To serve, arrange the roll-ups on a serving platter, or cover them with plastic wrap and refrigerate until serving time.

Each 2-piece serving contains approximately:
CAL: 68 PRO: 4g NET CARB: 1g FAT: 6g CHOL: 19mg SOD: 153mg

SERVES 8

# PORK RINDS
## WITH HOT SAUCE

As you may know, pork rinds are a favorite snack food for many low-carbers who crave a crunch. However, not everyone is an automatic fan just because they're low-carb. This recipe (actually more of a recommendation) is from a chef friend of Kim's, James Luster, who told Kim about it in an effort to alleviate her fear of pork rinds. If red Tabasco is too strong for your taste, try the green variety—it's less spicy.

**9** **pork rinds**

**1** **tablespoon Tabasco sauce**

Place the pork rinds into a bowl and drizzle with the Tabasco. That's it; they're ready! Enjoy with a glass of water and plenty of napkins.

Each serving contains approximately:
CAL: 51 PRO: 6g NET CARB: 0g FAT: 3g CHOL: 9mg SOD: 258mg

SERVES 1

# ENTERTAINING ALMONDS

Slightly spicy, with an unexpected twist of lemon, these almonds are a great match for classic martinis or an interesting complement to a cheese plate. Their flavor is improved by a day of aging, so prepare them the day before your company is expected, and cross one thing off your "to do" list.

2 cups raw whole almonds

**SPICED OIL**

2 tablespoons olive oil

1/4 teaspoon cayenne pepper

1/4 teaspoon paprika

Pinch of ground black pepper

1 teaspoon kosher salt

1 1/2 teaspoons lemon zest
(see page 33)

Preheat the oven to 300°F. Spread the almonds on a baking sheet and bake for 15 minutes, until lightly toasted.

**Meanwhile, make the Spiced Oil:** In a medium mixing bowl, using a rubber spatula, stir together the olive oil, cayenne, paprika, and black pepper until combined. When the almonds are done, remove them from the oven, leaving the oven on, and add them to the bowl with the spiced oil; stir, thoroughly coating them with the mixture. Return the almonds to the baking sheet, spread them in a single layer, and bake for an additional 5 minutes.

Return the almonds to the mixing bowl and let cool for 10 minutes, stirring once or twice. Sprinkle the salt over the almonds and stir with the spatula. Let cool completely, then toss with the lemon zest. Store in a covered container until ready to serve.

Each 1/4-cup serving contains approximately:
CAL: 239 PRO: 7g NET CARB: 4g FAT: 20g CHOL: 0mg SOD: 64mg

MAKES 2 CUPS; SERVES 8

# SWEET PECANS

Coated with a crunchy, cinnamon-flavored glaze, these pecans are almost candylike. They were a huge hit when we tried them out on friends, who gobbled them up by the handful. They're also good on top of cottage cheese or low-carb yogurt for breakfast, or sprinkled over a green salad along with some blue cheese. Although they're easy to prepare, be sure to watch them carefully so they don't overcook.

2 cups raw pecan halves

4 tablespoons butter

2 tablespoons Splenda Granular sweetener

1 tablespoon light brown sugar

1½ teaspoons ground cinnamon

Preheat the oven to 300°F. Place the pecans in a medium mixing bowl and set aside.

In a small saucepan over low heat, combine the butter, Splenda, brown sugar, and cinnamon. Cook and stir for about 2 minutes, until the butter is melted and the mixture is blended. Remove from the heat and pour the butter mixture over the pecans. Stir the pecans with a rubber spatula until they're well coated with the seasoned butter.

Transfer the pecans to a baking sheet and use the spatula to spread them into an even layer. Bake the pecans for 18 minutes, or until lightly browned. Let cool completely on the baking sheet.

When cool, use a metal spatula to scrape the pecans off the baking sheet. Store in a covered container or zip-top plastic bag for up to 10 days.

Each 1/4-cup serving contains approximately:
CAL: 236 PRO: 2g NET CARB: 5g FAT: 24g CHOL: 16mg SOD: 60mg

MAKES 2 CUPS; SERVES 8

# MAPLE WALNUTS

For some people, walnuts taste quite bitter, but their texture and nutritional benefits shouldn't be missed. So, we created this recipe for walnuts that features a great maple coating to remove any underlying bitterness. We love to eat these as a snack out of hand, but they also make a sweet addition to a homemade trail mix.

$1/4$ cup Splenda Granular sweetener

2 tablespoons butter, melted

2 tablespoons maple extract

1 tablespoon maple syrup

$1/8$ teaspoon vanilla extract

2 cups raw walnut halves

Preheat the oven to 300°F. In a medium mixing bowl, using a rubber spatula, mix together all of the ingredients except for the walnuts. Add the nuts to the bowl and mix until they are well coated with the maple mixture.

Transfer the nuts to a baking sheet and use the spatula to spread them into an even layer. Bake for 15 minutes, or until lightly toasted. Let cool completely on the baking sheet.

When cool, use a metal spatula to scrape the walnuts off the baking sheet. Store in a covered container or zip-top plastic bag for up to 10 days.

Each 1/4-cup serving contains approximately:
CAL: 193 PRO: 4g NET CARB: 5g FAT: 18g CHOL: 8mg SOD: 32mg

MAKES 2 CUPS; SERVES 8

# DIJON-AND-DILL SHRIMP SALAD BOATS

This elegant appetizer is a pleasant change from the usual shrimp cocktail, and its presentation is not only beautiful, it's convenient for party noshing (no utensils required!). The shrimp salad also makes a tasty sandwich filling or salad topping. Be sure to start the recipe early in the day or even a day ahead of time in order to let the shrimp salad flavors mingle.

Pinch of salt

1 pound raw small shrimp (36 to 45 per pound), peeled and deveined

**DRESSING**

2 tablespoons mayonnaise

2 tablespoons sour cream

1 tablespoon finely chopped fresh dill

2 teaspoons Dijon mustard

1/4 teaspoon kosher salt

1/4 teaspoon ground black pepper

8 leaves Belgian endive, washed and air-dried

In a large saucepan over high heat, stir together 2 quarts of water and the salt until the salt dissolves. Bring to a boil. Add the shrimp and reduce the heat to medium. Cook the shrimp just until they turn pink and curl, about 3 minutes. Drain the shrimp and let cool. Finely chop the shrimp and set aside.

**To make the dressing:** In a medium mixing bowl, whisk together all the dressing ingredients until well blended.

Add the chopped shrimp to the dressing and stir with a wooden spoon to thoroughly coat the shrimp. Refrigerate the salad at least 6 hours or preferably overnight.

To serve, spoon 2 tablespoons of the salad on each endive leaf. Arrange on a platter and serve cold.

Note

Precooked salad shrimp could be used in this recipe, but the chopped medium shrimp have a better presentation, and shrimp you cook yourself at home have much better flavor.

Each serving (1 piece) contains approximately:
CAL: 91 PRO: 12g NET CARB: 0.5g FAT: 4g CHOL: 114mg SOD: 197mg

SERVES 8

# HALLOUMI WITH GRAPE TOMATOES

Halloumi cheese, a Greek product, can be found in most cheese stores and natural-food stores. You may have had this in a Greek restaurant before. The cheese is amazing because it doesn't lose its shape when heated, and it browns beautifully in a skillet. This is one of Kim's favorite "easy but impressive" recipes.

2 tablespoons olive oil

One 8-ounce package Halloumi cheese, cut into 8 equal slices

1 pint grape tomatoes, halved

1/4 teaspoon kosher salt

Pinch of ground black pepper

2 teaspoons fresh lemon juice

4 small, fresh mint sprigs for garnish (optional)

In a large skillet or sauté pan over medium heat, warm the olive oil. When hot, add the Halloumi (it may splatter a bit) and cook for about 3 minutes, or until browned on the bottom. Using tongs, flip the cheese slices and slide them to one side of the pan.

Add the tomato halves to the empty side of the pan; sprinkle with the salt and pepper and cook, stirring, for 3 minutes, or until they soften. Check the Halloumi to see if it's browned on the second side. When the cheese is nicely browned on both sides and the tomatoes are soft and heated through, remove from the heat. Add the lemon juice to the tomatoes, stirring to combine.

Transfer 2 cheese slices to each of 4 plates. Spoon the tomatoes over and alongside the cheese. Garnish each plate with a mint sprig, if desired.

Each 2-piece serving contains approximately:
CAL: 250 PRO: 13g NET CARB: 2g FAT: 21g CHOL: 43mg SOD: 659mg

SERVES 4

# STUFFED CUBANELLE PEPPERS

Cubanelle peppers are bright green, beautiful peppers that contain very little "heat." In this recipe they work perfectly as a vessel for chopped ham and Cheddar. If you want a spicier appetizer, feel free to substitute poblano peppers for the cubanelles, but be sure to wear gloves when seeding and cutting them.

Cooking spray

One 8-ounce package cream cheese, softened

2 cups (8 ounces) shredded Cheddar cheese

6 thin slices (about 5 ounces) boiled ham, chopped

1/2 teaspoon Tabasco sauce

6 cubanelle peppers, cut in half lengthwise, seeds and membranes removed

3/4 cup Low-Carb Buttered Bread Crumbs (page 294)

Preheat the oven to 375°F. Coat a baking sheet with cooking spray; set aside.

In a medium mixing bowl, using an electric mixer on medium speed, beat the cream cheese with the Cheddar. Add the ham and Tabasco and mix until well blended.

Using a small spoon, stuff the cheese mixture into the pepper halves; transfer the stuffed peppers to the prepared baking sheet. Sprinkle each pepper half with about 1 tablespoon of the bread crumbs.

Bake for 30 to 35 minutes, until soft. Let cool for 10 minutes. Using a sharp knife, cut each pepper into 4 pieces and serve immediately.

Each 2-piece serving contains approximately:
CAL: 102 PRO: 5g NET CARB: 2g FAT: 8g CHOL: 26mg SOD: 200mg

SERVES 24

# JEN'S BACON AND CREAM CHEESE-STUFFED MUSHROOMS

The basics of this recipe—mushrooms, cream cheese, and bacon—came to us from Kitty's neighbor, Jennifer Benevides, who likes these appetizers for parties because of their simplicity and rich taste. We augmented the recipe only slightly with a little scallion and some pepper. These are best made with regular white button mushrooms and not larger "stuffing" mushrooms, because the filling is so decadent that a little goes a long way.

Cooking spray

One 10-ounce package button mushrooms, washed, stems removed

4 ounces cream cheese, softened

5 slices bacon, cooked crisp and finely chopped (about 1/2 cup)

1 scallion, finely chopped

1/8 teaspoon ground black pepper

Preheat the oven to 375°F. Coat a 9-by-9-inch baking pan with cooking spray and set aside. Place the mushroom caps, hollow side up, in the baking pan.

In a small bowl, combine the cream cheese, bacon, and scallion; mash together with a spoon until well mixed. Using a teaspoon, divide the filling between the mushroom caps, mounding it slightly in the center of each cap. Sprinkle the caps with the pepper.

Bake for 20 minutes, or until the mushrooms are cooked and the filling has melted; serve immediately.

Each serving contains approximately:
CAL: 106 PRO: 4g NET CARB: 1.5g FAT: 9g CHOL: 25mg SOD: 142mg

SERVES 6

# MUSSELS WITH LEMON AND PARSLEY

Even though she's from Maine, where cultured (and wild) mussels are abundant, Kim didn't fall in love with mussels until she vacationed in Normandy and Belgium. Now mussels are frequently served at Chez Mayone! Cooking the mussels in wine and garlic is a simple, classic treatment that infuses the mussels with extra flavor. Please note that mussels contain more carbs than most other types of seafood, so we suggest serving them as an appetizer.

3 tablespoons butter

6 cloves garlic, minced (about 1 tablespoon)

1 fresh lemon, cut into quarters, divided

1/4 teaspoon kosher salt

1/4 teaspoon ground black pepper

1/4 cup dry white wine

2 pounds mussels, beards removed, rinsed well

2 tablespoons finely chopped flat-leaf parsley

In a stockpot large enough to hold the mussels, melt the butter over medium-high heat. Add the garlic, 2 quarters of the lemon, the salt, and pepper; cook, stirring frequently, for 1 to 2 minutes, or until the garlic is fragrant.

Add the wine and raise the heat to high. Bring to a simmer, then add the mussels and parsley, stirring to coat the mussels with the wine mixture. Cover and cook until the mussels open, about 3 to 6 minutes.

Serve the mussels right out of the pot, or transfer them to individual bowls using tongs or a slotted spoon, discarding any mussels that failed to open. Cut the remaining 2 lemon quarters into thirds and use for garnish. Serve the mussels with plenty of napkins and a bowl to hold the empty shells.

Each serving contains approximately:
CAL: 318 PRO: 36g NET CARB: 12g FAT: 13g CHOL: 100mg SOD: 637mg

SERVES 6

# MUSSELS WITH TOMATOES AND CREAM

This recipe strays from the classic lemon and white wine combination, and the result is decidedly Italian in flavor.

- 1 tablespoon olive oil
- 4 cloves garlic, minced (about 2 teaspoons)
- 1/4 teaspoon ground black pepper
- 1/8 teaspoon kosher salt
- 1/2 teaspoon crushed red pepper flakes (optional)
- 1 cup canned crushed tomatoes
- 1/4 cup heavy cream
- 1 tablespoon red wine
- 2 pounds mussels, beards removed, rinsed well
- 1 tablespoon finely chopped fresh basil leaves

In a stockpot large enough to hold the mussels, warm the olive oil over medium-high heat. Add the garlic, pepper, salt, and red pepper flakes, if using. Cook for 1 to 2 minutes, or until the garlic is fragrant.

Stir in the tomatoes, cream, and wine, then raise the heat to high. Bring the mixture to a simmer, then add the mussels and basil, stirring to coat the mussels with the tomato mixture. Cover and cook until the mussels open, about 3 to 6 minutes.

Serve the mussels right out of the pot, or transfer them to individual bowls using tongs or a large ladle, discarding any mussels that failed to open. Serve the mussels with plenty of napkins and a bowl to hold the empty shells.

### Note

Although this recipe doesn't contain much basil, it really does add essential flavor to the dish. (You can use some of the extra basil leaves as a garnish, too.) Do not substitute dried basil; the flavor won't be correct.

Each serving contains approximately:
CAL: 304 PRO: 37g NET CARB: 13g FAT: 11g CHOL: 92mg SOD: 591mg

SERVES 6

# AUNT NANCY'S BUFFALO WINGS

Kim was able to convince her aunt, Nancy Schultz, to give away her "secret" Buffalo wing recipe. Apparently, Aunt Nancy got the recipe from a friend in the Rochester, New York, area, who claims it's the "original" recipe. Even if it's not, we think it's one of the best! There's a bit of prep work and basting involved, but these wings are definitely worth it.

**SPICE MIX**

1/2 cup Atkins Bake Mix

2 tablespoons garlic powder

1 tablespoon onion powder

1 tablespoon poultry seasoning

1 teaspoon cayenne pepper

1/2 teaspoon kosher salt

Cooking spray

2 1/2 pounds fresh "party" chicken wings (also called drumettes)

**BASTING SAUCE**

2/3 cup Tabasco sauce

1/4 cup butter

Blue cheese or ranch dressing for garnish (optional)

Celery stalks for garnish (optional)

Preheat the oven to 375°F.

To make the spice mix: In a large mixing bowl, stir together all the ingredients until blended.

Coat a large baking sheet with cooking spray; set aside. Working with 6 wings at a time, toss the wings in the spice mix until well coated. Shake the excess off the wings and place them on the prepared baking sheet, skin side down. Repeat with the remaining wings and spice mixture, then discard any excess spice mixture. (The wings can be placed tightly together on the baking sheet, as they shrink during cooking.) Bake for 45 minutes.

Meanwhile, make the basting sauce: In a small saucepan over medium-low heat, combine the Tabasco and butter. Stir until melted and blended. Remove from the heat and set the sauce aside until the wings have baked for 45 minutes.

Remove the wings from the oven and, using a pastry brush, baste them with the sauce. Using tongs or a spatula, flip the wings over and baste them again. Return to the oven to bake an additional 20 minutes, or until the wings are sizzling and the skin is crispy.

Place the wings on a platter and drizzle any remaining sauce over them if extra saucy wings are desired; otherwise discard the remaining sauce. Serve with dressing for dipping and celery stalks, if desired.

Each serving contains approximately:
CAL: 546 PRO: 41g NET CARB: 5g FAT: 41g CHOL: 164mg SOD: 476mg

SERVES 6

# ASIAN WINGS

Kim's daughter, Sophia, is one of the fussiest eaters on the planet, yet after tasting these wings, she asked, "Can I have these for supper every night?" Even if you're not a picky eater, we think you'll enjoy the slightly sweet, salty, and garlicky flavor of these wings. Note that the wings need to marinate at least 6 hours, or preferably overnight.

## MARINADE

- 3 tablespoons soy sauce
- 3 tablespoons Splenda Granular sweetener
- 2 tablespoons hoisin sauce
- 2 tablespoons low-carb ketchup
- 12 cloves garlic, minced (about 2 tablespoons)
- 1 tablespoon vegetable oil
- 2 teaspoons rice vinegar

2 1/2 pounds fresh "party" chicken wings (also called drumettes)

Cooking spray

**To make the marinade:** In a medium mixing bowl, whisk together all the ingredients until blended.

Place the chicken wings in a gallon-sized, zip-top plastic bag; pour the marinade over the wings. Seal the bag and refrigerate the wings for at least 6 hours, or preferably overnight.

Preheat the oven to 375°F. Coat a large baking sheet with cooking spray; set aside.

Remove the wings from the refrigerator; drain and discard the excess marinade. Place the wings on the prepared baking sheet, skin side down. (The wings can be placed tightly together on the baking sheet, as they shrink during cooking.) Bake for 45 minutes. Remove from the oven and, using tongs or a spatula, flip the wings over, then return them to the oven to bake for an additional 20 minutes, or until the skin is nicely browned.

Each serving contains approximately:
CAL: 465 PRO: 35g NET CARB: 4g FAT: 35g CHOL: 143mg SOD: 800mg

SERVES 6

# CHAPTER

# 3

## SALADS AND DRESSINGS

## CHANCES ARE, SINCE YOU'VE BEEN LOW-CARBING, YOU'VE BEEN EATING MORE SALAD THAN YOU EVER HAVE IN YOUR LIFE.

Good for you; keep it up! Having a great salad to accompany your low-carb entrée is an easy way to incorporate more vegetables into your diet, as well as adding welcome texture and flavor to your meals. All our salads are paired with appropriate homemade dressing recipes (salad recipe analyses include the amount of dressing called for), and we're sure you'll find more ways to utilize the dressings.

Whether you opt for an easy favorite such as Classic Iceberg Lettuce Wedges with Blue Cheese Dressing, a festive appetizer salad such as the Baby Spinach Salad with Cranberries, Chèvre, and Hazelnuts, or a quick and refreshing chopped salad like our Veggie Slaw, this chapter's got the variety of salads you'll need to complement any low-carb meal. We've even got a few entrée salads, such as Mom's All-in-One Salad or the Italian Sandwich Salad—both of which feature meat, cheese, and vegetables for a one-dish approach to low-carb eating.

Feel free to experiment with abandon when it comes to salads and dressing. Your diet can always use more variety—and more vegetables. Plus, it's hard to really ruin a salad! The key to enjoying lots of salads in your eating plan is making them taste super-delicious with plenty of seasoning and bold flavors, and to incorporate lots of variety—don't make the same salad all the time; mix it up a bit!

# ASPARAGUS AND AVOCADO SALAD

Kim was served a salad similar to this at a catered business luncheon in California. Ever since, it's been one of her favorite salads. For parties or large gatherings, simply serve it in a big salad bowl instead of on individual plates.

1 bunch (about $3/4$ pound) asparagus, ends trimmed, cut into $1\frac{1}{2}$-inch pieces

6 ounces mixed salad greens

1 ripe Haas avocado, peeled, pitted, and chopped

$1/4$ medium red onion, thinly sliced, cut into 1-inch-long pieces (about $1/2$ cup)

1 navel orange, peeled, seeded, and sectioned, each section cut in half crosswise

$1/2$ cup Basic Red Wine Vinaigrette (facing page) or bottled red wine vinaigrette

Kosher salt and ground black pepper (optional)

In a medium saucepan over high heat, bring $1\frac{1}{2}$ inches of water to a boil. Add the asparagus, cover, and cook for 3 to 4 minutes, or until the asparagus is slightly tender (not limp) and bright green. Drain and run under cold water until cooled completely. Drain again and pat dry.

Divide the greens among 4 individual plates. Top each portion with one-fourth of the asparagus, avocado, onion, and orange pieces.

Drizzle each salad with 2 tablespoons of the vinaigrette. If desired, season the salads with the salt and pepper.

Each serving contains approximately:
CAL: 271 PRO: 4g NET CARB: 9g FAT: 24g CHOL: 0mg SOD: 26mg

SERVES 4

# BASIC RED WINE VINAIGRETTE

This mild dressing is a classic vinaigrette that's well suited to mixed green salads. The recipe doubles easily, and keeps well. Customize the recipe to your tastes by adding herbs, minced shallots, or a bit of Dijon mustard.

$1/_3$ cup olive oil (not extra-virgin)

2 tablespoons red wine vinegar

$1/_8$ teaspoon kosher salt

$1/_8$ teaspoon ground black pepper

Combine all the ingredients in a blender and process on medium speed until blended, about 20 to 30 seconds. Use immediately or refrigerate until ready to serve.

Each 2-tablespoon serving contains approximately:
CAL: 143 PRO: 0g NET CARB: 0.5g FAT: 16g CHOL: 0mg SOD: 16mg

MAKES ABOUT $1/_2$ CUP;
SERVES 4

# ENDIVE AND ARUGULA SALAD WITH PEARS, WALNUTS, AND BLUE CHEESE

This sophisticated salad offers an abundance of textures. The slight bitterness of the walnuts and the spiciness of the arugula are offset by the sweet pear and lemony dressing.

1 medium head Belgian endive, outer leaves removed, cored, and cut into 1-inch pieces

2 loosely packed cups (about 2 ounces) arugula

$1/3$ cup walnuts, toasted (see page 33) and coarsely chopped

1 ripe pear, cored and chopped

$3/4$ cup (about 3 ounces) crumbled blue cheese

$1/4$ cup Fresh Lemon and Walnut Oil Vinaigrette (following page), or bottled vinaigrette

Kosher salt and ground black pepper (optional)

In a medium mixing bowl, toss together the endive and arugula. Divide the lettuce mixture among 4 individual salad plates or bowls. Top each portion evenly with the walnuts, pear pieces, and blue cheese.

Drizzle each salad with 1 tablespoon of the vinaigrette. If desired, season the salads with salt and pepper.

Each serving contains approximately:
CAL: 349 PRO: 8g NET CARB: 9g FAT: 32g CHOL: 16mg SOD: 324mg

SERVES 4

# FRESH LEMON AND WALNUT OIL VINAIGRETTE

Available at natural-food stores and well-stocked supermarkets, walnut oil lends a distinctive flavor to this bright dressing. Be sure to refrigerate it after opening, as nut oils are expensive and tend to go rancid more quickly than other oils. This dressing nicely complements the Endive and Arugula Salad with Pears, Walnuts, and Blue Cheese (facing page).

$1/3$ cup walnut oil

1 tablespoon cider vinegar

1 tablespoon fresh lemon juice

$1/4$ teaspoon lemon zest
(see page 33)

$1/8$ teaspoon ground black pepper

$1/8$ teaspoon kosher salt

Combine all the ingredients in a blender and process on medium speed until blended, about 20 to 30 seconds. Use immediately or refrigerate until ready to serve.

Each 2-tablespoon serving contains approximately:
CAL: 146 PRO: 0g NET CARB: 0.5g FAT: 17g CHOL: 0mg SOD: 16mg

MAKES ABOUT $1/2$ CUP; SERVES 4

# APPLE AND ALMOND SALAD WITH POMEGRANATE SEEDS

This colorful salad has a lively, fresh flavor. It's a great starter for a meal of Creamy Carrot-Ginger Soup (page 110) and Maple-Baked Chicken Breasts (page 192).

1 large head Boston (butter) lettuce, cored, torn into bite-sized pieces

1 medium apple, cored and chopped (not peeled)

$1/2$ cup almonds, toasted (see page 33) and coarsely chopped

$1/4$ cup pomegranate seeds

$1/3$ cup Almond and Sherry Vinaigrette (facing page) or bottled vinaigrette

Kosher salt and ground black pepper (optional)

Divide the lettuce among 4 individual salad plates or bowls. Top each portion evenly with the apple pieces, almonds, and pomegranate seeds.

Drizzle each portion with $1/2$ tablespoons of the vinaigrette. If desired, season the salads with salt and pepper.

Each serving contains approximately:
CAL: 245 PRO: 4g NET CARB: 8g FAT: 22g CHOL: 0mg SOD: 18mg

SERVES 4

# ALMOND AND SHERRY VINAIGRETTE

Almond oil combines well with sherry vinegar to create an unusual vinaigrette. This dressing is great with a simple green salad, or with our Apple and Almond Salad with Pomegranate Seeds (facing page).

1/3 cup almond oil

1 tablespoon plus 2 teaspoons sherry vinegar

1/8 teaspoon kosher salt

1 teaspoon minced shallot

Pinch of ground black pepper

Combine all the ingredients in a blender and process on medium speed until blended, 20 to 30 seconds. Use immediately, or refrigerate until ready to serve.

Note

Almond oil is available at natural-food stores and well-stocked supermarkets. Be sure to refrigerate it after opening, as nut oils are expensive and tend to go rancid more quickly than other oils.

Each 2-tablespoon serving contains approximately:
CAL: 147 PRO: 0g NET CARB: 0g FAT: 16g CHOL: 0mg SOD: 17mg

MAKES ABOUT 1/2 CUP;
SERVES 4

# BABY SPINACH SALAD WITH CRANBERRIES, CHÈVRE, AND HAZELNUTS

The cranberries and hazelnuts give this salad an autumn feel, but it would be equally tasty in the winter or spring months.

One 6-ounce bag prewashed baby spinach

$3/4$ cup hazelnuts, toasted (see page 33) and coarsely chopped

One 4-ounce log chèvre (goat cheese), crumbled

$1/3$ cup sweetened dried cranberries

$1/2$ cup Hazelnut Vinaigrette (facing page) or bottled vinaigrette

Kosher salt and ground black pepper (optional)

Divide the spinach among 4 individual salad plates or bowls. Sprinkle each salad evenly with the hazelnuts, chèvre, and cranberries.

Drizzle each salad with 2 tablespoons of the vinaigrette. If desired, season the salads with salt and pepper.

Each serving contains approximately:
CAL: 427 PRO: 10g NET CARB: 11g FAT: 39g CHOL: 13mg SOD: 149mg

SERVES 4

# HAZELNUT VINAIGRETTE

The combination of hazelnuts and orange juice creates a sweet, tangy salad dressing. This vinaigrette is particularly good when paired with the Baby Spinach Salad with Cranberries, Chèvre, and Hazelnuts (facing page).

1/4 cup hazelnut oil

3 tablespoons vegetable oil

3 tablespoons fresh orange juice

2 tablespoons cider vinegar

1 tablespoon hazelnuts, toasted (see page 33) and chopped

1/4 teaspoon orange zest (see page 33)

1/8 teaspoon kosher salt

1/8 teaspoon ground black pepper

Combine all the ingredients in a blender and process on medium speed until blended, 20 to 30 seconds. Use immediately or refrigerate until ready to serve.

Note

Hazelnut oil is available at natural-food stores and well-stocked supermarkets. Be sure to refrigerate it after opening, as nut oils are expensive and tend to go rancid more quickly than other oils.

Each 2-tablespoon serving contains approximately:
CAL: 152 PRO: 0g NET CARB: 1g FAT: 17g CHOL: 0mg SOD: 11mg

MAKES ABOUT 3/4 CUP;
SERVES 6

# CLASSIC ICEBERG LETTUCE WEDGES WITH BLUE CHEESE DRESSING

In this age of fancy lettuces, iceberg can still hold its own, especially when paired with Blue Cheese Dressing (facing page). This salad is a great starter for a BBQ or steak dinner, and is super-easy for entertaining.

1 head iceberg lettuce, outer leaves removed, cored

1 pint grape tomatoes

1/2 medium red onion, thinly sliced and cut into 1-inch long pieces (about 3/4 cup)

1 cup Blue Cheese Dressing (facing page)

5 slices bacon, cooked crisp and chopped (about 1/2 cup) for garnish (optional)

Kosher salt and ground black pepper (optional)

Using a long, sharp knife, cut the lettuce into eight wedges; place each wedge on an individual salad plate. Sprinkle the tomatoes and onion pieces over the lettuce wedges.

Top each salad with 2 tablespoons of the dressing. Sprinkle each portion with a tablespoon of the bacon pieces, if using, and season with salt and pepper, if desired.

Each serving contains approximately:
CAL: 116 PRO: 4g NET CARB: 5g FAT: 9g CHOL: 11mg SOD: 187mg

SERVES 8

# BLUE CHEESE DRESSING

Blue cheese dressing is one of our all-time faves. Serve it over salad, as a dip for Aunt Nancy's Buffalo Wings (page 78) or with Crispy Chicken Strips (page 200). For best flavor, bring the dressing to room temperature before serving.

$^3/_4$ cup low-fat plain yogurt

$^1/_2$ cup mayonnaise

$^1/_4$ teaspoon kosher salt

$^1/_4$ teaspoon black pepper

1 cup (about 4 ounces) crumbled blue cheese

In a small mixing bowl, using a wooden spoon, mix together the yogurt, mayonnaise, salt, and pepper until smooth. Add the cheese and stir gently to mix. Refrigerate overnight so the flavors can mingle.

Each 2-tablespoon serving contains approximately:
CAL: 94 PRO: 3g NET CARB: 1g FAT: 9g CHOL: 12mg SOD: 176mg

MAKES ABOUT 1$^3/_4$ CUPS;
SERVES 14

# VEGGIE SLAW

A bag of broccoli "slaw" is handy to have on hand at all times. In this dish it's combined with a beautiful mixture of sweet peppers and a zingy dressing; it can also be used in a quick stir-fry, added to a soup, or just sprinkled on top of a tossed salad for extra crunch and nutrition. Kitty's kids love it no matter how it's fixed, which has earned it a "most favored vegetable" award at her house.

One 16-ounce bag broccoli "slaw" mix

1 medium (about 8 ounces) red bell pepper, seeded, thinly sliced, and cut into 1-inch pieces

1 medium (about 8 ounces) yellow bell pepper, seeded, thinly sliced, and cut into 1-inch pieces

$1/4$ medium red onion, grated or very finely chopped (about $1/2$ cup)

$3/4$ cup Dijon Vinaigrette (facing page) or bottled vinaigrette

In a medium bowl, combine the slaw mix with the peppers and onion; toss to combine. Just before serving, pour the vinaigrette over the slaw and toss until the slaw is well coated with dressing. Serve immediately.

Each serving contains approximately:
CAL: 152 PRO: 1g NET CARB: 6.5g FAT: 13g CHOL: 0mg SOD: 151mg

SERVES 8

# DIJON VINAIGRETTE

This classic dressing adds a little zing to any salad, and it's perfect with our Veggie Slaw (facing page).

1/2 cup extra-virgin olive oil

1/4 cup balsamic vinegar

1/4 cup Dijon mustard

1/4 cup canola oil

4 cloves garlic, minced (about 2 teaspoons)

1/4 teaspoon kosher salt

1/4 teaspoon paprika

1/8 teaspoon ground black pepper

Combine all ingredients in a blender and process on medium speed until blended, about 20 to 30 seconds. Use immediately or refrigerate until ready to serve.

Each 2-tablespoon serving contains approximately:
CAL: 162 PRO: 0g NET CARB: 3g FAT: 17g CHOL: 0mg SOD: 165mg

MAKES ABOUT 1 1/4 CUPS;
SERVES 10

# JICAMA SALAD WITH PUMPKIN SEEDS

Jicama, a crisp-textured Mexican root vegetable, is readily available at most supermarkets. Here, the delicate flavor of the jicama is complemented by our Lime Vinaigrette (facing page) and roasted pumpkin seeds. Together these ingredients make for an eye-catching salad.

1 jicama (12 to 14 ounces), peeled, thinly sliced, and cut into 1/4-inch wide strips

1/2 medium green bell pepper, chopped

1/2 medium red bell pepper, chopped

1/4 medium red onion, thinly sliced and cut into 1-inch pieces (about 1/2 cup)

1/2 cup chopped baby carrots

1/2 cup Lime Vinaigrette (facing page)

1/3 cup roasted pumpkin seeds (spicy or regular)

2 tablespoons finely chopped fresh cilantro (optional)

Kosher salt and ground black pepper (optional)

Divide the jicama among 6 individual salad plates. Sprinkle the green and red pepper pieces, onion, and carrots evenly over each portion.

Drizzle the vinaigrette over the salads and sprinkle with the roasted pumpkin seeds. If desired, sprinkle the salads with the cilantro and season with salt and pepper.

Note

After much trial and error, we've found that using a sharp paring knife to peel the jicama yields the best results.

Each serving contains approximately:
CAL: 143 PRO: 1g NET CARB: 5g FAT: 12g CHOL: 0mg SOD: 34mg

SERVES 6

# LIME VINAIGRETTE

Perfect for a Mexican-inspired meal, this dressing works wonderfully on a simple salad of lettuce, avocado, tomatoes, and chopped almonds. It's also quite tasty drizzled over grilled chicken.

$1/3$ cup vegetable oil

2 tablespoons lime juice

1 teaspoon white vinegar

$1/2$ teaspoon lime zest (see page 33)

$1/4$ teaspoon Tabasco sauce

Pinch of garlic powder

Pinch of kosher salt

Pinch of ground black pepper

Combine all the ingredients in a blender and process on medium speed until blended, about 20 to 30 seconds. Use immediately or refrigerate until ready to serve.

Each 2-tablespoon serving contains approximately:
CAL: 146 PRO: 0g NET CARB: 1g FAT: 16g CHOL: 0mg SOD: 14mg

MAKES ABOUT $1/2$ CUP; SERVES 4

# FENNEL AND RED ONION SALAD

Chef Paul Charpentier, a colleague of Kim's at Southern Maine Community College, developed this recipe and was kind enough to let us "borrow" it. We're both new fans of fennel in salad, and think you'll agree that this combination is simple, sophisticated, and utterly delicious. Note that the salad needs to mingle with the dressing for at least four hours before serving.

2 large fennel bulbs (about 20 ounces), ends and brown spots trimmed

1 medium red onion, halved and thinly sliced (about 1$\frac{1}{4}$ cups)

## DRESSING

$\frac{1}{4}$ cup vegetable oil

2 tablespoons rice vinegar

1 tablespoon olive oil

$\frac{3}{4}$ teaspoon kosher salt

$\frac{1}{4}$ teaspoon ground black pepper

Cut the fennel bulbs into $\frac{1}{4}$-inch-thick slices. In a medium mixing bowl, toss the fennel and onion slices together; set aside.

To make the dressing: Combine all the dressing ingredients in a blender and process on medium speed until blended, about 20 to 30 seconds.

Pour the dressing over the fennel and onion mixture; tossing to coat the vegetables with the dressing. Refrigerate the salad for at least 4 hours, or preferably overnight, before serving.

Each serving contains approximately:
CAL: 132 PRO: 1g NET CARB: 4g FAT: 12g CHOL: 0mg SOD: 101mg

SERVES 6

# COLESLAW
## WITH A TWIST
A touch of fresh lemon really brightens up traditional slaw. For convenience, we've used preshredded cabbage.

**DRESSING**

1/4 cup mayonnaise

1/4 cup Splenda Granular sweetener

2 tablespoons white vinegar

1 1/2 teaspoons fresh lemon juice

1 teaspoon lemon zest
(see page 33)

1/4 teaspoon celery salt

1/4 teaspoon Tabasco sauce

Pinch of ground black pepper


One 8-ounce bag shredded
"coleslaw mix" cabbage

**To make the dressing:** Stir together all the dressing ingredients in a small bowl; refrigerate for at least 4 hours.

Combine the cabbage and dressing in a medium mixing bowl and mix well. Serve immediately or refrigerate until ready to serve.

Each serving contains approximately:
CAL: 115 PRO: 1g NET CARB: 3g FAT: 11g CHOL: 8mg SOD: 165mg

SERVES 4

# MOM's ALL-IN-ONE SALAD

This is a version of an entrée salad that Kitty's mother, Shirlee Broihier, used to feed the family on summer nights when it was just too hot to cook. Her mom always likes to say that this salad has "everything you need in a meal," which is true (although we've eliminated the macaroni that used to be in Mom's version). This makes a nice lunch or light dinner, and is also good for toting along to potluck dinners.

One 15 $1/2$-ounce can dark red kidney beans, rinsed and drained

6 ounces ham steak or leftover cooked ham, cut into $1/4$-inch dice (about 1 cup)

$3/4$ cup frozen petite peas (no need to thaw)

6 ounces Colby-Jack cheese, cut into $1/4$-inch dice (about $3/4$ cup)

$2/3$ cup low-carb mayonnaise-type dressing

$1/4$ medium red onion, finely chopped (about $1/2$ cup)

2 stalks celery, chopped

2 hard-boiled eggs, chopped

1 tablespoon pickle relish

$1/4$ teaspoon Tabasco sauce

6 cups shredded iceberg lettuce

In a large mixing bowl, using a wooden spoon, stir together all ingredients except for the lettuce. Refrigerate the salad mixture for at least 2 hours.

To serve, divide the lettuce among 6 individual plates or bowls, then top with 1 cup of the salad mixture.

Each serving contains approximately:
CAL: 344 PRO: 21g NET CARB: 10g FAT: 21g CHOL: 124mg SOD: 867mg

SERVES 6

# TUNA AND EGG MACARONI SALAD

Kim's aunt, Donna Unger, is always asked to bring her macaroni salad to cookouts. We've taken her basic recipe and modified it by using low-carb pasta. This is an excellent salad to serve with BBQ, or as a main dish when served over a bed of greens.

**DRESSING**

- 3/4 cup mayonnaise
- 2 stalks celery, finely chopped
- 1/8 medium red onion, finely chopped (about 1/4 cup)
- 2 tablespoons prepared brown mustard
- 2 tablespoons cider vinegar
- 3/4 teaspoon kosher salt
- 1/4 teaspoon ground black pepper
- 1/4 teaspoon Tabasco sauce

- 1 1/2 cups low-carb elbow macaroni, cooked according to package directions and drained
- 3 hard-boiled eggs, chopped
- Two 6-ounce cans water-packed tuna, drained and flaked
- 1/2 teaspoon paprika for garnish (optional)

**To make the dressing:** In a medium mixing bowl, stir together all the ingredients until combined.

Add the cooked macaroni and chopped eggs to the bowl with the dressing. Using a wooden spoon, mix to coat with the dressing. Add the tuna and stir to combine.

Cover and refrigerate the salad for at least 4 hours, or as long as overnight, before serving. Garnish with the paprika, if desired.

Each side dish serving contains approximately:
CAL: 306 PRO: 22g NET CARB: 5g FAT: 21g CHOL: 103mg SOD: 493mg

SERVES 8 AS A SIDE DISH;
4 AS A MAIN DISH

# ROASTED RED PEPPER AND FRESH MOZZARELLA SALAD

The simplicity of fresh mozzarella is complemented by the big flavors of Kalamata olives and roasted red peppers. Fresh thyme and a balsamic vinaigrette complete the dish.

## DRESSING

$1/4$ **cup olive oil**

2 **tablespoons extra-virgin olive oil**

1 **tablespoon red wine vinegar**

1 **tablespoon balsamic vinegar**

$1/2$ **teaspoon ground black pepper**

$1/4$ **teaspoon kosher salt**

$1/4$ **teaspoon anchovy paste**

$1/8$ **teaspoon crushed red pepper flakes**

1 $1/2$ **cups prepared roasted red peppers, drained, and patted dry**

$3/4$ **pound tiny fresh mozzarella balls (*bocconcini*), cut in half (about 2 cups)**

1 $1/2$ **cups Kalamata olives, pitted and cut in half lengthwise**

$1/4$ **medium red onion, thinly sliced and cut into 1-inch pieces (about $1/2$ cup)**

2 **tablespoons capers, drained and minced**

2 **tablespoons minced fresh thyme**

To make the dressing: Combine all the dressing ingredients in a blender and process on medium speed until blended, 20 to 30 seconds; set aside.

Cut the peppers into strips $1/4$ inch wide and 1 inch long. In a medium mixing bowl, using a wooden spoon, mix together the roasted peppers, mozzarella, olives, onions, capers, and thyme. Arrange the salad mixture on a platter or divide among individual plates, and drizzle with the reserved dressing. Serve at room temperature.

Each serving contains approximately:
CAL: 436 PRO: 13g NET CARB: 8g FAT: 37g CHOL: 41mg SOD: 1,059mg

SERVES 6

# ITALIAN
## SANDWICH SALAD

Visitors to Maine sometimes wonder why signs along the road proclaim: "Loaded Italians Inside!" To a Mainer, an "Italian" is a sandwich containing sliced green peppers, sweet onions, black olives, pickles, tomatoes, salami, and cheese. Here we've turned those ingredients into a tasty salad that delivers all the flavor of the sandwich, but without the carb-heavy roll.

¼ pound sliced provolone cheese, chopped

¼ pound sliced salami, chopped

1 medium (about 8 ounces) green bell pepper, seeded and chopped

½ medium Vidalia or other sweet onion, chopped (about ¾ cup)

¾ cup hamburger chip pickles, drained and chopped

One 2¼-ounce can sliced black olives, drained

1 cup grape tomatoes, halved

3 tablespoons olive oil

2 teaspoons red wine vinegar

½ teaspoon kosher salt

¼ teaspoon ground black pepper

In a large mixing bowl, combine all the ingredients and toss well. That's it!

Each serving contains approximately:
CAL: 229 PRO: 10g NET CARB: 4g FAT: 19g CHOL: 28mg SOD: 934mg

SERVES 6

# MUFFULETTA SALAD

This salad is inspired by the famous sandwich of New Orleans, which is stuffed with salami, cheese, and a relish-like olive salad. Of course, we've eliminated the bread to create a salad version, but otherwise we've stuck to the classic ingredients. If desired, serve the salad over some simple greens for a little crunch and contrast to this flavorful mixture. To ease some of the prep, ask the deli to slice the meats thickly (about $1/4$-inch slices) for neater chopping.

| | |
|---|---|
| $1/2$ | pound fresh mozzarella cheese, patted dry, cut into bite-sized pieces |
| $1/4$ | pound smoked ham, roughly chopped |
| $1/4$ | pound Genoa salami, roughly chopped |
| One | 12-ounce jar roasted red peppers, drained, patted dry, and cut into strips $1/4$ inch thick and 1 inch long |
| 2 | stalks celery, finely chopped |
| 1 | cup sliced, pimiento-stuffed olives, drained |
| One | $2 1/4$-ounce can sliced black olives, drained |
| $1/2$ | small Vidalia or other sweet onion, cut into $1/4$-inch slices (about $1/2$ cup) |
| $1/4$ | cup finely minced flat-leaf parsley |
| 3 | cloves garlic, minced (about $1 1/2$ teaspoons) |
| $1/2$ to $3/4$ | teaspoon crushed red pepper flakes (optional) |
| $1/4$ | teaspoon ground black pepper |
| 3 | tablespoons olive oil |
| 1 | tablespoon extra-virgin olive oil |

In a medium bowl, using a wooden spoon, stir together all ingredients except the olive oils. Pour both the olive oils over the salad mixture and stir gently to coat all the ingredients with the oil.

Refrigerate for at least 6 hours. Remove from the refrigerator about 15 minutes before serving to bring the salad to room temperature.

**Each serving contains approximately:**
CAL: 447 PRO: 20g NET CARB: 9g FAT: 35g CHOL: 69mg SOD: 1,560mg

SERVES 5

# MINTED YOGURT DRESSING

**Perfect for Greek-inspired menus, a spoonful of this refreshing dressing over chopped cucumbers and tomatoes couldn't be simpler or more delicious.**

1 cup whole-milk plain yogurt

2 tablespoons olive oil

2 tablespoons finely chopped fresh mint

1 tablespoon honey

2 teaspoons minced dried onion

$1/4$ teaspoon dried oregano

$1/2$ clove garlic, minced (about $1/4$ teaspoon)

$1/8$ teaspoon kosher salt

$1/8$ teaspoon ground black pepper

In a small mixing bowl, using a wooden spoon, mix together all the ingredients until well blended. Refrigerate the dressing overnight so the flavors can mingle.

Each 2-tablespoon serving contains approximately:
CAL: 48 PRO: 1g NET CARB: 3g FAT: 4g CHOL: 3mg SOD: 18mg

MAKES ABOUT $1^{1}/_{4}$ CUPS;
SERVES 10

# CRÈME FRAÎCHE DRESSING

Kim calls this dressing "fancy ranch," but you needn't reserve it just for special occasions. It's equally at home served alongside veggies, as a simple sauce for grilled chicken, or spooned over a crunchy summer salad.

$2/3$ cup Crème Fraîche (page 310)

3 tablespoons minced fresh chives

3 tablespoons minced flat-leaf parsley

2 tablespoons cider vinegar

$1/8$ teaspoon kosher salt

$1/8$ teaspoon ground black pepper

In a small mixing bowl, using a wooden spoon, mix together all the ingredients until well blended. Use immediately, or refrigerate until ready to serve.

Each 2-tablespoon serving contains approximately:
CAL: 56 PRO: 1g NET CARB: 1g FAT: 2g CHOL: 18mg SOD: 9mg

MAKES ABOUT 1 CUP; SERVES 8

# 4

CHAPTER

SOUPS, STEWS, AND CHILIS

ONE-POT WONDERS—SOUPS, STEWS, AND CHILIS—ARE ESSENTIAL IN ANY BUSY COOK'S REPERTOIRE. HAPPILY, THESE FAVORITES ARE ALSO RELATIVELY EASY TO MAKE LOW-CARB.

Leftovers like cooked poultry or ham form the basis for many of the soups in this chapter, such as the Turkey-Cabbage Soup and Easy Ham Soup, making them ideal recipes to cook up after holidays. When cooking meat in a simple fashion—roast turkey, broiled beef, or sautéed chicken—it pays to think "double duty" by cooking a little extra and saving it for soup, stew, or chili for later in the week.

Although most of us associate soups with cool weather, a good bowl of soup can make a satisfying meal on its own, for lunch or dinner, any season of the year. In the springtime, when leeks are widely available, try the Cheesy Broccoli-Leek Soup; in the summer, utilize some of your garden's bounty in the Vegetable and Bean Soup. The fall and winter months may induce you to prepare heartier stews and chilis, such as our Beef, Mushroom, and Swiss Chard Stew or Weeknight Pork and Black Soybean Chili.

# BEER AND CHEESE SOUP

This creamy, cheesy soup is accented with beer and dotted with carrots and celery. It's delicious and filling; serve with just a green salad.

2 cups light cream

1 tablespoon all-purpose flour

2 tablespoons butter

1/2 cup finely chopped baby carrots

1/2 medium onion, finely chopped (about 1/2 cup)

1/4 teaspoon kosher salt

1/8 teaspoon ground black pepper

1/4 teaspoon paprika

One 14 1/2-ounce can chicken broth

1 cup low-carb beer

1/4 teaspoon Tabasco sauce

3/4 cup (3 ounces) shredded Monterey Jack cheese

3/4 cup (3 ounces) shredded Cheddar cheese

In a 1-cup liquid measuring cup, or a small bowl, whisk together the cream and flour; set aside.

In a stockpot over medium heat, melt the butter. Add the carrots, onion, salt, pepper, and paprika. Cook, stirring, for about 8 minutes, or until the vegetables are softened. Add the cream mixture, bring to a simmer, and cook, stirring constantly, until the mixture thickens, about 5 minutes.

Reduce the heat to medium-low and add the broth, beer, and Tabasco. Bring to a simmer and cook for 10 minutes more, stirring occasionally. Remove from the heat and stir in the cheeses until melted. Ladle into bowls and serve.

Each serving contains approximately:
CAL: 506 PRO: 15g NET CARB: 10g FAT: 44g CHOL: 139mg SOD: 841mg

SERVES 4

# CHEESY BROCCOLI-LEEK SOUP

**This soup is for everyone who likes their broccoli with cheese . . . the bacon doesn't hurt, either.**

- 2 tablespoons butter
- 1 medium leek, white and light green parts, thoroughly cleaned and chopped (about 1 cup)
- One 16-ounce bag frozen cut broccoli, thawed
- One 14 1/2-ounce can chicken broth
- 3/4 cup water
- 1/4 teaspoon ground black pepper
- 1 1/4 cups light cream
- 3 slices bacon, cooked crisp and chopped, divided (about 1/3 cup)
- 1 cup (4 ounces) shredded Cheddar cheese

In a large saucepan over medium heat, melt the butter. Add the leek and cook, stirring, for 3 minutes, or until the leeks are soft. Stir in the broccoli, broth, water and pepper. Bring to a simmer and cook for 5 minutes, or until the broccoli is tender. Remove from the heat.

Using an immersion blender, blend the mixture until smooth but still thick. Alternatively, transfer the hot mixture to a blender in batches and purée until smooth—keep the top vent open to let out the steam.

Add the cream and 1/4 cup of the bacon pieces to the soup. Return to medium heat and continue to cook until heated through, stirring occasionally. Remove from the heat and stir in the cheese until melted.

Ladle the soup into bowls, garnish each portion with the remaining bacon, and serve immediately.

**Each serving contains approximately:**
CAL: 402 PRO: 15g NET CARB: 9g FAT: 34g CHOL: 102mg SOD: 807mg

SERVES 4

# CREAMY CARROT-GINGER SOUP

Yes, you can have carrots on a low-carb diet! They do contain carbohydrates, but you needn't shun them; just use them smartly, as we've done here. This recipe delivers 12 appetizer-sized servings—think cups, not bowls.

1 tablespoon butter

1 tablespoon vegetable oil

2 medium onions, chopped (about 2 cups)

2 tablespoons peeled and minced fresh ginger

1/2 teaspoon kosher salt

1/4 teaspoon ground black pepper

2 pounds baby carrots

7 cups chicken broth, divided

1 teaspoon soy sauce

1 tablespoon honey

1 tablespoon Splenda Granular sweetener

3/4 cup light cream

Chopped fresh chives for garnish (optional)

In a stockpot over medium heat, melt the butter with the oil. Add the onions, ginger, salt, and pepper; cook for about 5 minutes, or until the onions soften. Add the carrots and cook for another 5 minutes, then stir in 4 cups of the broth and bring the mixture to a simmer.

Cover and simmer, stirring occasionally, for 20 to 25 minutes, or until the carrots are soft. Stir in the soy sauce, honey, and Splenda.

Remove from the heat and let cool for 10 minutes. Using an immersion blender, purée the carrot mixture until smooth. Alternatively, transfer the hot mixture to a blender in batches and process until smooth—keep the top vent open to let out steam.

Return to medium heat and add the remaining 3 cups broth and the cream. Simmer for 5 minutes, ladle into small bowls, and serve, garnished with chopped chives, if desired.

**Each serving contains approximately:**
CAL: 116 PRO: 2g NET CARB: 9g FAT: 8g CHOL: 16mg SOD: 675mg

SERVES 12

# VEGETABLE AND BEAN SOUP

Vegetable soup is one of Kim's all-time favorites—it's delicious, nutritious, and incredibly flexible. In this recipe, we've used our favorite vegetables, but feel free to use what's in season in your area. If you haven't tried canned white soybeans yet, seek them out at your natural-foods store; they give the soup added protein, fiber, and texture.

2 tablespoons olive oil

1/2 medium onion, chopped (about 1/2 cup)

4 cloves garlic, minced (about 2 teaspoons)

1 carrot, peeled and chopped (about 1/2 cup)

One 10-ounce package button mushrooms, washed and sliced

3/4 teaspoon celery salt

1/4 teaspoon ground black pepper

1/2 teaspoon dried thyme

1/2 teaspoon dried oregano

1 medium (about 8 ounces) red bell pepper, seeded and chopped

1 medium zucchini, chopped (about 1 1/3 cups pieces)

1 medium summer squash, chopped (about 1 1/3 cups pieces)

4 cups vegetable broth

2 cups frozen cut green beans, thawed

One 15-ounce can white soybeans, rinsed and drained

1/2 teaspoon Tabasco sauce

Grated Parmesan cheese for garnish (optional)

In a large stockpot over medium heat, warm the olive oil. Add the onion, garlic, carrot, mushrooms, celery salt, pepper, thyme, and oregano. Cook, stirring, for 5 to 8 minutes, or until the onions are soft and the mushrooms have given off some of their liquid.

Add the bell pepper, zucchini, and summer squash and cook, stirring, for 3 to 5 minutes, until the vegetables begin to soften. Add the broth, green beans, and soybeans and bring to a gentle simmer, stirring occasionally. Simmer, uncovered, for 20 minutes. Test the carrot and bell pepper for desired doneness. If they aren't tender enough, cook for an additional 5 to 10 minutes and test again. Stir in the Tabasco, ladle into bowls, and serve immediately, with a sprinkling of Parmesan cheese, if desired.

Each serving contains approximately:
CAL: 140 PRO: 8g NET CARB: 11g FAT: 7g CHOL: 326mg SOD: 601mg

SERVES 8

# LAZY LOBSTER BISQUE

In an ideal world, whenever we desired lobster bisque, we'd make it the old-fashioned way—by simmering lobster shells to make our own stock, and slowly reducing it. Heck, we'd probably even go catch our own lobsters (we do live in Maine)! However, we actually live in the real world, which means we don't have the time or inclination—or a lobster trap—to do that. Hence, this recipe allows us to indulge in a rich lobster bisque while still leaving us time to create a side dish to serve with it (try the Green Beans with Almonds, Onions, and Bacon, page 278). What's the secret? Lobster stock created from a pastelike bouillon called Better Than Bouillon (they also sell chicken, beef, and other bouillon flavors). Check your supermarket or specialty-foods stores for it.

2 **tablespoons sherry**

2 **teaspoons lobster bouillon (such as Better Than Bouillon)**

2 **cups hot water**

1 **tablespoon tomato paste**

1 **teaspoon Splenda Granular sweetener**

3 **tablespoons butter, divided**

1/2 **medium onion, chopped (about 1/2 cup)**

1 **teaspoon kosher salt**

2 **tablespoons whole-wheat pastry flour**

1/4 **cup heavy cream**

1/2 **pound cooked lobster meat, chopped**

In a small pitcher or 1-quart liquid measuring cup, whisk together the sherry, bouillon, hot water, tomato paste, and Splenda until the bouillon and tomato paste are dissolved; set aside.

In a large saucepan over medium heat, melt 1 tablespoon of the butter. Add the onion and salt and cook, stirring, for 5 minutes, or until the onions begin to soften. Add the remaining 2 tablespoons butter to the pan and whisk until melted; whisk in the flour and cook, whisking constantly, for 3 minutes, or until thickened and lightly browned. Slowly pour in about one-fourth of the bouillon mixture, whisking to combine with the butter mixture (it will thicken quickly). Add another one-fourth of the bouillon mixture and whisk again until thick. Slowly pour in the remaining liquid and whisk thoroughly.

Cook the bisque, stirring occasionally, for another 5 to 8 minutes, until slightly thickened. Stir in the cream and lobster meat and cook for 3 minutes more, until heated through. Ladle into bowls and serve.

Each serving contains approximately:
CAL: 211 PRO: 13g NET CARB: 5g FAT: 15g CHOL: 84mg SOD: 1,115mg

SERVES 4

# CHICKEN SOUP WITH TOMATOES AND PENNE

We're big fans of dishes that give new life to leftover chicken. We're also fans of flavorful soups that come together in a hurry, which is how this soup came to be created. Full of vegetables (diced tomatoes, celery, mushrooms, carrots) and filled out with plenty of low-carb penne pasta, this chicken soup tastes anything but typical.

2 tablespoons olive oil

$1/2$ medium onion, chopped (about $1/2$ cup)

4 cloves garlic, minced (about 2 teaspoons)

4 stalks celery, chopped

2 carrots, peeled and chopped (about 1 cup)

One 10-ounce package button mushrooms, washed and quartered

$1/4$ teaspoon kosher salt

$1/4$ teaspoon ground black pepper

One $14 1/2$-ounce can petite diced tomatoes

Three $14 1/2$-ounce cans chicken broth

3 cups cubed cooked chicken meat (see page 32)

$1 1/2$ cups low-carb penne pasta (uncooked)

2 tablespoons finely chopped flat-leaf parsley

$1/4$ cup extra-virgin olive oil (optional)

Grated Parmesan cheese for garnish (optional)

In a stockpot over medium heat, warm the olive oil. Add the onion, garlic, celery, carrots, mushrooms, salt, and pepper. Cook, stirring, for 3 to 5 minutes, or until the onions soften and the mushrooms have given off some of their liquid.

Add the tomatoes and bring the mixture to a simmer, stirring occasionally and scraping up any browned bits from the bottom of the pot. Add the broth and chicken and stir to combine. Return the mixture to a simmer, stirring occasionally.

Stir in the pasta, return the mixture to a simmer again, and cook for 4 to 5 minutes more, or until the pasta is tender. Stir in the parsley; ladle into bowls, and serve, garnished with the extra-virgin olive oil and Parmesan, if desired.

Each serving contains approximately:
CAL: 265 PRO: 28g NET CARB: 8g FAT: 11g CHOL: 49mg SOD: 926mg

SERVES 8

# TURKEY-CABBAGE SOUP

A healthful way to use up leftover turkey from a holiday meal, this soup is easy on the cook. Feel free to substitute leftover chicken if you prefer, or purchase cooked turkey or chicken and start from scratch.

2 tablespoons olive oil

1 large onion, chopped (about 1 1/4 cups)

2 cloves garlic, minced (about 1 teaspoon)

1 carrot, peeled and chopped (about 1/2 cup)

1/2 medium head green cabbage, chopped (about 4 cups)

6 cups chicken broth

3 cups cooked, chopped turkey (see page 32)

1/2 teaspoon caraway seeds, crushed

1/2 teaspoon ground black pepper

Grated Parmesan cheese for garnish (optional)

In a stockpot over medium heat, warm the olive oil. Add the onion and garlic and cook, stirring frequently, about 3 to 5 minutes, or until the onion softens.

Add the carrot and cook for 1 minute more, stirring. Add the cabbage, broth, turkey, caraway seeds, and pepper and bring to a simmer. Cover and cook for 20 minutes, or until the cabbage and carrot are tender.

Ladle into bowls and serve, garnished with the Parmesan, if desired.

---

Each serving contains approximately:
CAL: 236 PRO: 23g NET CARB: 6g FAT: 12g CHOL: 58mg SOD: 1,071mg

SERVES 6

# EASY HAM SOUP

**Full of fresh, flavorful ingredients, this soup is a snap to prepare. Save yourself even more time by preparing it on the weekend, and then serve it during the week when you're pressed for time.**

2 tablespoons olive oil

$1/2$ medium onion, chopped (about $1/2$ cup)

1 carrot, peeled and chopped (about $1/2$ cup)

$1 1/2$ cloves garlic, minced (about $3/4$ teaspoon)

$3/4$ teaspoon dried oregano

$1/2$ teaspoon celery salt

$1/2$ teaspoon ground black pepper

One 10-ounce package button mushrooms, washed and quartered

Three $14 1/2$-ounce cans chicken broth

3 cups (about $1 1/2$ pounds) diced ham

$3/4$ cup prepared roasted red peppers, drained and chopped

1 medium (about 8 ounces) yellow bell pepper, seeded and chopped

One 6-ounce bag baby spinach, coarsely chopped

$1/4$ teaspoon Tabasco sauce

Grated Parmesan cheese for garnish (optional)

In a stockpot over medium heat, warm the olive oil. Add the onion, carrot, garlic, oregano, celery salt, and pepper. Cook, stirring, for 3 to 5 minutes, or until the onions soften. Add the mushrooms and cook for 5 minutes more, or until the mushrooms have given off some of their water.

Add the broth, ham, roasted peppers, bell pepper, spinach, and Tabasco and bring to a simmer. Simmer for 15 to 20 minutes, or until the carrot and bell pepper are tender. Ladle into bowls and serve, garnished with Parmesan, if desired.

Each serving contains approximately:
CAL: 221 PRO: 21g NET CARB: 6g FAT: 12g CHOL: 41mg SOD: 1,922mg

SERVES 6

# ASIAN BEEF NOODLE BOWL

**When you want a change from stir-fry, consider this easy soup. It's beautiful to look at, warming, and flavorful; it's also weeknight friendly.**

4 ounces low-carb spaghetti noodles, cooked according to package directions and drained

2 teaspoons toasted sesame oil

1 pound beef sirloin steak, trimmed of excess fat

$1/4$ teaspoon kosher salt

$1/8$ teaspoon ground black pepper

2 tablespoons vegetable oil, divided

3 cloves garlic, minced (about $1^1/2$ teaspoons)

3 scallions, chopped (about $1/3$ cup)

2 cups packaged broccoli "slaw" mix

Two 14 $1/2$-ounce cans beef broth

2 cups water

3 tablespoons tamari or soy sauce

2 teaspoons rice-wine vinegar

1 small head bok choy, chopped (about 5 cups)

In a small mixing bowl, toss the cooked noodles with the sesame oil; set aside.

Season the steak on both sides with the salt and pepper. In a stockpot over medium-high heat, warm 1 tablespoon of the oil. Add the steak and cook for about 3 minutes, until the bottom is browned. Using tongs, flip the steak and cook for another 2 minutes, until browned on the second side but not cooked through. The center of the steak will still be quite pink. Transfer the steak to a cutting board to cool.

Reduce the heat to medium and add the remaining 1 tablespoon oil, the garlic, scallions, and broccoli "slaw." Cook, stirring, for about 5 minutes, or until the broccoli slaw is tender. Add the broth, water, tamari, and vinegar. Cook, stirring occasionally, until the soup comes to a boil. While waiting for the soup to boil, cut the beef on the diagonal into $1/4$-inch slices.

When the soup boils, stir in the sliced beef and the bok choy; cook about 2 minutes, until heated through.

To serve, place one-fourth of the cooked noodles in the bottom of each of 4 bowls, then ladle the soup mixture over the noodles.

---

Each serving contains approximately:
CAL: 423 PRO: 48g NET CARB: 9g FAT: 18g CHOL: 81mg SOD: 1,739mg

SERVES 4

# BEEF STEW WITH PEPPERS AND ONIONS

Though it routinely contains potatoes, beef stew is just as tasty (not to mention lower in carbs!) without them. Our version features plenty of colorful bell peppers and a generous amount of onions, all seasoned with a rich, flavorful broth.

2 tablespoons olive oil

2 pounds beef chuck stew meat, trimmed of excess fat

2 medium white onions, thinly sliced (about 2 cups)

1 tablespoon all-purpose flour

2 cloves garlic, minced (about 1 teaspoon)

1 teaspoon dried oregano

1/2 teaspoon ground black pepper

1/2 teaspoon chili powder

1/4 teaspoon celery salt

1/4 teaspoon dry mustard

2 cups beef broth

1 teaspoon Worcestershire sauce

1 teaspoon soy sauce

1 medium (about 8 ounces) red bell pepper, seeded and thinly sliced, cut into 1-inch pieces

1 medium (about 8 ounces) yellow bell pepper, seeded and thinly sliced, cut into 1-inch pieces

1 medium (about 8 ounces) green bell pepper, seeded and thinly sliced, cut into 1-inch pieces

Shredded Cheddar cheese for garnish (optional)

Tabasco sauce (optional)

In a stockpot over medium-high heat, warm the olive oil. Add the stew meat, onions, flour, garlic, oregano, pepper, chili powder, celery salt, and mustard. Cook, stirring, for 5 to 7 minutes, or until the beef is lightly browned.

Add the broth, Worcestershire, and soy sauce and stir well. Bring to a simmer, then cover and reduce the heat to low. Cook for 1 hour, stirring occasionally.

Stir in the bell peppers; cover and simmer for about 30 minutes more. Check the peppers to see if they're tender. If not, cook for 5 to 10 minutes more until the peppers are soft. Ladle into bowls and serve, garnished with Cheddar cheese, if using. Pass the Tabasco at the table, if desired.

Each serving contains approximately:
CAL: 394 PRO: 44g NET CARB: 6.5g FAT: 20g CHOL: 134mg SOD: 848mg

SERVES 6

# BEEF, MUSHROOM, AND SWISS CHARD STEW

Chard is actually a beet that's been cultivated so that its leaves and stalks develop instead of the root. Not actually native to Switzerland, Swiss chard is sometimes known simply by the name "leaf beet." In many recipes, you'll see that either the stalks or the leaves of the chard are used—not both together. In this recipe, we use the leaves, which, along with mushrooms, contribute an earthy flavor to this hearty stew.

1 bunch (about 1 1/2 pounds) Swiss chard, washed well

2 tablespoons olive oil

1 1/2 pounds chuck stew meat, trimmed of excess fat

1 medium onion, chopped (about 1 cup)

2 stalks celery, chopped

4 cloves garlic, minced (about 2 teaspoons)

2 slices bacon, cooked crisp and chopped (about 1/4 cup)

1 tablespoon all-purpose flour

1 teaspoon dried thyme

1 teaspoon dried oregano

1/2 teaspoon ground black pepper

1/4 teaspoon kosher salt

One 10-ounce package button mushrooms, washed and quartered

2 cups beef broth

2 tablespoons dry red wine

2 tablespoons tomato paste

2 teaspoons soy sauce

1/2 teaspoon Worcestershire sauce

1 bay leaf

Cut away the stems of the chard and remove any thick stems from the leaves. Chop the leaves into bite-sized pieces and set aside.

In a stockpot over medium-high heat, warm the olive oil. Add the stew meat, onion, celery, garlic, bacon, flour, thyme, oregano, pepper, and salt. Cook, stirring, for 5 to 7 minutes, or until the beef is lightly browned.

Stir in the mushrooms and cook for another 5 minutes, or until the mushrooms have given off some of their liquid. Add the broth, wine, tomato paste, soy sauce, Worcestershire, and bay leaf and stir well. Bring to a simmer, then cover and reduce heat to low. Cook for 1 hour, stirring occasionally.

Stir in the Swiss chard, cover, and cook for 30 minutes more, or until the chard is tender. Discard the bay leaf, ladle into bowls, and serve.

**Each serving contains approximately:**
CAL: 347 PRO: 36g NET CARB: 9g FAT: 17g CHOL: 98mg SOD: 1,094mg

SERVES 6

# VEAL STEW WITH ESCAROLE AND WHITE BEANS

This out-of-the-ordinary stew features tender veal, a rich broth, and plenty of vegetables. Feel free to substitute baby spinach for the escarole. This stew freezes very well.

2 tablespoons olive oil

1 1/2 pounds veal stew meat, trimmed of excess fat

1 medium onion, finely chopped (about 1 cup)

6 cloves garlic, minced

1/4 teaspoon celery salt

1/2 teaspoon ground black pepper

1/2 teaspoon dried thyme

1 teaspoon dried oregano

One 10-ounce package Baby Bella or button mushrooms, washed and sliced

2 tablespoons dry white wine

One 14 1/2-ounce can petite diced tomatoes

1 cup chicken broth

1 cup canned small white beans, rinsed and drained

1 small head escarole, washed well, cored and chopped (about 6 cups)

In a stockpot over medium-high heat, warm the olive oil. Add the stew meat and brown the pieces on all sides, about 6 minutes. Using a slotted spoon, remove the veal from the pot and set it aside on paper towels to drain.

Add the onion, garlic, celery salt, pepper, thyme, oregano, and mushrooms to the pot. Reduce the heat to medium and cook, stirring occasionally, for 5 to 8 minutes, or until the onions are soft and the mushrooms have given off some of their liquid.

Add the wine and bring the mixture to a simmer, stirring occasionally and scraping up any browned bits from the bottom of the pot. When it reaches a simmer, return the veal to the pot along with the tomatoes and broth. Return to a simmer again and stir well.

Reduce the heat to low, cover, and cook for 1 1/2 hours, stirring occasionally. Add the beans and escarole, then mix well and cook, uncovered, for about 30 minutes more, or until the beans are heated through and the escarole is tender. Ladle into bowls and serve.

Each serving contains approximately:
CAL: 316 PRO: 39g NET CARB: 12g FAT: 10g CHOL: 138mg SOD: 453mg

SERVES 6

# CHICKEN CHILI

Prepared with ground chicken, white soybeans, and a healthy dose of spices, this chili is a nice change of pace from the standard beef version.

## SPICE MIX

- 1 tablespoon chili powder
- 1 teaspoon ground cumin
- 1 teaspoon dried oregano
- 3/4 teaspoon ground black pepper
- 1/2 teaspoon celery salt
- 1/4 teaspoon kosher salt
- 1/8 teaspoon crushed red pepper flakes

<br>

- 2 tablespoons vegetable oil
- 1 medium onion, chopped (about 1 cup)
- 6 cloves garlic, minced (about 1 tablespoon)
- 2 pounds ground chicken
- 1 medium (about 8 ounces) green bell pepper, seeded and chopped
- 2 tablespoons tomato paste
- One 14 1/2-ounce can chicken broth
- Two 15-ounce cans white soybeans, rinsed and drained
- 1/2 teaspoon Tabasco sauce

**To make the spice mix:** In a small mixing bowl, stir together the spice mix ingredients.

In a stockpot over medium heat, warm the oil. Add the spice mix, onion, garlic, and chicken. Cook, stirring, for 5 to 8 minutes, or until the chicken is cooked through. Add the bell pepper, tomato paste, and broth and stir to combine.

Bring the mixture to a simmer and cook for 5 to 8 minutes, or until the peppers are tender and the tomato paste is dissolved. Add the soybeans and Tabasco and cook, stirring occasionally, for 10 minutes more. Ladle into bowls and serve.

---

Each serving contains approximately:
CAL: 451 PRO: 50g NET CARB: 12g FAT: 21g CHOL: 111mg SOD: 622mg

SERVES 6

# WEEKNIGHT PORK AND BLACK SOYBEAN CHILI

This recipe, which combines tender pork, black soybeans, and a packet of chili seasoning, can be made in less than 30 minutes, so it's a good option for a weeknight dinner. Any leftovers make a hearty, low-carb lunch.

One 1¼-ounce packet chili seasoning (such as McCormick's)

1 teaspoon dried oregano

¼ teaspoon ground black pepper

¼ teaspoon ground cumin

2 tablespoons vegetable oil

1 medium onion, finely chopped (about 1 cup)

6 cloves garlic, minced (about 1 tablespoon)

2 pounds boneless center-cut pork chops, trimmed of excess fat, cut into 1-inch cubes

One 4-ounce can chopped green chiles

One 14½-ounce can petite diced tomatoes

One 14½-ounce can chicken broth

Two 15-ounce cans black soybeans, rinsed and drained

Shredded Cheddar cheese for garnish (optional)

Sour cream for garnish (optional)

In a small mixing bowl, stir together the chili seasoning, oregano, pepper, and cumin.

In a stockpot over medium heat, warm the oil. Add the spice mixture, onion, garlic, and pork. Cook, stirring, for 3 to 5 minutes, or until the onions soften. Add the chiles and tomatoes and stir, scraping up any browned bits from the bottom of the pot.

Bring the mixture to a simmer, then stir in the broth and soybeans. Return to a simmer, then check the doneness of the pork by cutting into one cube. If not opaque throughout, cook for a few minutes more and test again.

To serve, ladle into bowls and garnish with Cheddar cheese and sour cream, if desired.

### Note

Black soybeans are perfect for low-carb cooking because of their low-carb, high-protein nutritional profile. They're a good stand-in for black beans in any favorite recipe, too.

Each serving contains approximately:
CAL: 476 PRO: 52g NET CARB: 10g FAT: 22g CHOL: 110mg SOD: 885mg

SERVES 6

# TEXAS CHILI

Traditional Texas chili is prepared without tomatoes or beans, which is perfect for low-carb dining. Our version is spicy, but by no means is it "five alarm." If you want it spicier, increase the amount of red pepper flakes, or pass hot sauce at the table. Some Texans like to garnish their chili with sour cream and a lime wedge, which tends to mellow the chili's flavor. Either way you like it, try serving it with a simple green salad and our Southwestern Corn Bread (page 273).

## SPICE MIX

- 1/4 cup mild chili powder
- 1 teaspoon dried oregano
- 1/2 teaspoon celery salt
- 1/2 teaspoon ground cumin
- 1/2 teaspoon ground black pepper
- 1/2 teaspoon crushed red pepper flakes

- 2 pounds beef chuck stew meat, trimmed of excess fat
- 2 tablespoons all-purpose flour
- 2 tablespoons vegetable oil
- 1 medium onion, finely chopped
- One 4-ounce can chopped green chiles
- 2 strips bacon, cooked crisp and chopped
- 1/2 teaspoon Worcestershire sauce
- 8 cloves garlic, minced
- 1 1/2 cups beef broth

To make the spice mix: In a small mixing bowl, stir together all the ingredients; set aside.

Pat the beef dry with paper towels. In a gallon-sized, zip-top plastic bag, combine the beef and flour and shake until coated; discard any excess flour.

In a stockpot over medium heat, warm the vegetable oil. Add the beef and the onions, and cook, stirring frequently, for 5 minutes, or until the beef browns slightly and the onions soften. Add the spice mix, chiles, bacon, Worcestershire, and garlic and stir the mixture well. Stir in the beef broth, scraping up any browned bits from the bottom of the pot; mix well to combine all ingredients.

Bring to a simmer, then reduce the heat to low and cover the pot. Cook for 1 1/2 hours, stirring occasionally. Ladle into bowls and serve.

Each serving contains approximately:
CAL: 554 PRO: 58g NET CARB: 10g FAT: 29g CHOL: 175mg SOD: 1,175mg

SERVES 4

# 5

# SANDWICHES, WRAPS, AND SALAD TOPPERS

WHILE WE HAVE NOTHING AGAINST LETTUCE LEAVES, USING THEM IN PLACE OF BREAD HAS ONLY LIMITED APPEAL TO US. WE'RE THRILLED WITH THE INTRODUCTION OF A VARIETY OF LOW-CARB BREADS AND ROLLS—A GOOD SANDWICH IS NO LONGER JUST A FOND MEMORY!

This chapter features sandwich fillings such as Lemon Chicken Salad, Curried Turkey Salad, and Lobster Salad—all of which are great on their own served with greens, or as sandwich filling; you choose. Keeping a bowl of one of these sandwich fillings/salad toppers prepared in your refrigerator is an easy way to ensure that a decent low-carb meal is always within reach. If wrap-type sandwiches are more to your liking, feel free to use low-carb tortillas instead of bread (or instead of lettuce leaves!). However, be careful, label readers, as not all tortillas and other wraps are low in carbs.

# LEMON CHICKEN SALAD

Combining some leftover chicken meat with our Lemon-Caper Crudité Dip (page 64) yields a quick and delicious salad that's perfect atop a bed of greens or sandwiched between two slices of low-carb bread.

2 cups cubed, cooked chicken meat (see page 32)

$2/3$ cup Lemon-Caper Crudité Dip (page 64)

$1/4$ medium (about 8 ounces) red, green, or yellow bell pepper, finely chopped (about $1/4$ cup)

2 scallions, chopped (about $1/4$ cup)

1 stalk celery, finely chopped

$1/8$ teaspoon poultry seasoning

$1/4$ teaspoon celery seed

Combine all the ingredients in a medium mixing bowl and stir well. Refrigerate the salad mixture for at least 4 hours or preferably overnight, so the flavors can mingle. Stir the salad before serving.

Each 1-cup serving contains approximately:
CAL: 352 PRO: 28g NET CARB: 2g FAT: 25g CHOL: 102mg SOD: 261mg

SERVES 3

# CURRIED TURKEY SALAD

Looking for something different to do with post-holiday turkey leftovers? Try this salad, which is packed with texture and flavor from slivered almonds, scallions, raisins, and a creamy curry dressing. If you'd rather use cooked chicken instead of turkey, that's fine, too.

2 cups chopped, cooked turkey meat (see page 32)

4 scallions, chopped (about 1/2 cup)

1/3 cup slivered almonds

3 tablespoons mayonnaise

3 tablespoons nonfat plain yogurt

2 tablespoons loosely packed raisins

3/4 teaspoon curry powder

1/4 teaspoon kosher salt

1/4 teaspoon Tabasco sauce

1/8 teaspoon ground black pepper

Using a fork, combine all the ingredients in a medium mixing bowl and stir well. Refrigerate the salad mixture for at least 4 hours or preferably overnight, so the flavors can mingle. Stir the salad before serving.

Each 1-cup serving contains approximately:
CAL: 376 PRO: 32g NET CARB: 8g FAT: 24g CHOL: 80mg SOD: 201mg

SERVES 3

# CLASSIC
# TUNA SALAD

When it comes to classic tuna salad, we've found there are two camps: the Miracle Whip camp and the mayonnaise camp. Kitty prefers to use the low-carb "whipped salad dressings" that are currently on the market, which taste more like Miracle Whip to her. If you'd rather use plain old mayo, feel free. Also, we've called for less expensive chunk light tuna in water as opposed to albacore or solid white tuna, since the tuna basically gets mashed with the other ingredients anyway; but again, feel free to use whichever tuna you like best. This recipe yields enough to top a couple of salads or make two big, full sandwiches or four smaller "lettuce wraps."

Two 6-ounce cans chunk light tuna in water, drained

1 stalk celery, finely chopped

1/4 medium onion, finely chopped (about 1/4 cup)

2 tablespoons pickle relish

2 tablespoons low-carb mayonnaise-type dressing

2 teaspoons fresh lemon juice

1/4 teaspoon celery seed

1/4 teaspoon kosher salt

1/8 teaspoon ground black pepper

Using a fork, in a small mixing bowl, combine all the ingredients until well mixed. Use immediately, or cover and refrigerate until ready to serve.

Each serving contains approximately:
CAL: 220 PRO: 30g NET CARB: 7g FAT: 6g CHOL: 40mg SOD: 688mg

SERVES 2

# TUNA SALAD
## WITH LEMON
## AND OLIVE OIL

When you're living low-carb, canned tuna is an economical, nutritious, and convenient fact of life. In this recipe, we use chunk light tuna packed in olive oil, dress it with a lemony olive oil, and season it with capers, red onion, and pepper. This salad has a fresh, bright taste that's perfect over greens or in a low-carb wrap (it's especially good paired with some roasted red peppers). Although it can be served immediately, the flavors in this salad really pop out with some refrigerator time.

One 6-ounce can chunk light tuna in olive oil

1 tablespoon fresh lemon juice

2 teaspoons minced red onion

2 teaspoons olive oil

1 1/2 teaspoons lemon zest (see page 33)

1/4 teaspoon capers, drained and finely chopped

1/4 teaspoon ground black pepper

1/8 teaspoon kosher salt

Using a fork, in a small mixing bowl, combine all the ingredients until well mixed. Refrigerate at least 4 hours before serving, if possible, so the flavors can mingle.

Each serving contains approximately:
CAL: 213 PRO: 25g NET CARB: 1g FAT: 12g CHOL: 15mg SOD: 348mg

SERVES 2

# LOBSTER SALAD

This is a classic New England preparation for lobster salad. It's a supremely simple treatment, so it really showcases the lobster. Here in Maine, you'll find lobster rolls on practically every restaurant menu during the summer months. Normally they're served on grilled, top-split (aka "New England Style") hot-dog rolls. To make a low-carb version, toast a low-carb hot-dog roll, then spoon in the lobster salad and a little lettuce, if you like.

1½ cups (8 ounces) cooked lobster meat, coarsely chopped

2 tablespoons Hellmann's mayonnaise (see note)

Pinch of kosher salt

Pinch of ground black pepper

Using a fork, in a small mixing bowl, combine all the ingredients until well mixed. Use immediately, or cover and refrigerate until ready to serve.

Note

Hellmann's mayo is the brand traditionally used in classic New England lobster rolls; however, feel free to substitute your favorite brand or any low-carb, mayonnaise-type dressing, if you prefer.

Each serving contains approximately:
CAL: 210 PRO: 23g NET CARB: 2g FAT: 12g CHOL: 90mg SOD: 533mg

SERVES 2

# REUBEN SANDWICH

For Kitty, one of the worst things about going low-carb was giving up Reuben sandwiches. Therefore, when low-carb rye bread hit the supermarket shelves, she was all over it. Kitty prefers her Reubens without the dressing, which can make the low-carb bread a tad soggy. If you like the dressing, by all means use it, and see the altered nutritional information in the note below. Serve with a pickle or Coleslaw with a Twist (page 97).

2 teaspoons butter, softened

2 slices low-carb rye bread

3 thin slices (2 ounces) corned beef

½ cup sauerkraut, lightly rinsed, water squeezed out

One 1-ounce slice Swiss cheese

2 teaspoons bottled Thousand Island dressing (optional)

Warm a medium skillet or sauté pan over medium heat. While waiting for the pan to heat, spread the butter on one side of each bread slice.

Place 1 slice of the bread, butter side down, in the hot skillet. Top the bread with the corned beef, then the sauerkraut (mound it in the middle to keep it from falling off the bread), the cheese, and finally the dressing, if using. Place the second slice of bread on top, butter side up.

Cook for 1 to 2 minutes, until the bottom is golden brown. Using a spatula, flip the sandwich, briefly press down on it lightly with the spatula, and cook for 2 minutes more, or until the second side is browned.

**Note**

Using the dressing changes the approximate nutritional content to:

CAL: 381 PRO: 26g NET CARB: 12g FAT: 24g CHOL: 77mg SOD: 1,670mg

Each serving (without dressing) contains approximately:
CAL: 341 PRO: 26g NET CARB: 10g FAT: 20g CHOL: 75mg SOD: 1,597mg

SERVES 1

# GRILLED BACON, AVOCADO, AND CHEDDAR SANDWICH

This is our grown-up version of a grilled cheese sandwich. It gets extra flavor from the bacon, and the slices of creamy avocado provide a nice contrasting texture. Add a little green salad and you've got a complete meal.

2 teaspoons butter, softened

2 slices low-carb white bread

1/4 ripe avocado, peeled, pitted and thinly sliced

2 slices bacon, cooked crisp and cut in half crosswise

One 1-ounce slice Cheddar cheese

Warm a medium skillet or sauté pan over medium heat. While waiting for the pan to heat, spread the butter on one side of each bread slice.

Place 1 slice of bread, butter side down, in the hot skillet. Top the bread with the avocado slices, then the bacon, and finally the cheese. Place the second slice of bread on top, butter side up.

Cook for about 1 to 2 minutes, until the bottom is golden brown. Using a spatula, flip the sandwich; press down on it lightly with the spatula, and cook for another 1 to 2 minutes, until the second side is browned.

Each serving contains approximately:
CAL: 476 PRO: 26g NET CARB: 8g FAT: 35g CHOL: 61mg SOD: 701mg

SERVES 1

# BUFFALO CHICKEN WRAPS

One can only eat so many Buffalo wings, right? Here's an easy new way to get the same flavors in an easy-to-eat (and less messy) form! These wraps are quick to make and easy to personalize with added ingredients such as thinly sliced onions, shredded Monterey jack cheese, or sliced tomatoes. For a party platter, cut each wrap in half and arrange them on a platter—they won't last long!

SANDWICHES, WRAPS, AND SALAD TOPPERS

2$\frac{1}{2}$ cups cooked chicken breast meat, shredded (see page 32)

$\frac{1}{4}$ cup bottled Buffalo-wing sauce

4 large low-carb tortillas (about 8$\frac{1}{2}$ inches in diameter)

1$\frac{1}{2}$ cups shredded iceberg lettuce

$\frac{1}{4}$ cup Blue Cheese Dressing (page 91) or bottled blue cheese or ranch dressing

In a medium mixing bowl, using a wooden spoon, stir the chicken and Buffalo-wing sauce together; toss well. (This step can be done up to 1 day ahead of time; refrigerate chicken until ready to serve.)

Working with 1 tortilla at a time, place one-fourth of the lettuce in the center of the tortilla, then top with one-fourth of the prepared chicken and top with 1 tablespoon dressing. Fold in the sides of the tortilla, then roll from the bottom up, to make a neat, closed wrap. To make the wraps easier to eat, you may want to wrap each one in aluminum foil or waxed paper.

Each serving contains approximately:
CAL: 429 PRO: 48g NET CARB: 11g FAT: 18g CHOL: 99mg SOD: 1,318mg

SERVES 4

# FRIED
# BOLOGNA
# SANDWICHES

Apparently there's a diner in the Midwest that specializes in fried bologna sandwiches. According to a TV program that Kim watched, people drive for miles to get their hands on these sandwiches. Intrigued (even though she's never been a bologna fan), Kim decided to try out the recipe on her family. It was a huge hit, although the condiments remain a point of debate: Kim favors red onions, pickles, and mustard, but her brother prefers ketchup and horseradish.

$^1/_2$   cup hamburger chip pickles, drained

$^1/_3$   medium red onion, thinly sliced (about $^1/_3$ cup)

$^1/_4$   cup prepared yellow mustard

Cooking spray

One   12-ounce package Hebrew National beef bologna, cut into 8 slices about $^3/_4$ inch thick

4   low-carb burger buns or sandwich rolls

Place the pickles, onion, and mustard into separate small serving bowls; set aside.

Coat a large skillet or sauté pan with cooking spray and place over medium heat. When hot, add the bologna slices and cook for 2 to 3 minutes, until lightly browned on the bottom. Using tongs, flip the bologna and cook for another 2 to 3 minutes, until browned on the second side.

Serve 2 slices of bologna with a sandwich roll, and let each person assemble their own sandwich, passing the pickles, onion, and mustard at the table.

**Note**

Hebrew National beef bologna can be found near the kielbasa and hot dogs at most well-stocked supermarkets.

Each serving contains approximately:
CAL: 432 PRO: 22g NET CARB: 6g FAT: 24g CHOL: 46mg SOD: 1,242mg

SERVES 4

# 6

## FIVE INGREDIENTS
### OR LESS

## THIS IS ONE OF OUR FAVORITE CHAPTERS IN THIS BOOK.

It appeals not only because the ingredient lists and recipes are blessedly brief, but because there's something innately appealing about being able to cook a recipe completely from memory. Many of us can probably remember certain recipes that our mothers or grandmothers used to prepare frequently, without using a recipe. We hope that once you've prepared these dishes a few times, you'll be able to shop for and make these dishes quickly and easily—practically at a moment's notice, if need be.

We designed these 11 recipes to be easy to cook from memory, so they each contain only five or fewer ingredients (not counting common pantry staples such as salt, pepper, garlic, and olive oil). For more ideas and tips on keeping your low-carb cooking simple with a well-stocked pantry, see "Stocking the Low-Carb Kitchen" (pages 28–29).

# POACHED HALIBUT WITH LEEKS

If you've never poached fish before, don't let the technique intimidate you. It's really very easy and quick, and you'll be amazed at how flavorful the fish becomes when cooked this way. This recipe uses just a few ingredients that you're likely to have on hand: leeks, chicken broth, and Parmesan cheese. If you don't have the leeks, substitute a few chopped scallions—you won't need many, since they're stronger in flavor than leeks. This recipe is easily doubled.

2 tablespoons olive oil

1 large leek, white and light green parts thoroughly cleaned and thinly sliced (about $1\frac{1}{2}$ cups)

$\frac{1}{2}$ teaspoon kosher salt

$\frac{1}{4}$ teaspoon ground black pepper

2 cloves garlic, minced (about 1 teaspoon)

2 cups chicken broth

Two 8-ounce halibut fillets, each about 1 inch thick

4 small pimiento-stuffed olives, thinly sliced

2 tablespoons grated Parmesan cheese

In a small, deep skillet over medium heat, warm the olive oil. When hot, add the leeks, salt, and pepper. Cook, stirring constantly, for about 2 minutes, then add the garlic and cook and stir for another 2 minutes, or until the leeks are softened. Add the broth and cook, stirring occasionally, about 5 minutes, until the broth comes to a simmer.

Using a spatula, carefully slide the fish into the hot poaching liquid. (The fish should just be covered with the poaching liquid; if not, add enough hot water to cover the fish.) Reduce the heat to low, cover the skillet, and cook for 10 to 15 minutes, or until the fish is opaque throughout.

Using a slotted spoon or spatula, transfer the fish to individual plates. Scoop out the leeks and arrange them alongside the fish. Sprinkle each portion with the olives and Parmesan and serve immediately.

**Each serving contains approximately:**
CAL: 450 PRO: 41g NET CARB: 9g FAT: 25g CHOL: 75mg SOD: 1,147mg

SERVES 2

# SQUID WITH TOMATOES AND OLIVES

Kitty's family loves squid, and this is one of their favorite ways to prepare it. Some people (including Kitty and her kids!) aren't fans of squid tentacles, so this recipe calls for squid rings only. However, using the tentacles along with the rings certainly won't hurt the dish at all. Leftovers reheat nicely in the microwave for lunch the next day.

2 tablespoons olive oil

1/2 medium onion, chopped (about 1/2 cup)

One 28-ounce can diced tomatoes with basil, garlic, and oregano

1/2 cup pimiento-stuffed green olives, drained and halved

1 1/2 pounds cleaned squid, cut into rings (if frozen, thaw first)

Kosher salt and freshly ground black pepper (optional)

1/4 cup grated Parmesan cheese

In a stockpot over medium heat, warm the olive oil. Add the onion and cook, stirring often, for about 5 minutes, or until soft. Stir in the tomatoes and olives. Bring to a simmer and cook for 5 minutes, stirring occasionally.

Stir in the squid, cover, and cook for 5 minutes, or until the squid is opaque throughout. (Do not overcook or the squid will be tough.) Taste and season with salt and pepper, if desired.

Ladle the mixture into individual bowls, top each serving with Parmesan, and serve.

Each serving contains approximately:
CAL: 381 PRO: 32g NET CARB: 15g FAT: 21g CHOL: 5mg SOD: 2,770mg

SERVES 4

# ITALIAN CHICKEN SKILLET SUPPER

With a few pantry ingredients, a bag of frozen vegetables, and some chicken breasts, you can whip up a one-dish meal that's easy on the cook and family friendly, too. Marinate the chicken early in the day so it will be ready by dinnertime.

1½ pounds skinless, boneless chicken breasts, trimmed of excess fat and cut into 1-inch cubes

2 tablespoons olive oil

1 packet dry Italian dressing mix (such as Kraft Good Seasons)

One 16-ounce bag frozen broccoli, cauliflower, and red pepper mixture or favorite frozen vegetable combination, thawed

½ cup chicken broth

¼ cup grated Parmesan or Romano cheese

In a medium mixing bowl, using clean hands or a wooden spoon, toss the chicken with the olive oil and Italian dressing mix until the chicken is thoroughly coated. Cover the bowl with plastic wrap and refrigerate for at least 4 hours. (Alternatively, combine the chicken, olive oil, and dressing mix in a gallon-sized, zip-top plastic bag, shake to combine, and refrigerate for at least 4 hours.)

Heat a large, dry nonstick skillet or sauté pan over medium-high heat. Add the chicken and cook, stirring often, for 8 minutes, or until the chicken is lightly browned and nearly opaque throughout (test doneness by cutting into one of the cubes). Add the vegetables and broth, reduce the heat to medium, cover the skillet, and cook for about 7 minutes, or until the vegetables are crisp-tender.

Sprinkle the Parmesan over the chicken mixture and serve from the skillet.

Each serving contains approximately:
CAL: 441 PRO: 53g NET CARB: 2g FAT: 22g CHOL: 149mg SOD: 443mg

SERVES 4

# CHICKEN WITH BANANA PEPPERS AND JACK CHEESE

This easy dish uses banana pepper rings, available in the pickle aisle of any well-stocked supermarket (choose hot or mild to suit your taste). If you've never tried them, do branch out—you'll be surprised at how tasty and versatile these zesty peppers are! In this recipe, the peppers mingle with chunks of tender chicken breast and are smothered with melted cheese. The tanginess of the dish can be mellowed with the addition of some sour cream, if you like.

2 tablespoons vegetable oil

1 medium onion, chopped (about 1 cup)

$1/2$ teaspoon chili powder

$1/2$ teaspoon kosher salt

Pinch of ground black pepper

$1^1/2$ pounds skinless, boneless chicken breasts, trimmed of excess fat, cut into 1-inch cubes

$1^1/2$ cups banana pepper rings, drained (mild or hot)

1 cup (4 ounces) shredded Monterey Jack cheese

Sour cream for garnish (optional)

In a large skillet or sauté pan over medium heat, warm the oil. When hot, add the onion, chili powder, salt, and pepper. Cook, stirring, for 3 to 5 minutes, or until the onions are soft.

Add the chicken and cook and stir for another 5 to 8 minutes, or until the chicken is nearly opaque throughout. Stir in the banana pepper rings and cook for 3 minutes more, or until heated through. Sprinkle the cheese over the top and cover the pan for about 1 minute, until the cheese is melted. Serve from the skillet, passing the sour cream at the table, if desired.

Each serving contains approximately:
CAL: 441 PRO: 53g NET CARB: 2g FAT: 22g CHOL: 149mg SOD: 443mg

SERVES 4

# LAZY TURKEY PARMESAN

This kid-friendly dish is just the thing on a busy weeknight—the whole dish is ready in about 10 minutes. The turkey cutlets, topped with garlicky tomatoes, mozzarella, and Parmesan cheese, are a nice change from chicken. However, if you'd rather use chicken, simply purchase thin-cut chicken cutlets, or pound chicken breast halves until they're about 1/4 inch thick.

1 tablespoon olive oil

1 clove garlic, minced (about 1/2 teaspoon)

4 turkey cutlets (about 1 1/4 pounds total weight)

One 14 1/2-ounce can petite diced Italian-seasoned tomatoes, drained

Four 1/4-inch-thick slices part-skim mozzarella cheese (about 4 ounces)

2 tablespoons grated Parmesan cheese

In a large skillet or sauté pan over medium heat, warm the olive oil. When hot, add the garlic and cook, stirring, for 1 minute, until fragrant.

Add the turkey cutlets and cook for 2 minutes, or until lightly browned. Using tongs, flip the cutlets and cook for another 2 minutes, or until browned on the second side. Pour the tomatoes over the turkey, reduce the heat to medium-low, cover, and cook for 5 minutes, or until the turkey is opaque throughout.

Remove the cover and top each cutlet with a slice of mozzarella. Replace the cover and cook for 1 minute longer, or until the mozzarella is melted. Sprinkle the cutlets with the Parmesan and serve hot.

Each serving contains approximately:
CAL: 303 PRO: 44g NET CARB: 5g FAT: 11g CHOL: 115mg SOD: 659mg

SERVES 4

# HAM STEAK WITH APPLE-MUSTARD SAUCE

Nothing could be quicker than a ham steak, so this is an entrée that we both prepare frequently. It's also handy that most kids like ham, so if you're feeding a hungry family, feel free to double the recipe. If you have time, make the sauce in the morning (or even a day ahead of time) and let the flavors mingle in the refrigerator until serving time.

½ cup (4 ounces) unsweetened natural applesauce

2 tablespoons Dijon mustard

One 1-pound, reduced-sodium ham steak, trimmed of excess fat

In a small bowl, stir together the applesauce and mustard; set aside.

Prepare the ham steak according to the package directions (panfry, grill, or microwave according to your preference). Serve with the apple-mustard sauce alongside.

Each serving contains approximately:
CAL: 347 PRO: 29g NET CARB: 13g FAT: 20g CHOL: 101mg SOD: 2,709mg

SERVES 2

# KIELBASA AND GREEN BEANS WITH MUSTARD-CREAM SAUCE

When Kim was in college, one of her friends used to make this recipe, using egg noodles instead of the lower-carb green beans. Like any good college recipe, it's delicious, inexpensive, and easy—and makes great leftovers!

$^1/_2$ cup heavy cream

2 tablespoons prepared brown mustard

$^1/_4$ teaspoon Tabasco sauce

Cooking spray

1 pound "light" kielbasa, sliced on the diagonal into $^1/_2$-inch "coins"

One 16-ounce bag frozen cut green beans

3 tablespoons water

$^1/_8$ teaspoon kosher salt

In a small mixing bowl, stir together the cream, mustard, and Tabasco; set aside.

Coat a large skillet or sauté pan with cooking spray and warm over medium heat. Add the kielbasa and cook for 2 minutes, until browned on the bottom. Using tongs, flip the pieces and cook for 2 minutes more, until browned on the second side. Remove from the heat and cover the pan to keep the kielbasa warm.

In a second large skillet or sauté pan over medium heat, combine the green beans, water, and salt. Cook for 5 minutes, or until the beans are crisp-tender, then stir in the cream mixture and bring to a simmer. Cook, stirring frequently, for 2 to 3 minutes, or until the sauce reduces slightly.

To serve, divide the green-bean mixture among individual bowls, and top each portion with some of the kielbasa slices.

Each serving contains approximately:
CAL: 357 PRO: 21g NET CARB: 8g FAT: 28g CHOL: 110mg SOD: 1,141mg

SERVES 4

# SKILLET KIELBASA AND CABBAGE

This super-easy supper dish provides a generous portion of cabbage and meat—perfect for a busy fall evening. Serve with cold low-carb beer.

Cooking spray

- 1 pound "light" kielbasa, sliced on the diagonal into $1/2$-inch "coins"
- 1 cup water
- $3/4$ cup unsweetened applesauce
- 2 teaspoons Splenda Granular sweetener
- 1 teaspoon caraway seeds, crushed
- $1/2$ teaspoon kosher salt
- $1/4$ teaspoon ground black pepper
- Two 10-ounce bags finely shredded cabbage or cole slaw mix

Coat a large skillet or sauté pan with cooking spray and warm over medium heat. Add the kielbasa and cook for 2 minutes, until browned on the bottom. Using tongs, flip the pieces and cook for 2 minutes more, until browned on the second side. Remove from the heat and transfer the kielbasa pieces to a plate and cover with aluminum foil to keep warm. Reserve the skillet.

In a large mixing bowl, stir together the water, applesauce, Splenda, caraway seeds, salt, and pepper. Add the cabbage and toss gently to combine.

Return the skillet to medium heat. When hot, add the cabbage mixture. Cover and cook for 5 minutes, or until the cabbage is tender. Return the kielbasa to the skillet and stir and cook for 1 minute, or until the kielbasa is heated through.

Each serving contains approximately:
CAL: 280 PRO: 21g NET CARB: 13g FAT: 17g CHOL: 69mg SOD: 1,160mg

SERVES 4

# STOVE-TOP COUNTRY-STYLE PORK RIBS

This recipe yields great barbecue flavor, without the hassle of actually firing up the grill. We call for bone-in ribs, but boneless ribs will work fine, too. Serve with Veggie Slaw (page 92) for a crisp contrast.

3 pounds bone-in, country-style pork ribs, trimmed of excess fat

1 teaspoon garlic powder

1 teaspoon kosher salt

1/2 teaspoon ground black pepper

1 tablespoon vegetable oil

1 large onion, halved and thinly sliced (about 1 1/4 cups)

1/4 cup water

1/2 cup low-carb barbecue sauce (such as Carb Options), divided

Season the ribs on both sides with the garlic powder, salt, and pepper. In a large skillet or sauté pan over medium-high heat, warm the oil. Add the ribs and cook for 4 minutes, or until browned. Using tongs, flip the ribs and cook for another 4 minutes, or until browned on the second side.

Reduce the heat to medium-low, sprinkle the onions over the ribs, and add the water to the skillet. Cover and cook for 15 minutes.

Using tongs, flip the ribs over, then brush them with 1/4 cup of the barbecue sauce. Re-cover and cook for another 15 to 20 minutes, adding 1 or 2 tablespoons water to the skillet if the liquid evaporates, until the pork is just a little pink in the center when cut with a knife.

Transfer the ribs to a platter. Scoop the onions out of the liquid with a slotted spoon and place them on top of the ribs. If you like, you can pour the cooking liquid over the top of the ribs as well. Brush the ribs with the remaining 1/4 cup barbecue sauce and serve.

Each serving contains approximately:
CAL: 477 PRO: 47g NET CARB: 7g FAT: 28g CHOL: 152mg SOD: 553mg

SERVES 4

# HOISIN PORK

Hoisin sauce, a Chinese condiment made from beans, garlic, and chiles, can be found in most supermarkets in the ethnic foods aisle. Here, the slightly sweet flavor of hoisin complements the pork, and the scallions offer a super color and texture contrast as well as brighten up the flavor of the dish. Let the tenderloin warm at room temperature for 15 minutes before beginning the recipe to make cooking quicker. Be sure to trim off the tough, pearly membrane, called the "silver skin," before cutting the tenderloin.

**SAUCE**

$1/4$ cup chicken broth

1 tablespoon hoisin sauce

1 tablespoon soy sauce

1 tablespoon butter

1 tablespoon vegetable oil

One 16-ounce pork tenderloin, silver skin removed, cut into 9 equal slices (1 to $1/2$ inches thick)

2 scallions, green parts only, chopped (about 2 tablespoons)

**To make the sauce:** In a small mixing bowl, whisk together the sauce ingredients until combined; set aside.

In a large skillet or sauté pan over medium heat, melt the butter with the oil. Add the pork slices and cook for 3 to 5 minutes, or until lightly browned on the bottom. Using tongs, flip the pork slices. Add the sauce and bring to a simmer. Using tongs, flip the pork again to coat both sides with the sauce. Cook for another 2 to 3 minutes, until the pork is opaque throughout and the sauce reduces slightly.

Remove from the heat and let the pork rest in the pan for 2 minutes. Transfer the pork slices to a serving platter, stir the sauce and pan drippings together, and pour the mixture over the pork slices. Sprinkle the scallion pieces over the top and serve.

Each serving contains approximately:
CAL: 311 PRO: 39g NET CARB: 4g FAT: 15g CHOL: 115mg SOD: 623mg

SERVES 3

# CHEESEBURGER MACARONI

A favorite among kids and adults (though some of us may hesitate to admit it), this dish is supremely cheesy, and not a soul will know you used low-carb macaroni.

- 1 pound 90% lean ground beef
- 1/2 teaspoon kosher salt
- 1/4 teaspoon ground black pepper
- 1 tablespoon plus 1 teaspoon minced dried onions
- One 8-ounce package Velveeta cheese food, cut into 1/2-inch cubes
- 1/4 cup skim milk
- 1 cup low-carb elbow macaroni, cooked according to package directions and drained
- 1/8 teaspoon Tabasco sauce, or more to taste

In a large skillet or sauté pan over medium heat, combine the ground beef, salt, pepper, and onions and cook, stirring, for 5 to 10 minutes, until the beef is completely cooked through.

Add the Velveeta and stir until melted, about 5 minutes. Stir in the milk to thin the cheese to a saucelike consistency. Stir in the cooked macaroni and Tabasco to taste.

Each serving contains approximately:
CAL: 553 PRO: 51g NET CARB: 11g FAT: 31g CHOL: 132mg SOD: 1,025mg

SERVES 4

# 7

CHAPTER

CASSEROLES:
CLASSIC AND CURRENT

# CASSEROLES HAVE COME A LONG WAY SINCE YOU PERHAPS LAST GAVE THEM ANY THOUGHT.

The old "hot dish" or "one-dish wonder" has had a facelift, so to speak. For one thing, casseroles now often include fresh protein—fish, chicken, sausage, or beef—and pasta, while once the main ingredient, now generally takes a supporting role, if present at all.

Without deviating from the basic casserole principle that makes an easy dinner-in-a-dish appeal to people of all ages, we've created 8 fresh recipes that are bound to change your mind about casseroles. Yes, we still used some convenience foods, otherwise the recipes wouldn't be . . . well, convenient. But we've also used fresh vegetables, interesting seasonings, and updated ingredient combinations.

If Tuesday night's "Tuna Surprise" is something you've been missing since going low-carb, surprise yourself with our Updated Tuna Casserole. Fool your friends into thinking you've slaved over the Easy Lobster Bake. Make "taco night" even easier than it already is with our Layered Taco Pie. Use up leftover cooked poultry with any of the chicken or turkey casseroles we've included—they're so delicious that you might want to cook up the poultry just for the casserole.

# EASY
# LOBSTER BAKE

This is a special way to stretch a little lobster—and if you have guests joining you, they'll be none the wiser, as the dish is so rich. The lobster really shines in this dish, where the delicate butter sauce provides flavor and moisture, but isn't at all heavy. This is a quick dish to prepare, provided you have all the ingredients on hand; you can be eating in 15 minutes flat.

1 **pound cooked lobster meat, coarsely chopped**

3 **tablespoons butter**

2 **cloves garlic, minced (about 1 teaspoon)**

$1/4$ **cup dry white wine**

. $1/4$ **cup heavy cream**

$1/4$ **teaspoon kosher salt**

$1/4$ **teaspoon ground black pepper**

1 **tablespoon Low-Carb Buttered Bread Crumbs (page 294)**

1 **tablespoon grated Parmesan cheese**

Preheat the oven to 400°F. Place the lobster in a 1-quart casserole dish; set aside.

Place the butter and garlic in a microwavable dish and microwave on low power for 1 minute, or until the butter is melted. Pour the butter and garlic mixture over the lobster.

Add the wine, cream, salt, and pepper to the dish and toss all the ingredients gently to combine. Sprinkle the bread crumbs and Parmesan over the top of the casserole.

Bake for 10 minutes, or until heated through. Serve immediately.

Each serving contains approximately:
CAL: 268 PRO: 25g NET CARB: 3g FAT: 16g CHOL: 127mg SOD: 601mg

SERVES 4

# UPDATED TUNA CASSEROLE

If you've never been a fan of tuna casserole before, brush aside your previous impressions and give this one a chance! We've created an upscale mélange of fresh tuna, cream sauce, bacon, and Asiago cheese, combined with colorful veggies and a buttered bread-crumb topping. Fresh tuna can be pricey, but you'll only need 1 pound for this scrumptious dish.

**SAUCE**

- 1 cup heavy cream
- 1 egg yolk
- 1/4 teaspoon kosher salt
- 1/4 teaspoon ground black pepper

Pinch of cayenne pepper

Cooking spray

- 4 tablespoons Low-Carb Buttered Bread Crumbs, divided (page 294)
- 1 small zucchini, ends trimmed, thinly sliced (about 1 1/2 cups)
- 4 tablespoons (1 ounce) shredded Asiago cheese
- 1 pound fresh tuna, cut into 1-inch cubes
- 1/2 medium (about 8 ounces) red bell pepper, chopped (about 1/2 cup)
- 2/3 cup frozen green peas, thawed
- 1 teaspoon minced dried onion
- 3 strips bacon, cooked crisp and crumbled
- 2 scallions, finely chopped (about 1/4 cup)

Preheat the oven to 350°F.

**To make the sauce:** In a medium mixing bowl, whisk together all the sauce ingredients until combined.

Coat a 10-inch pie plate with cooking spray and sprinkle with 1 tablespoon of the bread crumbs. Place the zucchini slices in the pie plate, then sprinkle with another 1 tablespoon bread crumbs and 1 tablespoon of the cheese. Top with the tuna, then the bell pepper, then the peas. Top with another 1 tablespoon cheese, then sprinkle the onion, bacon, and scallions over all.

Pour the sauce over the casserole. Sprinkle the top with the remaining 2 tablespoons bread crumbs and 2 tablespoons cheese. Bake for 35 to 45 minutes, until the zucchini is tender and the tuna is cooked through but not dry. Let rest for 5 to 8 minutes, then serve hot.

Each serving contains approximately:
CAL: 434 PRO: 34g NET CARB: 6g FAT: 30g CHOL: 163mg SOD: 217mg

SERVES 5

# MEXICAN CHICKEN BAKE

Who doesn't love a cheesy casserole? This one, which contains a blend of shredded cheese commonly referred to as "Mexican blend" and Velveeta, makes its own cheese sauce as it cooks—all you need to do is stir it a couple of times. If you like *queso* dip, you'll like this dish. Serve it with a green salad dressed with Lime Vinaigrette (page 95).

Cooking spray

8 ounces Velveeta cheese food, cut into 1/2-inch cubes

One 4-ounce can diced green chiles

5 cups cubed, cooked chicken breast meat (see page 32)

2 tablespoons low-carb whole milk or light cream

3/4 cup bottled salsa

1/2 cup (2 ounces) shredded Mexican-blend cheese

One 2 1/4-ounce can sliced black olives, drained

2 scallions, chopped (about 1/4 cup)

Sour cream for garnish (optional)

Shredded lettuce for garnish (optional)

Low-carb tortilla chips for garnish (optional)

Preheat the oven to 350°F. Coat a 2-quart casserole dish with cooking spray; set aside.

In a large mixing bowl, using a wooden spoon, stir together the Velveeta, chiles, chicken, and milk. Transfer the mixture to the prepared casserole dish.

Bake for 30 minutes, then stir well with a clean spoon. Top the casserole with spoonfuls of the salsa and sprinkle with the shredded cheese, olives, and scallions. Bake for another 5 to 10 minutes, or until the sauce is bubbling. Let rest for 5 minutes before serving. Serve with sour cream, lettuce, and tortilla chips, if desired.

Each serving contains approximately:
CAL: 370 PRO: 45g NET CARB: 7g FAT: 17g CHOL: 132mg SOD: 1,122mg

SERVES 6

# EASY CHICKEN AND GREEN BEAN BAKE

This recipe is a play on the classic green bean casserole that many people grew up having at holiday meals. It's still a family favorite, and we've added chicken to make it more substantial. If you're tired of green beans, this dish is equally good with broccoli. It's a great make-ahead entrée; mix it up and keep it refrigerated until you're ready to bake it.

Cooking spray

- 4 cups cubed, cooked chicken breast meat (see page 32)
- One 16-ounce bag frozen cut green beans, thawed
- One 10$\frac{1}{2}$-ounce can condensed cream of mushroom soup
- $\frac{1}{3}$ cup low-carb whole milk
- 2 tablespoons light cream
- 2 tablespoons minced dried onions
- $\frac{1}{2}$ teaspoon kosher salt
- $\frac{1}{2}$ teaspoon Tabasco sauce
- $\frac{1}{4}$ teaspoon ground black pepper
- $\frac{1}{2}$ cup French's French Fried Onions

Preheat the oven to 350°F. Coat a 2-quart casserole dish with cooking spray; set aside.

In a large mixing bowl, using a wooden spoon, stir together all the ingredients except for the fried onions, until well combined. Transfer the mixture to the prepared dish.

Bake for 30 minutes. Stir well and sprinkle the top of the casserole with the fried onions. Return to the oven and bake for 5 to 10 minutes more, or until bubbling. Let rest for 5 minutes before serving.

---

Each serving contains approximately:
CAL: 330 PRO: 39g NET CARB: 10g FAT: 13g CHOL: 106mg SOD: 627mg

SERVES 5

# GREEK CHICKEN
## CASSEROLE
This beautiful layered casserole is one of our favorites. It requires some precooking, but if you like, you can prepare it ahead of time, keep it refrigerated, and bake it later. This casserole adapts easily for entertaining; just double the ingredients and use a 13-by-9-inch baking dish.

Cooking spray

**SPINACH LAYER**

One 10-ounce package frozen, chopped spinach, thawed, water squeezed out

1/2 cup (2 ounces) crumbled feta cheese

1 egg

1 tablespoon minced dried onion

1/4 teaspoon ground black pepper

**CHICKEN MIXTURE**

1 tablespoon olive oil

1 1/2 pounds skinless, boneless chicken breasts, trimmed of excess fat, cut into 1-inch cubes

6 cloves garlic, minced (about 1 tablespoon)

1 1/2 teaspoons dried oregano

**TOPPING**

1/2 cup canned crushed tomatoes

1/2 cup (2 ounces) crumbled feta cheese

One 2 1/4-ounce can sliced black olives, drained

Preheat the oven to 325°F. Coat a 9-by-9-inch baking dish with cooking spray; set aside.

To make the spinach layer: In a medium mixing bowl, stir together the spinach layer ingredients until combined. Spread the mixture loosely in the prepared baking dish (it won't completely cover the bottom of the dish).

To make the chicken mixture: In a large skillet or sauté pan over medium heat, warm the olive oil. Add the chicken, garlic and oregano. Cook, stirring, for 5 minutes, or until the outside of the chicken is cooked—the chicken pieces will not be completely cooked through. Spoon the chicken mixture over the spinach layer.

To make the topping: Spoon the tomatoes over the chicken mixture (it will not completely cover the chicken), then sprinkle on the feta and top with the olives.

Bake for 30 minutes, or until the chicken is opaque throughout. If not done, cook for 5 minutes more, then recheck. Let rest for 5 minutes before serving.

Each serving contains approximately:
CAL: 345 PRO: 39g NET CARB: 9g FAT: 16g CHOL: 157mg SOD: 741mg

SERVES 4

# TURKEY AND CAULIFLOWER GRATIN WITH TOASTED HAZELNUTS

This dish takes a little more effort to prepare than most of our recipes, but it's a complete meal. Once it goes into the oven, all you have to do is set the table and have a glass of wine while you wait!

2 teaspoons butter, softened

1 head cauliflower, cut into florets (about 5$\frac{1}{2}$ cups)

1 teaspoon kosher salt

2 cups Basic White Sauce (page 306)

$\frac{1}{2}$ cup light cream

$\frac{1}{2}$ cup (2 ounces) shredded Swiss cheese, divided

$\frac{1}{2}$ teaspoon minced dried onion

$\frac{1}{4}$ teaspoon ground black pepper

$\frac{1}{8}$ teaspoon mild chili powder

2$\frac{3}{4}$ cups chopped, cooked turkey meat (see page 32)

$\frac{1}{4}$ cup Low-Carb Buttered Bread Crumbs (page 294)

$\frac{1}{3}$ cup hazelnuts, toasted (see page 33) and finely chopped

Preheat the oven to 375°F. Grease a 13-by-9-inch casserole dish with the butter; set aside.

Combine the cauliflower and salt in a large saucepan and fill with water to cover. Bring the mixture to a simmer over high heat and cook for 8 minutes, or until the cauliflower is tender. Drain and set aside.

In a small saucepan over medium heat, whisk together the Basic White Sauce with the cream, $\frac{1}{4}$ cup of the Swiss cheese, the dried onion, pepper, and chili powder. Bring to a simmer, then remove from the heat.

In a large mixing bowl, using a wooden spoon, stir together the cauliflower and turkey. Transfer the turkey mixture to the prepared casserole, spreading to cover the bottom of the dish. Pour the sauce mixture over the turkey and cauliflower. Sprinkle the top with the remaining $\frac{1}{4}$ cup Swiss cheese, the bread crumbs, and the hazelnuts.

Bake for 30 to 35 minutes, or until bubbly. Let rest for 5 minutes before serving.

Each serving contains approximately:
CAL: 409 PRO: 31g NET CARB: 9.5g FAT: 27g CHOL: 112mg SOD: 543mg

SERVES 6

# SAUSAGE, MOZZARELLA, AND PASTA BAKE

This is a low-carb version of a classic baked pasta dish, featuring slices of sweet Italian sausage, chunks of stewed tomatoes, a creamy tomato sauce, and a generous amount of cheese. It's a great potluck dish—one that will discreetly ensure at least one low-carb offering!

**SAUCE**

Two 14 1/2-ounce cans Italian-style stewed tomatoes, drained

3/4 cup prepared low-carb pasta sauce (such as Carb Options)

3/4 cup heavy cream

1 teaspoon dried oregano

1 teaspoon minced dried onion

2 cloves garlic, minced (about 1 teaspoon)

1/4 teaspoon ground black pepper

Cooking spray

2 pounds sweet Italian sausage links, parboiled (see page 31)

2 1/4 cups low-carb *mezze* penne or penne pasta, cooked according to package directions and drained

One pound part-skim mozzarella cheese, cut into 1/2-inch cubes

2 tablespoons Low-Carb Buttered Bread Crumbs (page 294)

1/4 cup grated Parmesan cheese

Preheat the oven to 350°F.

**To make the sauce:** In a medium mixing bowl, using a wooden spoon, stir together all the sauce ingredients until blended; set aside.

Coat an 11-by-15-inch lasagna pan with cooking spray. Cut each parboiled sausage link into 6 chunks and add the sausage to the lasagna pan, along with the pasta and cheese cubes. Mix well with a wooden spoon. Pour the sauce over the mixture and stir to coat all ingredients with the sauce. Sprinkle the bread crumbs and Parmesan over the top.

Bake for 30 minutes, or until bubbling. Let rest for 10 minutes before serving.

Each serving contains approximately:
CAL: 659 PRO: 46g NET CARB: 10g FAT: 48g CHOL: 135mg SOD: 1,749mg

SERVES 8

# LAYERED
# TACO PIE

This easy recipe boasts all the taco flavors you love—you won't even miss the taco shells! The spicy beef "crust" is put together like a meatloaf, pressed into a pie plate and baked, then topped with crunchy lettuce, shredded cheese, and ripe tomatoes. Feel free to alter the toppings to suit your taste (sliced black olives, chopped scallions, and sour cream are nice additions).

Cooking spray

1 1/2 pounds lean ground beef

1 egg

One 1 1/4-ounce packet taco seasoning (such as Ortega)

1 tablespoon minced dried onions

1/2 cup bottled salsa, at room temperature

3 cups shredded lettuce

One 8-ounce bag shredded Mexican-blend cheese or Cheddar cheese, at room temperature

1 small tomato, cored and chopped (about 1/2 cup)

Preheat the oven to 350°F. Coat a 9- or 10-inch pie plate with cooking spray; set aside.

In a large mixing bowl, using clean hands or a wooden spoon, mix together the beef, egg, taco seasoning, and dried onions until combined. Press the mixture into the bottom and up the sides of the prepared pie plate, forming an even layer. Bake about 20 minutes, or until the beef is cooked through. Remove from the oven and pour off any fat.

Working quickly, top the beef "crust" with the salsa, spreading it with a rubber spatula or spoon. Top with the lettuce, spreading it almost to the edge, then mound the cheese in the middle and spread it slightly. Lastly place the chopped tomatoes in the center. Cut the pie into wedges and serve immediately.

Each serving contains approximately:
CAL: 454 PRO: 36g NET CARB: 7.5g FAT: 30g CHOL: 164mg SOD: 939mg

SERVES 6

CHAPTER

# 8

## VEGETARIAN ENTRÉES

## SOMETIMES VEGETARIANS FEEL LEFT OUT OF THE LOW-CARB HOOPLA, BUT IT NEEDN'T BE SO AT ALL.

In developing this book, we found that many recipes in which we originally intended to include meat were actually better without it! The Stuffed Bell Peppers and the Spaghetti Squash with Tomato, Mushroom, and Olive Sauce are two such recipes.

Granted, the traditional vegetarian practice of using lots of grains runs contrary to many low-carb regimens (many grains are very high in carbs, but they're also high in fiber), so we've limited grains in many of our vegetarian recipes. If your diet plan allows for increased whole grains, by all means, include them; adding them to these recipes would work fine in many cases. But for the most part, we've relied on good old vegetables to carry these dishes, along with cheese and the occasional dose of soy crumbles.

Nonvegetarians, don't skip this chapter! These recipes are fine for you, too, as main or side dishes—for example, the Spanakopita or the Layered Vegetable Casserole. Going meatless a few times a week is a good way to work more variety into your diet, too.

# BEAN AND FENNEL SALAD

Stuck in a heat wave? Prepare this lovely salad in the morning or a day ahead, then ignore your stove. Crisp fennel, creamy white beans, and bright green edamame are tossed with an olive oil and lemon dressing. For a little intrigue, we added ricotta salata, a very mild Italian cheese.

## DRESSING

- 1/2 cup vegetable oil
- 1/2 cup olive oil
- 1/4 cup red wine vinegar
- 1/4 cup fresh lemon juice
- 2 teaspoons lemon zest (see page 33)
- 3/4 teaspoon kosher salt
- 3/4 teaspoon ground black pepper

- 2 large fennel bulbs (about 20 ounces), ends and brown spots trimmed
- 1/2 medium red onion, thinly sliced (about 3/4 cup)
- 1 cup canned small white beans, rinsed and drained
- 1/4 cup finely chopped flat-leaf parsley
- 1 cup frozen edamame beans, cooked according to package directions and drained
- 2/3 cup (about 2 ounces) shredded ricotta salata

Kosher salt and ground black pepper (optional)

**To make the dressing:** In a small mixing bowl, whisk together all the dressing ingredients; set aside.

Cut the fennel bulbs in half lengthwise, then cut crosswise into thin slices. Layer the ingredients in an 8-cup mixing bowl as follows: first the fennel, then the onion, white beans, parsley, and edamame, and finally the ricotta. Pour the dressing over the salad. Cover with plastic wrap and refrigerate for at least 4 hours or preferably overnight to let the flavors mingle.

Remove from the refrigerator about 30 minutes before serving, to bring to room temperature. Toss well and season with salt and pepper, if desired.

Each serving contains approximately:
CAL: 549 PRO: 9g NET CARB: 13g FAT: 49g CHOL: 12mg SOD: 395mg

SERVES 5

# WHEAT BERRY AND BROCCOLI SALAD

Wheat berries, the whole kernels of wheat, are an often-overlooked grain. They take a while to cook, but when done they're plump, chewy, and full of healthful fiber. They add lots of texture and help to fill out salads such as this balsamic-dressed one. This recipe yields 4 entrée-sized portions, but it could also serve 8 as an unusual side dish or potluck offering. Serve at room temperature for the best flavor.

$1/2$ cup wheat berries, rinsed and picked over

1 cube vegetable bouillon

$1^1/_2$ cups water

**DRESSING**

5 tablespoons olive oil

2 tablespoons balsamic vinegar

2 teaspoons soy sauce

1 teaspoon Dijon mustard

$1/2$ teaspoon kosher salt

$1/2$ teaspoon Tabasco sauce

$1/4$ teaspoon ground black pepper

1 pound fresh broccoli, cut into florets (about 4 cups), blanched and shocked (see page 31)

1 medium (about 8 ounces) yellow bell pepper, seeded and chopped

$1/4$ medium red onion, finely chopped (about $1/2$ cup)

2 tablespoons finely chopped flat-leaf parsley

In a small saucepan over high heat, combine the wheat berries, bouillon, and water; bring to a boil. Reduce the heat to low, cover, and cook for $1^1/_2$ hours, or until the wheat berries are tender yet chewy. Drain and set aside. (This step may be completed 1 day ahead of time.)

**To make the dressing:** Combine all the dressing ingredients in a medium mixing bowl and whisk until well blended. Alternatively, process the ingredients briefly in a blender.

Using paper towels, pat the broccoli dry. In a large mixing bowl, combine the broccoli, bell pepper, onion, parsley, and wheat berries; stir well. Add the dressing and stir to combine.

Each serving contains approximately:
CAL: 254 PRO: 8g NET CARB: 14g FAT: 18g CHOL: 0mg SOD: 531mg

SERVES 4

# BLUE CHEESE GREEN BEANS WITH ROASTED SOY NUTS

Kim's friend Craig Hobbs created this tasty dish that we treat as a warm salad. The warmth of the green beans softens the blue cheese and the soy nuts add great crunch. This recipe yields 2 entrée portions, but it can make a nice side dish for 4 as well.

1 tablespoon olive oil

One 16-ounce bag frozen green beans

$1/4$ teaspoon kosher salt

$1/4$ teaspoon ground black pepper

2 teaspoons balsamic vinegar

$1/2$ cup (2 ounces) crumbled blue cheese, at room temperature

$1/2$ cup unsalted roasted soy nuts

In a large skillet or sauté pan over medium heat, warm the olive oil. Add the green beans, salt, and pepper and cook, stirring, for 4 to 6 minutes, or until the beans are heated through.

Remove from the heat and add the vinegar, stirring to coat the beans. Divide the beans among individual bowls and top with the crumbled blue cheese and soy nuts.

Each serving contains approximately:
CAL: 436 PRO: 24g NET CARB: 14g FAT: 29g CHOL: 26mg SOD: 681mg

SERVES 2

# SESAME FRIED TEMPEH
## WITH SCALLIONS
If you're not a tofu lover but want to embrace the health benefits of soy, try tempeh, which can be found in the produce section of well-stocked grocery and natural-food stores. Full of great sesame flavor and with the added texture of sesame seeds, this tempeh dish makes a great entrée, wrap filler, or salad topper.

**Two** 8-ounce blocks of multi-grain tempeh

**2** teaspoons toasted sesame oil

**1** tablespoon soy sauce

**2** teaspoons sesame seeds

**2** tablespoons peanut oil

**2** scallions, chopped (about $\frac{1}{4}$ cup)

Cut each block of tempeh into 40 cubes (7 cuts crosswise and 4 cuts lengthwise); set aside.

In a small bowl, mix together the sesame oil, soy sauce and sesame seeds; set aside.

In a medium skillet over medium heat, warm the peanut oil. Add the tempeh cubes and fry for 5 to 8 minutes, stirring occasionally, until golden in color. Remove from the heat. Add the sesame oil mixture to the pan and stir. Sprinkle the scallions over the top and serve.

Each serving contains approximately:
CAL: 212 PRO: 15g NET CARB: 13g FAT: 12g CHOL: 0mg SOD: 177mg

SERVES 6

# TOFU FRIED "RICE"

Using Cauliflower "Couscous" (page 280) as a base, here we've re-created a Chinese classic that tastes amazingly like the real thing. Baked tofu, scrambled eggs, and mushrooms give this "rice" more substance, and green bell peppers and scallions lend it color, texture, and additional flavor.

2 tablespoons peanut oil

2 cloves garlic, minced (about 1 teaspoon)

4 ounces button mushrooms, washed and sliced

$1/2$ cup matchstick-cut carrots

$1/2$ medium (about 8 ounces) green bell pepper, chopped

3 eggs, lightly beaten

4 ounces Oriental- or Asian-style baked tofu, cut into strips $1/4$ inch wide and 1 inch long (about 1 cup)

4 scallions, chopped (about $1/2$ cup)

2 cups Cauliflower "Couscous" (page 280)

$1/4$ cup soy sauce

In a large wok or skillet with high sides, over medium high heat, warm the oil. Add the garlic, mushrooms, carrots, and bell pepper. Cook, stirring frequently, for 3 to 4 minutes, or until the mushrooms have given off some of their liquid.

Remove from the heat. Add the eggs and stir for about 45 seconds, or until the eggs are cooked but a bit runny (the mixture may stick to the bottom of the pan; just scrape it all up).

Return to medium heat and add the tofu, scallions, and Cauliflower "Couscous." Cook and stir for about 4 minutes, or until heated through. Remove from heat, stir in the soy sauce, and serve.

Each serving contains approximately:
CAL: 324 PRO: 16g NET CARB: 13g FAT: 23g CHOL: 185mg SOD: 1,429mg

SERVES 4

# FOUR "P" PASTA DINNER

Penne pasta, portobello mushrooms, roasted red peppers, and a creamy pesto sauce form the basis of this easy Italian dish. If penne isn't your passion, feel free to substitute a different low-carb pasta cut.

- 2 tablespoons olive oil
- 2 portobello mushroom caps (about 4 ounces), cut into strips $1/4$ inch wide and 1 inch long
- $1/2$ medium onion, thinly sliced (about $1/2$ cup)
- 2 cloves garlic, minced (about 1 teaspoon)
- $1/2$ teaspoon kosher salt
- $1/4$ teaspoon ground black pepper
- $1/8$ teaspoon crushed red pepper flakes
- 1 cup prepared roasted red peppers, drained and chopped
- 2 tablespoons dry white wine
- $1/2$ cup heavy cream
- $1/2$ cup prepared pesto
- 2 cups low-carb penne pasta, cooked according to package directions and drained

In a large skillet or sauté pan over medium heat, warm the olive oil. Add the mushrooms, onion, garlic, salt, black pepper, and red pepper flakes. Cook, stirring frequently, for 5 to 6 minutes, or until the onions soften.

Stir in the roasted red peppers and cook for another minute. Raise the heat to medium-high and stir in the wine. Cook until the wine simmers, then stir in the cream and pesto and bring the mixture to a fast simmer.

Add the penne to the pan and stir until the pasta is coated with the sauce and the ingredients are combined and warmed through, about 4 minutes. Serve immediately.

Each serving contains approximately:
CAL: 474 PRO: 26g NET CARB: 15g FAT: 35g CHOL: 48mg SOD: 558mg

SERVES 4

# SPAGHETTI SQUASH
## WITH TOMATO, MUSHROOM, AND OLIVE
### SAUCE Using soy crumbles and sliced mushrooms gives the sauce for this dish a little more substance than a plain marinara. If spaghetti squash is not to your liking, you can substitute low-carb pasta.

**TOMATO, MUSHROOM, AND OLIVE SAUCE**

- 1 teaspoon olive oil
- 2 cloves garlic, minced (about 1 teaspoon)
- 4 ounces button mushrooms, washed and sliced
- One 25 $\frac{3}{4}$-ounce can "light" spaghetti sauce (such as Hunt's)
- One 14 $\frac{1}{2}$-ounce can petite diced tomatoes
- $\frac{1}{2}$ cup sliced black olives, drained
- 1 cup frozen soy crumbles (such as Boca "ground burger")
- $\frac{1}{2}$ cup dry red wine
- $\frac{1}{2}$ teaspoon dried Italian seasoning

- 1 medium (about 3 $\frac{1}{2}$ pounds) spaghetti squash

Grated Parmesan cheese for garnish (optional)

**To make the sauce:** In a large saucepan over medium heat, warm the olive oil. Add the garlic and mushrooms and cook, stirring, for 5 minutes, or until the mushrooms have given off some of their liquid. Stir in the remaining sauce ingredients, then reduce the heat to low. Cook for another 20 minutes, stirring occasionally.

Meanwhile, prepare the squash: Using a long, sharp knife, carefully cut the squash in half lengthwise. Scrape out the seeds with a spoon. Place each squash half, cut side down, in a 2-quart, microwavable dish. Pour in 2 cups water and cover the dish with microwavable plastic wrap. Microwave on high for 10 minutes. Use a fork to check for tenderness; if not tender, microwave on high for 3 to 5 minutes more. Let the squash cool slightly, then scrape out the flesh with a fork. (This yields about 4 cups of spaghetti squash, enough for 6 servings.)

Divide the squash among individual bowls and top with the sauce. Garnish each portion with Parmesan, if desired.

Each serving contains approximately:
CAL: 146 PRO: 8g NET CARB: 16g FAT: 3g CHOL: 0mg SOD: 712mg

SERVES 6

# SPANAKOPITA
A refreshing change from salad-based vegetarian entrees, this Greek spinach and cheese pie boasts four kinds of cheese and plenty of spinach. Even kids seem to like spinach when it's delivered in this way.

Cooking spray

Two 10-ounce packages frozen, chopped spinach, thawed, water squeezed out

$1/2$ cup 1% low-fat cottage cheese

3 scallions, chopped (about $1/3$ cup)

2 eggs, lightly beaten

$1/2$ cup (2 ounces) crumbled feta cheese

$1/4$ cup grated Parmesan cheese

$1/4$ cup shredded part-skim mozzarella cheese

2 cloves garlic, minced (about 1 teaspoon)

$1/4$ teaspoon dried oregano

$1/2$ teaspoon kosher salt

Five 9-by-14-inch sheets phyllo dough, thawed and cut in half crosswise to make 10 half sheets

3 tablespoons butter, melted

Preheat the oven to 350°F. Coat an 8-by-8-inch baking dish with cooking spray; set aside. In a medium mixing bowl, stir together all ingredients except for the phyllo dough and butter; set aside.

Place 2 half-sheets of phyllo in the bottom of the prepared baking pan. (Keep the remaining sheets of phyllo dough covered with a piece of plastic wrap and a damp kitchen towel to prevent them from drying out.) Using a pastry brush, brush the top sheet lightly with some of the melted butter. Repeat with two more half-sheets of phyllo, brushing the top sheet with butter. Spoon the spinach mixture into the pan on top of the phyllo, patting it down with a rubber spatula until it nearly touches the edges of the pan. One at a time, place the remaining half-sheets of phyllo over the top of the spinach mixture, brushing each lightly with butter. Tuck the edges of the phyllo sheets down along the edges of the pan.

Bake for 30 minutes, or until nicely browned. Let cool for 5 to 10 minutes before cutting into 4 large squares.

Each serving contains approximately:
CAL: 243 PRO: 15g NET CARB: 11g FAT: 14g CHOL: 122mg SOD: 577mg

SERVES 4

# SPINACH AND CHEESE ENCHILADAS

These cheesy enchiladas will nip a Tex-Mex craving in the bud! Because these enchiladas are nice and plump, you can get by with just 1 enchilada per person, as long as you fill out the meal with a nice side dish, such as the Jicama Salad with Pumpkin Seeds (page 94). The key to keeping these enchiladas low-carb is finding the right tortilla. We prefer the tortillas produced by La Tortilla Factory. There are a few varieties to choose from (the basic whole-wheat variety works well with this recipe) and they are soft, not too big, and only contain 3 net carbs (see page 30). If you're using tortillas with more carbs, be sure to adjust your total carb count for this recipe accordingly.

Cooking spray

1 1/2 cups canned green enchilada sauce

2 tablespoons butter

1/2 small onion, chopped (about 1/4 cup)

5 cloves garlic, minced (about 1 1/2 teaspoons)

1 teaspoon kosher salt

1/4 teaspoon ground black pepper

1/2 teaspoon taco seasoning (such as Ortega)

3/4 cup heavy cream

Two 10-ounce packages frozen chopped spinach, thawed, water squeezed out

1/2 cup 1% low-fat cottage cheese

6 small low-carb tortillas (such as La Tortilla Factory)

1 cup (4 ounces) shredded Mexican-blend cheese or Cheddar cheese

Sour cream for garnish (optional)

Chopped tomatoes for garnish (optional)

Preheat the oven to 400°F. Coat a 9-by-9-inch baking dish or casserole dish with cooking spray. Pour $1/4$ cup of the enchilada sauce into the dish and spread to coat the bottom with a thin layer of the sauce; set aside.

In a medium skillet or sauté pan over medium heat, melt the butter. Add the onion, garlic, salt, pepper, and taco seasoning and cook, stirring, until the onion softens, about 5 minutes. Add the cream and cook, stirring, for 2 minutes, until the mixture comes to a boil. Remove from the heat and stir in the spinach; mix well. Let cool for 10 minutes, then stir in the cottage cheese.

Place a tortilla on a clean work surface. Using a measuring cup, scoop about $1/2$-cup of the spinach mixture and place it toward one end of the tortilla. Roll the tortilla up, then place it in the prepared baking pan. Continue with the remaining tortillas and filling to make 6 enchiladas. When all the enchiladas are in the pan, gently press them down to evenly distribute the filling within each enchilada (do not press so hard that the spinach comes out the ends of the enchiladas).

Pour the remaining $1 1/4$ cups enchilada sauce over the top of the enchiladas. Bake for 20 to 25 minutes, until the sauce is bubbling. Remove from the oven and sprinkle with the cheese. Let rest for 5 minutes before serving. Serve with a dollop of sour cream and a sprinkle of chopped tomatoes, if desired.

Each serving contains approximately:
CAL: 343 PRO: 16g NET CARB: 10g FAT: 25g CHOL: 69mg SOD: 768mg

SERVES 6

# LAYERED VEGETABLE CASSEROLE

The combination of ricotta, provolone, and Romano cheeses along with a garlicky, creamy tomato sauce gives this multilayered casserole the flavor and consistency of vegetable lasagna. It's substantial enough for an entrée, but could also double as a special side dish for company.

Cooking spray

**SAUCE**

1 cup low-carb pasta sauce (such as Carb Options)

$1/2$ cup heavy cream

5 cloves garlic, minced (about 1 $1/2$ teaspoons)

$1/2$ teaspoon kosher salt

$1/4$ teaspoon ground black pepper

**Pinch of crushed red pepper flakes**

1 tablespoon olive oil

One 6-ounce package sliced portobello mushrooms

1 medium zucchini, ends trimmed, halved lengthwise, then cut crosswise into $1/4$-inch slices

$1/2$ small Vidalia or other sweet onion, thinly sliced (about $1/2$ cup)

$1/4$ pound provolone cheese, thinly sliced, divided

$1/4$ cup Low-Carb Buttered Bread Crumbs (page 294), divided

$1/2$ cup prepared roasted red peppers, thinly sliced

$1 1/4$ cups part-skim ricotta cheese

1 egg

One 10-ounce package frozen, chopped spinach, thawed, water squeezed out

$1/4$ cup shredded Romano cheese

Preheat the oven to 350°F. Coat a 9-by-9-inch baking dish or casserole dish with cooking spray; set aside.

**To make the sauce:** In a small mixing bowl, stir together the sauce ingredients until well mixed; set aside.

In a medium skillet or sauté pan over medium heat, warm the olive oil. Add the mushrooms and zucchini and cook, stirring, for 5 to 8 minutes, until the zucchini has softened and the vegetables have given off some of their liquid. Place the zucchini-mushroom mixture in the bottom of the prepared baking dish as the first layer.

Top with half of the onion slices, then half of the provolone cheese. Sprinkle with 2 tablespoons of the bread crumbs. Arrange the roasted red pepper slices and the remaining onions over the top.

In a small bowl, stir together the ricotta and egg until combined. Spoon the mixture over the casserole (no need to spread it evenly), then top with the remaining bread crumbs. Using clean hands, pull the spinach apart into small chunks and place them over the ricotta mixture. Place the remaining provolone slices over the spinach, then pour the tomato sauce over all, covering the top of the casserole.

Bake, uncovered, for 30 minutes, or until bubbling. Remove from the oven and sprinkle with the Romano cheese. Let rest for 5 minutes before serving.

Each serving contains approximately:
CAL: 345 PRO: 18g NET CARB: 11g FAT: 25g CHOL: 98mg SOD: 648mg

SERVES 6

# STUFFED BELL PEPPERS

Soy crumbles are such a versatile and tasty ingredient, creating an updated vegetarian version of the classic stuffed pepper wasn't difficult. We've made these even more interesting than usual by adding grated portobello mushrooms for a more flavorful filling. Be sure to take advantage of beautiful, mild-tasting red, orange, and yellow bell peppers for a nice change from the typical green ones.

Cooking spray

4 medium bell peppers (about 2 pounds)

2 tablespoons olive oil

$1/2$ medium onion, finely chopped (about $1/2$ cup)

2 portobello mushroom caps (about 4 ounces), coarsely grated

4 cloves garlic, minced (about 2 teaspoons)

1 teaspoon kosher salt

$1/4$ teaspoon ground black pepper

$1/2$ teaspoon dried oregano

$1/8$ teaspoon cayenne pepper

One 8-ounce package frozen soy crumbles (such as Boca "ground burger")

1 tablespoon tomato paste

One $5\,1/2$-ounce can tomato juice

$1/2$ cup (2 ounces) shredded Asiago cheese, divided

Preheat the oven to 350°F. Coat a 9-by-9-inch baking dish with cooking spray; set aside.

Using a sharp paring knife, remove the tops from the peppers. Remove any seeds and white membranes from the pepper "cups" and set them aside. Cut the stems out of the pepper tops and discard; finely chop the remaining pieces of the tops and set aside.

In a large skillet or sauté pan over medium heat, warm the olive oil. Add the chopped pepper pieces, onion, mushrooms, garlic, salt, black pepper, oregano, and cayenne. Cook, stirring, for 3 to 4 minutes, or until the onions soften.

Stir in the soy crumbles and cook another 2 minutes, then stir in the tomato paste and juice until well combined. Remove from the heat and stir in $1/4$ cup of the cheese. Using a tablespoon, spoon the filling into the peppers. (If desired, the stuffed peppers can now be refrigerated; when ready to cook, just add 15 minutes to the baking time.)

Place the stuffed peppers in the prepared baking dish and bake for 35 minutes. Remove from the oven, sprinkle 1 tablespoon of the cheese over each pepper, then return to the oven and bake for another 10 minutes. Let rest for 5 minutes before serving.

**Each serving contains approximately:**
CAL: 262 PRO: 18g NET CARB: 16g FAT: 12g CHOL: 12mg SOD: 553mg

SERVES 4

# 9

## FISH AND SHELLFISH ENTRÉES

# MANY PEOPLE WE KNOW ARE AFRAID TO COOK FISH AT HOME, PREFERRING INSTEAD TO ORDER IT AT RESTAURANTS.

We think this is unfortunate, as seafood is quick cooking and versatile, not to mention delicious. Yes, it's relatively expensive, but so are quality meats. Our advice: find a reputable fishmonger who can tell you what's the freshest, what's on sale, and how to cook it. Health professionals recommend eating seafood twice a week for its health benefits. Doing so will help break up the meat monotony that can occur with low-carb eating regimens.

If traditional fish preparations are your favorite, try our Crab Cakes, Panfried Scallops, or Crispy Parmesan Haddock. If you're more adventurous, the Spicy Portuguese Clams or Asian Salmon will probably be to your liking. Whichever you choose, keep in mind that some of these preparations can be used for more than one variety of seafood (see our notes for suggestions). Also, remember that some types of shellfish, such as mussels, are higher in carbs, and need to be consumed with discretion.

# THE BENEVIDES' SPICY PORTUGUESE CLAMS

Kitty's next-door neighbors, the Benevides family, are of Portuguese descent, and when they decide to cook Portuguese-inspired dishes, Kit's family always tries to wrangle an invitation. The food is generally a little spicy and full of great, fresh ingredients—this dish is no exception. Scott Benevides created this dish using Portuguese Chourico sausage, lots of garlic, parsley, onion, and local steamer clams. There's a bit of prep involve but the whole thing cooks quickly once it's on the stove. Served with a tossed green salad and some Almond-Stuffed Olives (page 61), this meal is a nice chang of-pace from plain steamed clams.

4 pounds steamer clams

1 teaspoon white vinegar

1 teaspoon olive oil

$\frac{1}{2}$ medium Spanish onion (about $\frac{1}{2}$ cup), divided

1 cup chopped flat-leaf parsley, divided

8 garlic cloves, 2 minced and the rest left whole

1 tablespoon bottled, crushed hot red peppers in liquid (such as Pastene)

$\frac{1}{2}$ pound Chourico sausage, cut into 1-inch chunks

Rinse the clams in a sink of cool water, filling the sink just enough to cover the clams. Drain the sink and fill again with fresh, luke-warm water. Add the vinegar to the water and soak the clams 10 to 15 minutes while preparing the water to boil the clams.

Fill a stockpot large enough to hold the clams, with about 2 inches of water. Add the olive oil, 1 tablespoon of the onion, 2 table-spoons of the parsley, half of the minced garlic, and the hot red peppers to the pot. Bring the mixture to a boil over high heat. Add the sausage chunks and bring to a boil again.

When the cooking liquid is boiling, layer half of the clams, half of the remaining onions, half of the remaining parsley, and 3 of the garlic cloves into the pot. Repeat the layers, using up the clams, onions and parsley; top it all with the remaining garlic cloves and minced garlic. With the heat still on high, cover the pot and cook for 10 to 12 minutes, or until the clams open up. Discard any clams that failed to open.

To serve, portion the clams onto plates or bowls. Serve some of the broth in a small bowl alongside each portion, for dipping.

Each serving contains approximately:
CAL: 481 PRO: 65g NET CARB: 13.5g FAT: 16g CHOL: 177mg SOD: 609mg

SERVES 8

# CRAB CAKES

There are many different versions of crab cakes in the world. Ours is very straightforward and simple, highlighting the flavor of fresh crabmeat. While you could use canned crabmeat that has been well drained, the quality and flavor of the finished product will not be as good. These large cakes are fantastic when served very simply with a fresh lemon wedge or tartar sauce. If you want something more fancy, try Spicy Lemon Mayonnaise (page 308) as an accompaniment. For a party appetizer, double the recipe and make miniature crab cakes.

1 pound fresh lump crabmeat, picked over for shell fragments

1 egg

2 tablespoons mayonnaise

1 teaspoon Worcestershire sauce

1 teaspoon fresh lemon juice

1/4 teaspoon Tabasco sauce

3 tablespoons Low-Carb Buttered Bread Crumbs (page 294)

2 tablespoons butter

2 tablespoons vegetable oil

In a medium mixing bowl, using a wooden spoon or clean hands, mix together all ingredients except for the butter and oil. Form the mixture into 4 loose patties.

In a large skillet or sauté pan, over medium heat, melt the butter with the oil. Add the crab cakes and cook for 4 to 7 minutes, until the bottoms are golden brown. Using a spatula, flip the cakes over and cook for another 3 to 5 minutes, until browned on the second side.

Transfer 2 cakes to each of 2 plates and serve immediately.

Each 2-cake serving contains approximately:
CAL: 652 PRO: 52g NET CARB: 3g FAT: 47g CHOL: 380mg SOD: 989mg

SERVES 2

# PANFRIED SCALLOPS

This is a simple recipe that really showcases the mild flavor and creamy texture of the scallops, so it pays to buy the best (see Note). These scallops are great on their own, but if you're looking for a flavor boost, try them with Spicy Sesame Sauce (page 303).

1 tablespoon grapeseed oil or other mild cooking oil

1¼ pounds dry sea scallops, side muscles removed

Kosher salt and ground black pepper

In a large skillet or sauté pan over medium-high heat, warm the oil. Add the scallops (try not to crowd them) and cook for 3 to 4 minutes, until nicely browned on the bottoms. Using tongs, flip the scallops over and cook for another 2 to 3 minutes, until opaque throughout. Season to taste with salt and pepper and serve immediately.

**Note**

Sea scallops are the larger scallops; bay scallops are the small ones. "Dry" scallops are those that are untreated, while "wet" or "water-added" scallops have been treated with sodium tripolyphosphate, a chemical that causes them to absorb water. Therefore, wet scallops weigh about 30 percent more than dry ones, but the weight is all water (which you're paying for). When wet scallops are cooked, much of this water is released, which can result in a less-than-desirable end product. Previously frozen scallops can be either wet or dry. It pays to read labels and ask your grocer or fishmonger. We recommend using dry scallops whenever possible.

Each serving contains approximately:
CAL: 181 PRO: 23g NET CARB: 3g FAT: 8g CHOL: 45mg SOD: 581mg

SERVES 4

# SHRIMP AND ASPARAGUS SAUTÉ WITH ASIAGO CHEESE

Take advantage of abundant springtime asparagus and whip up this quick sauté for dinner. The light Italian flavors complement the shrimp, but substitute boneless chicken breast strips if you prefer. If you don't have Asiago cheese on hand, use Parmesan.

1 bunch (about 1 pound) asparagus, trimmed, cut into 2-inch pieces, and blanched and shocked (see page 31)

3 tablespoons extra-virgin olive oil, divided

1/4 medium onion, chopped (about 1/4 cup)

4 cloves garlic, minced (about 2 teaspoons)

3/4 teaspoon kosher salt

1/4 teaspoon ground black pepper

2 tablespoons dry white wine

1 1/4 cups canned, crushed tomatoes

1 1/2 pounds large (21 to 30 per pound) shrimp, peeled and deveined

2 tablespoons finely chopped flat-leaf parsley

1/2 cup (2 ounces) shredded Asiago cheese

Let the asparagus drain in a colander in the sink until needed.

In a large skillet or sauté pan with high sides, warm 2 tablespoons of the olive oil over medium heat. Add the onion, garlic, salt, and pepper. Cook, stirring, for 2 minutes, or until fragrant. Stir in the wine and tomatoes and bring to a simmer.

Raise the heat to medium-high, add the shrimp, and return to a simmer, stirring occasionally. Simmer for 5 minutes, stirring frequently, or until the shrimp are pink. Add the asparagus to the pan and cook for 2 to 3 minutes more, or until the shrimp are opaque throughout and the asparagus is heated through.

Stir in the parsley. Divide the mixture among individual bowls. Drizzle with the remaining 1 tablespoon olive oil and sprinkle with the cheese. Serve immediately.

Each serving contains approximately:
CAL: 365 PRO: 43g NET CARB: 8g FAT: 16g CHOL: 343mg SOD: 642mg

SERVES 4

# SESAME SHRIMP STIR-FRY

This easy stir-fry can be tailored to your liking because it calls simply for 5 cups of green vegetables—you choose your favorites. We like to use snow peas, asparagus, and bok choy, but you could also use snap peas, broccoli, celery, zucchini, or Chinese cabbage, for example. You'll need to blanch the vegetables (except for the leafy greens) before adding them to the stir-fry so that all the ingredients are properly and evenly cooked. This recipe allows for generous portions, since you'll be eating it sans rice!

5 cups green vegetables, cut into 2-inch pieces

1$\frac{1}{4}$ pounds medium (31 to 35 per pound) raw shrimp, peeled and deveined

2 tablespoons toasted sesame oil

1 tablespoon toasted sesame seeds

$\frac{1}{2}$ cup chicken broth

$\frac{1}{2}$ cup cold water

$\frac{1}{4}$ cup tamari or soy sauce

2 tablespoons cornstarch

1 tablespoon hoisin sauce

2 tablespoons peanut oil

6 cloves garlic, minced (about 1 tablespoon)

2 scallions, chopped (about $\frac{1}{4}$ cup)

One 14-ounce can bean sprouts, drained, or 14 ounces fresh bean sprouts, rinsed and drained

Blanch and shock the green vegetables (see page 31), except for leafy greens such as cabbage or bok choy. Let the vegetables drain in a colander in the sink until needed.

In a small mixing bowl, using clean hands, mix together the shrimp, 1 tablespoon of the sesame oil, and the sesame seeds; set aside.

In a 2-cup liquid measuring cup or a small bowl, combine the broth and water; stir in the tamari, cornstarch, and hoisin sauce until blended; set aside.

In a large skillet or sauté pan or a medium wok over medium-high heat, warm the peanut oil and the remaining 1 tablespoon sesame oil. Add the garlic and cook, stirring, until fragrant, about 2 minutes. Add the scallions, bean sprouts, and the vegetables (including any leafy greens you may be using) to the pan. Raise the heat to high and cook, stirring, for 2 minutes, or until the vegetables are cooked through but still crispy (greens will be wilted). Transfer the vegetables to a plate and set aside.

Return the pan to the high heat and add the shrimp. Cook, stirring and tossing, for 5 minutes, until the shrimp are pink and opaque throughout. Add the cornstarch mixture and stir until just thickened, about 1 minute. Return the vegetables to the pan and stir to combine all the ingredients. Serve immediately.

**Each serving contains approximately:**
CAL: 355 PRO: 36g NET CARB: 12g FAT: 17g CHOL: 277mg SOD: 1,471mg

SERVES 4

# LEMON AND DILL SALMON

This recipe combines the classic flavors of lemon and dill with yogurt, creating great depth of flavor in the salmon. This is a nice recipe for a weeknight dinner; once the marinating is done, you can bake the fish in a matter of minutes.

**MARINADE**

- 1/2 cup chopped fresh dill
- 1 tablespoon lemon zest (see page 33)
- 1/3 cup plain low-fat yogurt
- 1/2 teaspoon kosher salt
- 1/2 teaspoon ground black pepper
- 1/4 teaspoon Tabasco sauce
- 1 tablespoon vegetable oil

- 1 1/2 pounds salmon fillet, skin removed, cut into 4 equal portions
- Cooking spray

**To make the marinade:** In a medium mixing bowl, whisk together all the ingredients until combined and smooth.

Place the salmon in a gallon-sized zip-top plastic bag; pour the marinade over the salmon, making sure all surfaces are coated. Seal the bag and refrigerate for 24 hours.

When ready to cook, preheat the oven to 400°F. Coat a medium baking pan with cooking spray; set aside. Remove the salmon pieces from the bag (discard the marinade) and arrange them in the prepared pan.

Bake for 15 to 22 minutes, or until the fish is opaque throughout (test by cutting into one piece with a sharp knife). Serve immediately.

Each serving contains approximately:
CAL: 301 PRO: 37g NET CARB: 2g FAT: 15g CHOL: 101mg SOD: 155mg

SERVES 4

# ASIAN SALMON

This recipe is a favorite for its ease and its Asian flavors that are both sweet and savory. The marinade is quickly stirred together in the morning so that the salmon can absorb it all day long. Once baked, the salmon will have a beautiful, glossy brown glaze.

## MARINADE

- 2 tablespoons Atkins Quick Quisine Teriyaki Sauce
- 2 tablespoons tamari or soy sauce
- 2 scallions, chopped (about 1/4 cup)
- 1 tablespoon rice wine vinegar
- 1 tablespoon sugar-free, orange marmalade (such as Smucker's Light)
- 1 tablespoon sesame oil
- 2 cloves garlic, minced (about 1 teaspoon)
- 1 teaspoon hoisin sauce
- 1 teaspoon ground ginger
- 1/4 teaspoon kosher salt
- 1/4 teaspoon ground black pepper

- 1 1/2 pounds salmon fillet, skin removed, cut into 4 equal portions
- Cooking spray

**To make the marinade:** In a medium mixing bowl, whisk together all the ingredients until combined. Place the salmon in a gallon-sized zip-top plastic bag; pour the marinade over the salmon, making sure all the surfaces are coated. Seal the bag and refrigerate for 8 to 12 hours.

When ready to cook, preheat the oven to 425°F. Coat a medium baking sheet with cooking spray. Remove the salmon pieces from the bag (reserve the marinade) and arrange them in the prepared pan. Pour the marinade over the fish pieces. Bake for 15 to 22 minutes, or until the fish is opaque throughout (test by cutting into one piece with a sharp knife). Serve immediately.

Each serving contains approximately:
CAL: 308 PRO: 37g NET CARB: 4g FAT: 16g CHOL: 100mg SOD: 686mg

SERVES 4

# CRISPY PARMESAN HADDOCK

A crispy, crunchy, cheesy bread crumb topping gives haddock a real flavor boost. This dish is so easy to put together, the kids can even help (maybe they'll be more inclined to eat it then, too)! To add another flavor to the dish, try serving it with some bottled low-carb pasta sauce on the side for dipping.

## TOPPING

- 1/4 cup Low-Carb Buttered Bread Crumbs (page 294)
- 1/4 cup grated Parmesan cheese
- 1/2 teaspoon dried Italian seasoning
- 1/4 teaspoon kosher salt
- 1/4 teaspoon ground black pepper

Cooking spray

- 1 1/2 pounds haddock fillet, cut into 4 portions
- 1 egg, lightly beaten
- 4 lemon wedges for garnish (optional)

Preheat the broiler and position the rack 6 to 8 inches from the heat source.

**To make the topping:** In a shallow bowl, stir together all the topping ingredients; set aside.

Coat a baking pan with cooking spray; set aside. Working with one portion of fish at a time, using a pastry brush, coat the top of the fish with the beaten egg. Press the coated side of the fish piece into the topping (do not coat the bottom of the fish). Place the fish on the prepared baking pan, topping side up. Continue with the remaining fish and topping.

Broil for 5 to 8 minutes, or until the topping is nicely browned. Turn off the broiler and turn on the oven to 375°F. Cook for another 10 to 15 minutes, or until opaque throughout (test by cutting into one piece with a sharp knife). Serve immediately, with the lemon wedges, if desired.

Each serving contains approximately:
CAL: 247 PRO: 41g NET CARB: 2g FAT: 7g CHOL: 168mg SOD: 351mg

SERVES 4

# SWORDFISH WITH OLIVE OIL AND LEMON

On Kim's travels in Italy she was impressed by the simplicity of some of the dishes. This recipe adopts that simple style of cooking. If you'd prefer something more elaborate, serve the fish with Olive and Caper Sauce (page 302), but eliminate the olive oil in the recipe below if you do so.

1½ pounds swordfish, cut into 4 portions

½ teaspoon kosher salt

½ teaspoon ground black pepper

Cooking spray

1 lemon, ends trimmed

4 tablespoons extra-virgin olive oil

Season the fish pieces on both sides with the salt and pepper.

Coat a large skillet or sauté pan with cooking spray. Heat the skillet over medium heat; when hot, add the fish and cover. Cook for 5 minutes to brown the bottoms. Using tongs or a spatula, flip the fish, re-cover, and cook for 4 to 5 minutes more, or until the fish is opaque throughout (test by cutting into one piece with a sharp knife).

While waiting for the fish to cook, quarter the lemon and remove any visible seeds; set aside.

When the fish is done, transfer the pieces to individual plates. Drizzle each serving with 1 tablespoon of the olive oil and serve with a lemon wedge on the side of each plate.

**Note**

This swordfish is also delicious when grilled. Coat the fish pieces with cooking spray before grilling.

Each serving contains approximately:
CAL: 343 PRO: 36g NET CARB: 1g FAT: 21g CHOL: 71mg SOD: 223mg

SERVES 4

# 10

## CHICKEN ENTRÉES

# CHICKEN, THAT UNIVERSAL FAVORITE, HAS A BIG PLACE IN THIS BOOK.

We like it for many reasons: affordability, availability, variety of cuts, and, of course, taste. Chicken can support a lot of flavorful ingredients, and can be easily transformed in myriad ethnic recipes, all of which points to its versatility.

You'll see that this chapter only focuses on chicken. It's not because we're turkey phobic—note, we do have a few turkey recipes elsewhere in the book. Turkey is just as good as chicken in many ways, but it's not available in as many cuts, nor as cheaply, as chicken. If you like, substitute turkey cutlets for the chicken breast in some of these recipes, but be aware that cooking times may then be altered (cutlets are thinner than chicken breasts, unless the chicken is pounded first, so turkey may cook more quickly).

For a crowd-pleasing entrée, you really can't beat chicken. It's kid approved, and practically every adult likes at least one chicken cut. This chapter includes such family-friendly fare as Crispy Chicken Strips, Oven "Fried" Chicken Drumsticks, and Maple-Baked Chicken Breasts. Visit faraway lands without leaving your kitchen, with Mediterranean Chicken, Pasta, and Olives; Coconut-Lime Chicken Legs; or Coriander Chicken with Olives and Almonds. If you're looking for something really special, don't automatically turn to the beef chapter! Our Apricot Chicken and Chicken with Mushrooms and Mozzarella are two of our taste-testers' absolute favorites.

# MAPLE-BAKED CHICKEN BREASTS

This update of the classic chicken breast uses a brine—a fancy word for a sweetened, saltwater marinade. The brine plumps up the chicken meat and keeps it very moist during baking; but don't worry, only a fraction of its sugar and salt are absorbed. These bone-in chicken breasts are finished with a sweet maple basting sauce, which adds color and flavor. Serve this dish with Celery Root and Carrot Purée (page 287), or prepare the Baby Spinach Salad with Cranberries, Chèvre, and Hazelnuts (page 88) while the chicken is cooking.

**BRINE**

- 6 cups water
- $2/3$ cup sugar
- $1/3$ cup kosher salt
- $1/3$ cup sugar-free maple syrup
- 1 tablespoon dried thyme
- 1 teaspoon maple extract
- $1/4$ teaspoon ground black pepper

- 4 split bone-in chicken breasts (about $2^3/4$ to 3 pounds)
- 2 tablespoons butter, melted

**BASTING SAUCE**

- $1/4$ cup sugar-free maple syrup
- 2 tablespoons unsweetened apple butter
- 1 tablespoon real maple syrup
- $1/2$ teaspoon dry mustard
- $1/4$ teaspoon maple extract

**To make the brine:** In a large mixing bowl, stir together all the brine ingredients until the salt and sugar are dissolved. Add the chicken breasts to the brine; cover and refrigerate for 3 hours. (At this point, you can remove the chicken from the brine, discarding the brine, and refrigerate the brined chicken as long as overnight, before cooking.)

When ready to cook, preheat the oven to 375°F. Place the chicken breasts in a 13-by-9-inch baking dish. Using a pastry brush, coat the breasts with the melted butter. The butter will solidify because the breasts are cold; don't worry, just continue to brush until all the butter is used.) Bake for 30 minutes.

**To make the basting sauce:** While the chicken is baking, stir together all the sauce ingredients in a small mixing bowl.

When the chicken has baked for 30 minutes, remove from the oven and brush the breasts with the sauce using a pastry brush. Return to the oven and bake for another 10 minutes. Baste again and bake for another 10 minutes, then check the chicken for doneness; the meat should show no pink when cut into at the thickest part. If done, remove from the oven, give the chicken a final baste and let rest in the pan for 5 minutes. If not done, bake for another 5 minutes and recheck. Transfer to individual plates and serve.

**Each serving contains approximately:**
**CAL: 372 PRO: 42g NET CARB: 9g FAT: 17g CHOL: 135mg SOD: 310mg**

SERVES 4

# CHICKEN WITH MUSHROOMS AND MOZZARELLA

Chicken Marsala is one of Kitty's favorites, and this version is served in her house when she's willing to prepare two different entrées—this chicken for the adults and something quick and easy for the kids. Be sure to have all ingredients prepped and waiting, as the actual cooking goes quite quickly.

1 tablespoon olive oil

1 egg white, lightly beaten

1 tablespoon water

$1/4$ cup Low-Carb Buttered Bread Crumbs (page 294)

2 tablespoons Atkins Bake Mix

$1/4$ teaspoon ground black pepper

$1/8$ teaspoon garlic powder

2 medium skinless, boneless chicken breast halves (about 6 ounces each), trimmed of excess fat, pounded $1/4$ inch thick

**SAUCE**

1 teaspoon cornstarch

$1/4$ cup Marsala wine

2 tablespoons butter

$1/2$ medium onion, thinly sliced (about $1/2$ cup)

One 8-ounce package sliced button mushrooms

$1/2$ cup chicken broth

$1/2$ teaspoon kosher salt

$1/4$ teaspoon ground black pepper

$1/4$ cup shredded part-skim mozzarella cheese

In a medium skillet or sauté pan over medium heat, warm the olive oil. Combine the egg white and water in a small bowl and stir together with a fork. On another small plate, using a spoon or clean hands, combine the bread crumbs, Atkins Bake Mix, pepper, and garlic powder. Dip each chicken breast half into the egg-white mixture, coating both sides, and then into the bread crumb mixture, coating both sides.

Place the chicken pieces into the hot oil and cook for 4 minutes, or until the bottoms are nicely browned. Using tongs, flip the chicken over and cook for another 4 minutes, until browned on the second side and opaque throughout. Using a spatula, transfer the chicken to a plate and cover with aluminum foil to keep warm while preparing the sauce.

**To make the sauce:** In a 1-cup liquid measuring cup, or a small bowl, stir together the cornstarch and Marsala; set aside.

In the same skillet the chicken was cooked in, melt the butter over medium heat. Add the onion and cook, stirring, for 3 minutes, or until softened. Add the mushrooms and cook for another minute, or until all the mushroom liquid has cooked off. Add the broth, salt, pepper, and cornstarch mixture; cook and stir until heated through and slightly thickened.

Return the chicken to the skillet and cook another minute to reheat. To serve, transfer the chicken pieces to individual plates, top each with half the mozzarella cheese, then spoon half the mushroom sauce over the top to melt the cheese.

Each serving contains approximately:
CAL: 688 PRO: 58g NET CARB: 12g FAT: 40g CHOL: 170mg SOD: 863mg

SERVES 2

# CORIANDER CHICKEN WITH OLIVES AND ALMONDS

After attending a lecture on spices at a culinary conference, Kim returned home with new inspiration for incorporating a wider variety of spices in her cooking; this is one of the resulting recipes. Here, ground coriander (the seeds of the same plant that gives us fresh cilantro), known for its slightly lemony flavor, delicately seasons the chicken and works nicely with the tangy olives.

$1^1/_4$ **teaspoons ground coriander**

2 **cloves garlic, minced (about 1 teaspoon)**

$^1/_2$ **teaspoon ground cumin**

$^1/_4$ **teaspoon kosher salt**

$^1/_8$ **teaspoon cayenne pepper**

**Pinch of ground black pepper**

4 **medium skinless, boneless chicken breast halves (about $1^1/_2$ pounds), trimmed of excess fat**

3 **tablespoons olive oil**

$^1/_4$ **cup almonds, chopped**

2 **tablespoons dry white wine**

$^1/_2$ **cup sliced, pimiento-stuffed olives, drained**

In a small bowl, stir together the coriander, garlic, cumin, salt, cayenne, and black pepper; set aside.

Cut each chicken breast half in half cross-wise. Place the chicken pieces in a gallon-sized, zip-top plastic bag. Seal the bag; using a rolling pin or the flat side of a meat mallet, flatten the chicken to a $^1/_4$-inch thickness. Open the bag and sprinkle in the spice mixture; seal the bag and massage the spice mixture into the chicken. (At this point the chicken can be covered and refrigerated for up to 1 day, if desired.)

In a large skillet or sauté pan over medium heat, warm the olive oil. Add the almonds and the chicken; cook for about 5 minutes, or until the chicken is golden brown on the bottom. Using tongs, flip the chicken pieces; cook another minute, then add the wine and olives. Bring the mixture to a simmer and cover. Cook another 3 to 4 minutes, until the chicken is opaque throughout.

To serve, transfer the chicken pieces to individual plates and spoon the olives, almonds, and sauce over the pieces.

Each serving contains approximately:
CAL: 410 PRO: 37g NET CARB: 5g FAT: 26g CHOL: 96mg SOD: 1,466mg

SERVES 4

# APRICOT CHICKEN

Kim and I like to call this a "date night" recipe—it's easy, yet looks beautiful and tastes like a top restaurant chef prepared it. Our recipe uses sugar-free apricot preserves, which can be found in the jelly section at your grocery store. Start your cook-to-impress dinner with the Endive and Arugula Salad with Pears, Walnuts, and Blue Cheese (page 84), and serve Spinach-Stuffed Mushroom Caps (page 291) alongside the chicken.

2 large skinless, boneless chicken breast halves (about 1 pound), trimmed of excess fat

1/4 cup Atkins Bake Mix

1 tablespoon butter

1 tablespoon vegetable oil

1 tablespoon finely minced shallot

1/8 teaspoon dry mustard

Pinch of ground black pepper

2 tablespoons dry white wine

1/4 cup water

3 tablespoons sugar-free apricot preserves (such as Smucker's Light)

1/4 teaspoon Tabasco sauce

Place the chicken in a gallon-sized, zip-top plastic bag. Seal the bag; using a rolling pin or the flat side of a meat mallet, flatten the chicken to a 3/4-inch thickness. Add the Atkins Bake Mix to the bag, seal it again, and shake the bag to coat the chicken pieces. Remove the chicken from the bag, shaking off any excess coating, and discard the bag.

In a large skillet or sauté pan over medium heat, melt the butter with the oil. Add the chicken and cook for 4 minutes, until nicely browned on the bottom. Using tongs, flip the chicken and cook another 4 minutes, until browned on the second side (the chicken will be nearly cooked through). Transfer to a plate and cover with aluminum foil.

Add the shallot, mustard, and pepper to the pan. Cook, stirring with a wooden spoon, for about 30 seconds, until the shallots begin to soften. Add the wine and bring the mixture to a simmer. Stir in the water, preserves, and Tabasco and cook, stirring, for 1 minute, or until slightly thickened.

Return the chicken to the pan, spoon the sauce over the chicken, and let cook for 1 to 2 minutes, or until opaque throughout. Transfer to individual plates and pour the sauce over each portion.

Each serving contains approximately:
CAL: 449 PRO: 58g NET CARB: 9g FAT: 19g CHOL: 160mg SOD: 245mg

SERVES 2

# CHICKEN SAUSAGE WITH ROASTED RED PEPPERS, VIDALIAS, AND ARUGULA

There are many varieties of chicken sausage available today, so it makes sense to shake up your sausage routine by trying a few of them. In this recipe, we used a sweet Italian chicken sausage, but substitute any type you like. This is a great dish for a busy springtime supper—it's quick to prepare, calls for bagged arugula and bottled red peppers, and you only dirty one pan! Plus, it makes great use of one of our favorite spring vegetables, Vidalia onions. Make this dish year round by substituting other varieties of sweet onions.

1 tablespoon olive oil

1½ pounds chicken sausage, cut into 1-inch chunks

1 medium Vidalia onion, halved and thinly sliced (about 1¼ cups)

½ teaspoon kosher salt

½ teaspoon ground black pepper

1 cup prepared roasted red peppers, drained, patted dry, and cut into strips ¼ inch thick and 1 inch long

One 5-ounce bag arugula, divided

In a large skillet or sauté pan over medium heat, warm the olive oil. Add the sausage, onion, salt, and pepper. Cook, stirring occasionally, for 8 minutes, or until the sausage is nearly cooked through. Add the red peppers and cook and stir for another 2 to 3 minutes, or until the sausage is thoroughly cooked.

Add half the bag of arugula and stir it into the sausage mixture. Let it cook down briefly. Stir in the remaining arugula, remove from the heat, and serve immediately.

Note

Chicken sausage can be difficult to cut easily with a knife; try using kitchen shears. Also, it can be helpful to freeze the sausage briefly (about 10 minutes) prior to cutting it.

Each serving contains approximately:
CAL: 257 PRO: 31g NET CARB: 10g FAT: 10g CHOL: 118mg SOD: 1,323mg

SERVES 4

# MEDITERRANEAN CHICKEN, PASTA, AND OLIVES

Both of us adore Mediterranean flavor combinations, and this chicken and pasta sauté—with its Kalamata olives, extra-virgin olive oil, oregano, and thyme—really delivers. We think it's best with the green beans, but broccoli works well, too.

- 2 tablespoons butter
- 3 tablespoons olive oil
- 1 pound skinless, boneless chicken breasts, trimmed of excess fat, cut into 1-inch cubes
- 4 cloves garlic, minced (about 2 teaspoons)
- 6 slices bacon, cooked crisp and crumbled
- 1 medium onion, finely chopped (about 1 cup)
- $1/2$ teaspoon dried oregano
- $1/4$ teaspoon dried thyme
- $1/8$ teaspoon crushed red pepper flakes
- $1/8$ teaspoon kosher salt
- $1/8$ teaspoon ground black pepper
- 2 cups (about 8 ounces) frozen cut green beans, thawed
- 2 cups low-carb fusilli pasta, cooked according to package directions and drained
- $1/2$ cup pitted Kalamata olives, chopped
- 2 tablespoons extra-virgin olive oil
- 4 tablespoons grated Parmesan cheese for garnish (optional)

In a large skillet or sauté pan with high sides, over medium heat, melt the butter with the olive oil. Add the chicken, garlic, bacon, onion, oregano, thyme, red pepper flakes, salt, and black pepper. Cook, stirring frequently, for about 3 minutes, or until the onion softens.

Add the green beans and cook for another 5 minutes, stirring frequently, until the chicken is opaque throughout. Stir in the fusilli and olives; cook for another minute, until heated through.

Drizzle the extra-virgin olive oil over the top, then divide the mixture among individual bowls. Sprinkle each portion with 1 table-spoon of the Parmesan, if desired.

Each serving contains approximately:
CAL: 546 PRO: 50g NET CARB: 13g FAT: 32g CHOL: 96mg SOD: 558mg

SERVES 4

# CRISPY CHICKEN STRIPS

Both kids and adults will find these strips a good substitute for fast-food chicken strips, which are much higher in carbs. Serve them with a dip such as Blue Cheese Dressing (page 91) or Crème Fraîche Dressing (page 105), or lay them atop a bed of greens for a substantial salad entrée.

1 pound skinless, boneless chicken breasts, trimmed of excess fat

$2/3$ cup panko (see Note) or Low-Carb Buttered Bread Crumbs (page 294)

$1/2$ cup grated Parmesan cheese

$1/2$ cup Atkins Bake Mix

2 tablespoons rotisserie chicken seasoning (such as McCormick)

2 egg whites, lightly beaten

$1/2$ cup vegetable oil, divided

Place half of the chicken in a quart-sized zip-top plastic bag. Seal the bag; using a rolling pin or the flat side of a meat mallet, flatten the chicken to a $1/4$-inch thickness. Remove from the bag and repeat with the remaining chicken breast. Transfer the flattened chicken to a cutting board and cut it into strips about 1 inch wide (you should have about 16 strips total). Discard the zip-top bag and set the chicken strips aside.

In a small bowl, stir together the panko, Parmesan, Atkins Bake Mix, and rotisserie seasoning. Pour the egg whites into another small bowl. Working with one chicken strip at a time, in assembly-line fashion, dip the chicken first into the egg whites, then into the panko mixture, pressing the crumbs onto the chicken and flipping to coat both sides of the strip. Transfer the coated chicken strips to a wire rack positioned over waxed paper (to catch drips and stray crumbs). Repeat until all the chicken strips have been coated with the mixture. Let stand on the rack for 20 to 30 minutes to dry.

In a large, heavy skillet over medium-high heat, warm $1/4$ cup of the oil. Place half of the chicken strips in the oil and cook for 2 minutes, or until nicely browned on the bottom. Using tongs, flip the strips and cook for another minute, or until browned on the second side. Transfer to paper towels to drain (cover with more paper towels to help keep them warm). Add the remaining oil to the pan, heat until hot, then cook the remaining chicken strips. Serve immediately.

**Note:** Panko, Japanese bread crumbs, is typically used for tempura and other deep-fried foods. Panko is very flaky, and therefore makes for a very crispy coating. Though they're not particularly low in carbs, when combined with other low-carb coating ingredients, such as the Atkins Bake Mix, a good compromise is achieved. Look for panko in the Asian section of your supermarket and at Asian markets. If you prefer not to use panko, Low-Carb Buttered Bread Crumbs (page 294) are a nice substitute. The finished recipe will be lower in carbs, though not as crispy.

**Each serving contains approximately:**
CAL: 434 PRO: 42g NET CARB: 10g FAT: 24g CHOL: 75mg SOD: 1,502mg

SERVES 4

# CHICKEN THIGHS WITH SPICY TOMATO SAUCE

Economical chicken thighs pair with a rich, spicy red sauce in this easy dish. Serve it with an equally easy salad that offers plenty of textural contrast, such as the Fennel and Red Onion Salad (page 96).

## SAUCE

- 1$\frac{1}{2}$ cups canned crushed tomatoes
- 2 slices bacon, cooked crisp and chopped (about $\frac{1}{4}$ cup)
- 2 tablespoons dry red wine
- 1 teaspoon minced dried onion
- $\frac{1}{2}$ teaspoon crushed red pepper flakes
- $\frac{1}{2}$ teaspoon dried oregano
- $\frac{1}{2}$ teaspoon kosher salt
- $\frac{1}{4}$ teaspoon dried rosemary, crushed between your fingers
- $\frac{1}{8}$ teaspoon ground black pepper

- 1 tablespoon olive oil
- 2 pounds chicken thighs (not skinless or boneless), trimmed of excess fat
- $\frac{1}{4}$ teaspoon garlic powder
- $\frac{1}{8}$ teaspoon ground black pepper

Cooking Spray

**To make the sauce:** In a medium mixing bowl, stir together all the sauce ingredients until combined; set aside.

Preheat the oven to 375°F. In a medium mixing bowl, using clean hands, toss together the olive oil and chicken thighs until the chicken is completely coated. Sprinkle the garlic powder and pepper over the chicken and toss again to distribute the seasoning.

Coat a 1$\frac{1}{2}$-quart casserole or baking dish with cooking spray. Spread the sauce in the bottom, then top with the chicken thighs, skin side up.

Bake, uncovered, for 40 to 45 minutes, or until the chicken is cooked through; the meat should show no pink when cut into at the thickest part. To serve, divide the chicken pieces among 4 plates and spoon some of the sauce over each portion.

Each serving contains approximately:
CAL: 384 PRO: 39g NET CARB: 5g FAT: 21g CHOL: 137mg SOD: 379mg

SERVES 4

# CHICKEN THIGHS BAKED WITH APPLES AND LEEKS

This recipe highlights classic flavors of the Normandy region of France, and it makes a delightful cold-weather supper. The combination of both fresh apple and unsweetened apple butter gives depth to the apple flavor. Look for the apple butter in the supermarket health-food or kosher sections.

$3/4$ cup chicken broth

$1/4$ cup dry white wine

1 tablespoon unsweetened apple butter

$1/8$ teaspoon dry mustard

Cooking spray

3 pounds chicken thighs (not skinless and boneless), trimmed of excess fat

1 tablespoon butter

1 medium leek, white part only, thoroughly cleaned and sliced (about $2/3$ cup)

$1/2$ Granny Smith apple, cored and finely chopped (about $1/2$ cup)

$1/2$ teaspoon dried thyme

$1/2$ teaspoon kosher salt

$1/4$ teaspoon ground black pepper

Preheat the oven to 375°F. In a small mixing bowl, whisk together the broth, wine, apple butter, and mustard until smooth; set aside.

Coat a large skillet or sauté pan with cooking spray and warm the pan over medium heat. Add half of the chicken thighs, skin side down; cook for 2 minutes to brown. Transfer the chicken to a 2-quart casserole dish, browned side up; set aside. Repeat with the remaining chicken.

Drain off any fat from the skillet and return to medium heat. Add the butter; when hot, add the leek, apple, thyme, salt, and pepper. Cook, stirring frequently, for 3 to 4 minutes, until the leek softens. Add the broth mixture to the pan and bring to a simmer. Pour the broth and leek mixture over and around the chicken thighs.

Bake for 45 minutes, or until the meat shows no pink when cut into at the thickest part. Using tongs, transfer the chicken to individual plates, then spoon some of the sauce over each portion.

Each serving contains approximately:
CAL: 504 PRO: 44g NET CARB: 8.5g FAT: 30g CHOL: 167mg SOD: 427 mg

SERVES 4

# OVEN "FRIED" CHICKEN DRUMSTICKS

This is a quick and easy way to have "fried" chicken—without the mess and hassle of deep-frying. Coleslaw with a Twist (page 97) provides a refreshing, crunchy contrast to the chicken.

3 tablespoons Low-Carb Buttered Bread Crumbs (page 294)

2 tablespoons Atkins Bake Mix

1 tablespoon dry Italian dressing mix (such as Kraft Good Seasons)

$1/2$ teaspoon garlic salt

$1/8$ teaspoon ground black pepper

3 pounds chicken legs (drumsticks only), skinned

**Cooking spray**

Preheat the oven to 450°F. Place the bread crumbs, Bake Mix, dressing mix, garlic salt, and pepper in a gallon-sized, zip-top plastic bag. Seal the bag and shake the ingredients to mix. Add the chicken legs to the bag and reseal it; shake to coat the chicken with the mixture.

Transfer the chicken legs to a baking sheet and discard any leftover coating mixture. Spray the chicken pieces on all sides with cooking spray.

Bake for 30 minutes, or until the chicken is cooked through; the meat should show no pink when cut into at the thickest part. If not done, bake another 5 to 10 minutes and recheck.

Each serving contains approximately:
CAL: 574 PRO: 91g NET CARB: 1g FAT: 20g CHOL: 294mg SOD: 631mg

SERVES 4

# HOT-AND-SOUR CHICKEN LEGS

We like chicken leg quarters because they are tasty, economical, and can be very easy to prepare. These are marinated in a spicy, sweet-and-sour liquid that also serves as a sauce, drizzled on after cooking. Serve these legs with Cauliflower "Couscous" (page 280) for a complete meal.

**MARINADE**

- 1/2 cup soy sauce
- 2 tablespoons fresh orange juice
- 2 tablespoons Worcestershire sauce
- 2 tablespoons low-carb ketchup
- 2 tablespoons peeled and grated fresh ginger
- 12 cloves garlic, minced (about 2 tablespoons)
- 1 tablespoon Splenda Granular sweetener
- 2 teaspoons rice vinegar
- 2 teaspoons hot chili paste, or more to taste

- 4 chicken leg quarters (about 2 1/2 pounds) trimmed of excess fat

Cooking spray

**To make the marinade:** In a medium mixing bowl, whisk together all the marinade ingredients until combined. Remove 1/3 cup of the marinade and refrigerate it, covered, until you're ready to cook the chicken.

Place the chicken legs in a gallon-sized, zip-top plastic bag; pour the remaining marinade over the chicken. Seal the bag, then flip it gently a few times to coat the chicken; refrigerate overnight. Flip the bag a few times during marinating, as well.

When ready to cook, preheat the oven to 375°F. Remove the reserved marinade from the refrigerator to bring it to room temperature. Coat a 13-by-9-inch casserole dish with cooking spray. Remove the chicken from the bag and discard the marinade. Place the chicken in a single layer in the prepared casserole dish, skin side down.

Bake for 30 minutes. Using tongs, flip the chicken legs. Bake for another 40 minutes, or until the chicken is cooked through; the meat should show no pink when cut into at the thickest part. If not done, bake for an additional 5 to 10 minutes and recheck. Pour the reserved 1/3 cup marinade through a fine mesh sieve; discard the solids.

Transfer the chicken legs to individual plates and drizzle the strained marinade over each portion.

---

Each serving contains approximately:
CAL: 369 PRO: 48g NET CARB: 4g FAT: 17g CHOL: 158mg SOD: 1,309mg

SERVES 4

# COCONUT-LIME CHICKEN LEGS

Marinated overnight in an aromatic mixture of coconut milk, fresh lime juice, garlic, and spices, these chicken legs are an easy way to put a taste of the tropics on your table. If you're in a grilling mood, cook over a medium-low fire.

**MARINADE**

- 2 tablespoons fresh lime juice, divided
- 1½ tablespoons lime zest (see page 33)
- One 14-ounce can unsweetened coconut milk (not cream of coconut)
- 1 tablespoon Splenda Granular sweetener
- 1 tablespoon vegetable oil
- 6 cloves garlic, minced (about 1 tablespoon)
- 2 teaspoons kosher salt
- ¼ teaspoon ground cumin
- ¼ teaspoon cayenne pepper

- 4 large chicken leg quarters (about 3½ pounds), skinned and trimmed of excess fat

**Cooking spray**

- 2 tablespoons unsweetened shredded coconut

**To make the marinade:** In a medium mixing bowl, whisk together 1 tablespoon of the lime juice and the remaining marinade ingredients until combined. Refrigerate the remaining lime juice until serving time.

Place the chicken quarters in a gallon-sized zip-top plastic bag; pour the marinade over the chicken and seal the bag. Flip the bag a few times to coat the chicken, then refrigerate the chicken for 24 hours. Flip the bag a few times during marinating, as well.

When ready to cook, preheat the oven to 375°F. Coat a 13-by-9-inch casserole dish with cooking spray. Remove the chicken from the bag and discard the marinade. Place the chicken in a single layer in the prepared dish with the plump, meaty side down.

Bake for 30 minutes. Using tongs, flip the chicken legs. Sprinkle the chicken with the coconut. Bake for another 40 minutes, or until the chicken is cooked through; the meat should show no pink when cut into at the thickest part. If not done, bake for another 5 to 10 minutes and recheck. Before serving, drizzle the reserved 1 tablespoon lime juice over the chicken.

Each serving contains approximately:
CAL: 417 PRO: 47g NET CARB: 0.5g FAT: 23g CHOL: 158mg SOD: 223mg

SERVES 4

# CUMIN ROASTED CHICKEN

A good roasted chicken recipe is a handy thing to have in your low-carb repertoire. After the initial prep you needn't touch the bird again until you're ready to serve, making it perfect for entertaining, or for nights when you're busy and don't have time to fuss in the kitchen. In this recipe, the chicken is rubbed with a pastelike mixture of cumin, orange peel and orange juice, garlic and chili powders, and salt and pepper. The result? A nicely spiced, faintly fruity, crispy-skinned bird that pairs well with Wilted Escarole with Almonds (page 283).

One 5- to 6$\frac{1}{2}$-pound roasting chicken, giblets removed

$\frac{1}{2}$ medium onion, peeled

$\frac{1}{2}$ orange

**SPICE PASTE**

2 tablespoons fresh orange juice

1 tablespoon olive oil

1$\frac{1}{2}$ teaspoons orange zest (see page 33)

1$\frac{1}{2}$ teaspoons ground cumin

1 teaspoon garlic powder

1 teaspoon chili powder

$\frac{1}{2}$ teaspoon ground black pepper

$\frac{1}{2}$ teaspoon kosher salt

Preheat the oven to 425°F. Trim the visible fat from the chicken (do not remove the skin), and rinse inside and out with cool water. Place the bird, breast side up, in a roasting pan and pat it dry with paper towels. Insert the onion and orange half into the cavity. If desired, tuck the wings back and under the bird, and tie the legs together with kitchen string; set aside.

To make the spice paste: In a small bowl, stir together the ingredients. Using clean hands, rub the paste over the surface of the bird, coating it heavily.

Roast for 30 minutes, then reduce the heat to 350°F and roast another 30 to 45 minutes, or until the juices run clear when meat is pierced with a fork and a meat thermometer inserted into the thigh away from the bone registers 180°F. Let rest for 5 to 10 minutes before carving.

Each serving contains approximately:
CAL: 387 PRO: 55g NET CARB: 1.5g FAT: 17g CHOL: 169mg SOD: 207mg

SERVES 6

CHAPTER

# 11

## PORK ENTRÉES

## BOTH OF US ARE BIG FANS OF PORK IN ALL ITS FORMS—SAUSAGE, CUTLETS, CHOPS, TENDERLOIN, AND ROASTS.

Like chicken, pork is a great way to banish the beef blues, so take another look at the pork section at your supermarket. Nearly every week there's a pork cut on sale, and this chapter gives you recipes that use almost all of them.

One of our favorite recipes in the book, Skillet Pork Chops with Mushrooms and Capers, is in this chapter. It's full of savory and salty flavors, isn't difficult to prepare, and is suitable for company or just family; don't miss it.

Pork frequently plays a starring role in Asian cooking, and we've carried on this tradition with a Pork and Peanut Stir-Fry, Miso and Garlic Pork Cutlets, and a Pork and Broccoli Slaw "Lo Mein" that utilizes bagged broccoli slaw. Although higher in fat than regular pork, pork sausage is delicious and earns a place in this chapter as well.

# SAUSAGE AND SAUERKRAUT

This is a version of a recipe obtained from a German friend of Kitty's mother. Hearty and quick to prepare, it's just what you need after a busy day raking fall leaves or shoveling snow in the winter.

1 pound sweet Italian sausage (if in casings, squeeze the sausage out of the casings, then break into small chunks)

Two 15-ounce cans sauerkraut, lightly rinsed and well drained

1 teaspoon caraway seeds, crushed between your fingers

3/4 cup sour cream (not nonfat)

In a medium skillet or sauté pan over medium heat, cook the sausage for 15 minutes, or until cooked through, breaking up the meat with a spoon or spatula while cooking. When the sausage is fully cooked, drain off any fat, then place the sausage pieces in a colander, and rinse them with hot water to remove additional fat. Return the sausage to the pan over medium heat.

Stir in the sauerkraut and caraway seeds until well mixed. Cook, uncovered, for about 5 minutes, or until the sauerkraut is heated through. Stir in the sour cream and heat an additional minute to warm the sour cream. Serve immediately.

Each serving contains approximately:
CAL: 415 PRO: 21g NET CARB: 4g FAT: 33g CHOL: 91mg SOD: 1,682mg

SERVES 4

# SPICY SAUSAGE WITH WHITE AND GREEN BEANS

Nothing beats a one-dish meal on a busy night. This skillet supper, which uses both canned and frozen beans, can be on the table in about 20 minutes (including prep time)!

1 tablespoon olive oil

1½ pounds spicy Italian sausage links, cut into 1-inch pieces

2 cups (about 8 ounces) frozen green beans (about 2 cups)

One 15-ounce can white soybeans, rinsed and drained

1 teaspoon minced dried onions

½ teaspoon kosher salt

¼ teaspoon ground black pepper

1 teaspoon dried oregano

⅛ teaspoon garlic powder

½ cup chicken broth

1 tablespoon tomato paste

¼ cup grated Parmesan cheese for garnish (optional)

In a large skillet or sauté pan over medium heat, warm the olive oil. Add the sausage and cook, stirring frequently, for 4 minutes, or until the sausage is lightly browned on all sides.

Stir in the green beans, soybeans, onions, salt, pepper, oregano, and garlic powder; cook for another 5 minutes. Stir in the broth and tomato paste and bring the mixture to a simmer, stirring to dissolve the tomato paste.

Test the doneness of the sausage by cutting into one piece with a knife (it should no longer be pink in the center). When done, divide the mixture among individual bowls, and garnish each portion with the Parmesan cheese, if desired.

Each serving contains approximately:
CAL: 471 PRO: 30g NET CARB: 7g FAT: 35g CHOL: 89mg SOD: 1,282mg

SERVES 5

# FRIED ITALIAN SAUSAGE WITH PEPPERS, MUSHROOMS, AND ONIONS

The classic combination of Italian sausage, peppers, and onions doesn't need much improvement. However, we prefer a more colorful version that features yellow and red peppers instead of the more typical green ones, and for extra texture we've added sliced mushrooms. To cut cooking time a bit, let the sausages warm up on the counter while you prep the vegetables.

1 medium (about 8 ounces) yellow bell pepper, seeded and thinly sliced

1 medium (about 8 ounces) red bell pepper, seeded and thinly sliced

1 medium onion, thinly sliced (about 1 cup)

One 8-ounce package sliced button mushrooms, washed

3 tablespoons olive oil, divided

1 1/2 pounds sweet Italian sausage links, halved crosswise

1 teaspoon kosher salt

1/2 teaspoon ground black pepper

Cut the pepper and onion slices into 1-inch pieces. Combine the peppers, onion, and mushrooms in a medium mixing bowl and set aside.

In a large skillet or sauté pan over medium heat, warm 1 tablespoon of the olive oil. When hot, add the sausage pieces. Reduce the heat to medium-low and cover the pan. Cook the sausages for 8 to 15 minutes, stirring occasionally, until they're no longer pink in the center (cut into one to check). Transfer to a plate and cover with aluminum foil to keep warm. Drain off any fat in the pan.

Raise the heat to medium and warm the remaining 2 tablespoons of olive oil in the pan. Add the vegetables, salt, and pepper. Cook and stir until the onions are soft and the peppers are crisp-tender, 6 to 8 minutes.

To serve, divide the vegetables among individual plates and top with the sausages.

Each serving contains approximately:
CAL: 595 PRO: 31g NET CARB: 10g FAT: 47g CHOL: 111mg SOD: 1,432mg

SERVES 4

# BROCCOLI RABE WITH SAUSAGE AND ONIONS

A classic Italian combination; the panfried sausage is a great match for the slightly bitter broccoli rabe.

2 tablespoons olive oil

1¹/₂ pounds sweet Italian sausage links, halved crosswise

1 medium onion, halved and cut into ¹/₄-inch-thick slices (about 1 cup)

4 cloves garlic, minced (about 2 teaspoons)

1 bunch broccoli rabe (about 1 pound), trimmed and cut into 2-inch long pieces

¹/₂ cup water

¹/₂ teaspoon ground black pepper

¹/₂ teaspoon Tabasco sauce

¹/₄ teaspoon kosher salt

Grated Parmesan cheese for garnish (optional)

In a large sauté pan or skillet over medium heat, warm the olive oil. When hot, add the sausage pieces. Cook, stirring occasionally, for 10 minutes, or until the sausage pieces are browned on all sides. Add the sliced onion; cook and stir for another 4 minutes, until the onion softens. Cut one sausage piece in half to see if it's cooked through; it should no longer be pink in the center. If not, cook 2 more minutes and recheck for doneness. Transfer the cooked sausages and onions to a platter and set aside.

Return the skillet to medium heat; add the garlic and stir for about 30 seconds, until fragrant. Add the broccoli rabe, water, pepper, Tabasco, and salt to the skillet. Cook, stirring and scraping up any browned bits from the bottom of the pan, until the broccoli rabe is soft and bright green, about 4 minutes. Spoon the broccoli rabe mixture over the sausage and onions on the platter; toss gently and serve, topped with Parmesan, if desired.

Each serving contains approximately:
CAL: 470 PRO: 28g NET CARB: 10.5g FAT: 36g CHOL: 89mg SOD: 1,110mg

SERVES 4

# PORK MEDALLIONS WITH BALSAMIC PAN SAUCE

Pork tenderloin is a great cut for the cook-in-a-hurry. It cooks in just minutes, and true to its name, it's very tender if you don't overcook it. Be sure to trim the tough, pearly membrane on the tenderloin (called the silver skin) before cutting it into medallions. Serve this pork with a side of Wilted Escarole with Almonds (page 283).

One 16-ounce pork tender-loin, silver skin removed

$1/2$ teaspoon kosher salt

$1/4$ teaspoon ground black pepper

2 tablespoons butter, divided

1 tablespoon olive oil

1 shallot, minced

1 clove garlic, minced (about $1/2$ teaspoon)

$1/2$ cup balsamic vinegar

$1/4$ cup chicken broth

$1/2$ teaspoon Italian seasoning

Cut the tenderloin on the diagonal into $3/4$-inch-thick slices (12 to 15 slices). Place the slices between pieces of plastic wrap. Using a rolling pin or the flat side of a meat mallet, pound them to a $1/2$-inch thickness. Sprinkle the pork with the salt and pepper; set aside.

In a large skillet or sauté pan over medium-high heat, melt 1 table-spoon of the butter with the olive oil. Add half the pork (so as not to crowd it in the pan) and cook for 2 minutes. Using tongs, flip the pork and cook for another 2 minutes, until nicely browned but not cooked through. Transfer the pork to a plate and cover with aluminum foil. Repeat with the remaining pork.

Add the shallot and garlic to the skillet and cook, stirring with a wooden spoon, for 1 to 2 minutes, or until the shallot softens. Add the vinegar and bring to a boil, scraping up any browned bits from the bottom of the pan. Boil the sauce for 4 minutes, or until it's reduced by half. Check the plate of pork for any juices that may have drained off, and add them to the skillet along with the chicken broth and Italian seasoning. Cook, stirring occasionally, for another 2 minutes, or until slightly reduced.

Return the pork to the skillet and cook for 2 minutes to heat through (do not overcook the pork; it will still be a little pink inside). Using clean tongs, transfer the pork to individual plates. Turn off the heat and stir the remaining 1 tablespoon butter into the sauce. Pour the sauce over each serving of pork and serve immediately.

Each serving contains approximately:
CAL: 391 PRO: 38g NET CARB: 13.5g FAT: 19g CHOL: 126mg SOD: 325mg

SERVES 3

# PORK AND PEANUT STIR-FRY

This dish gets its nutty flavor two ways—from the sauce, which utilizes low-carb peanut butter, and from a sprinkling of chopped peanuts as a garnish—ensuring both a good peanut flavor and a satisfying crunch. Check the ethnic-foods section of the grocery store for Chinese five-spice powder, if you can't find it in the regular spice section.

**SAUCE**

3/4 cup chicken broth

1/2 cup water

1/4 cup tamari or soy sauce

2 tablespoons low-carb peanut butter (such as Carb Options)

1 tablespoon cornstarch

1/2 teaspoon Chinese five-spice powder

1/2 teaspoon garlic powder

1 pound pork loin for stir-fry or pork cutlets, excess fat trimmed, cut in 1/4-by-2-inch strips

1 tablespoon toasted sesame oil

1 tablespoon minced, dried onions

2 cloves garlic, minced (about 1 teaspoon)

2 tablespoons peanut oil, divided

Two 16-ounce bags frozen stir-fry vegetable mixture, thawed

1/4 cup cocktail peanuts, chopped

**To make the sauce:** In a 4-cup liquid measuring cup, whisk together all the sauce ingredients until blended; set aside.

In a small mixing bowl, using a wooden spoon, combine the pork strips, sesame oil, dried onions, and garlic; set aside.

In a wok or large skillet with tall sides, over high heat, warm 1 tablespoon of the peanut oil. When hot, add the pork. Cook, stirring constantly, for 4 to 5 minutes, or until the pork is nearly cooked through. Transfer to a bowl and set aside.

Reduce the heat to medium-high and add the remaining 1 tablespoon peanut oil. When hot, add the stir-fry vegetable mixture. Cook, stirring constantly, for about 5 minutes, or until the vegetables are tender but not mushy. Raise the heat back to high and return the pork to the wok. Whisk the sauce briefly, then add it to the wok and cook for 2 minutes, until heated through and thickened. Divide among individual bowls and sprinkle each portion with the peanuts.

Each serving contains approximately:
CAL: 317 PRO: 25g NET CARB: 9g FAT: 19g CHOL: 49mg SOD: 794mg

SERVES 6

# PORK AND BROCCOLI SLAW "LO MEIN"

Packaged broccoli "slaw" substitutes for the noodles in this traditionally high-carb Chinese dish. Feel free to substitute another pork cut, such as tenderloin or boneless chops, or to use chicken or shrimp instead of the pork. Although the recipe looks complicated, it's mostly prep work; having everything ready for cooking is the key here. Note that the pork does not need to marinate long—just a few minutes while you get the dish started.

3 tablespoons soy sauce

12 cloves garlic, minced (about 2 tablespoons)

1 tablespoon peeled and grated fresh ginger

1 tablespoon Splenda Granular sweetener

2 teaspoons rice vinegar

$1\frac{1}{2}$ pounds pork cutlets, trimmed of excess fat, cut into $\frac{1}{4}$-inch strips

SAUCE

1 cup chicken broth

$\frac{1}{4}$ cup soy sauce

2 tablespoons sake

$1\frac{1}{2}$ teaspoons sesame oil

1 teaspoon Splenda Granular sweetener

$1\frac{1}{2}$ teaspoons low-carb thickener (such as Expert Foods' ThickenThin not/Starch)

$\frac{1}{8}$ teaspoon crushed red pepper flakes

2 tablespoons peanut oil, divided

One 12-ounce package broccoli slaw mix

3 ounces fresh shiitake mushrooms, thinly sliced (about $1\frac{1}{2}$ cups)

$\frac{1}{2}$ medium onion, thinly sliced and cut into 1-inch pieces (about $\frac{1}{2}$ cup)

In a medium mixing bowl, whisk together the soy sauce, garlic, ginger, Splenda, and vinegar. Add the pork to the marinade and stir with a wooden spoon to coat the pork with the mixture; set aside.

**To make the sauce:** In a small mixing bowl, whisk together all the sauce ingredients (the thickener will cause the sauce to gel immediately); set aside.

In a large skillet with high sides, or a wok over high heat, warm 1 tablespoon of the peanut oil. When hot, add the pork (discard the marinade). Cook and stir constantly for 4 to 5 minutes, or until the pork is nearly cooked through. Transfer the pork and any cooking juices to a bowl and set aside.

Reduce the heat to medium-high and add the remaining 1 table-spoon peanut oil. When hot, add the broccoli slaw, mushrooms, and onion. Cook, stirring constantly, for 3 to 4 minutes, or until the onion begins to soften. Raise the heat to high and return the pork and its cooking juices to the skillet. Stir in the sauce and cook for 2 minutes, until heated through. Serve immediately.

Each serving contains approximately:
CAL: 491 PRO: 40g NET CARB: 11g FAT: 29g CHOL: 115mg SOD: 2,180mg

SERVES 4

# MISO AND GARLIC PORK CUTLETS

Miso, a fermented soybean paste, can be found in most produce sections alongside the tofu. In addition to being the basis for classic Japanese miso soup, the paste can also lend seasoning to meats and seafood when used in a marinade. Here we've added sweet hoisin, garlic, and sake to the marinade, giving the pork a distinctively Asian flavor. Serve the dish with Bok Choy Stir-Fry (page 284) for a complete meal.

## MARINADE

- 2 tablespoons soy sauce
- 1 tablespoon yellow miso
- 6 cloves garlic, minced (about 1 tablespoon)
- 1 tablespoon hoisin sauce
- 1 tablespoon sake
- 1 teaspoon vegetable oil

- 2 pounds pork cutlets, trimmed of excess fat

Cooking spray

- 4 scallions, green parts only, chopped (about 1/3 cup) for garnish (optional)

**To make the marinade:** In a small mixing bowl, whisk together all the marinade ingredients until blended; set aside.

Place the pork cutlets in a gallon-sized, zip-top plastic bag. Pour in the marinade and seal the bag. Flip the bag gently to coat the pork with marinade. Refrigerate at least 6 hours or preferably overnight. Flip the bag a few times during marinating, too.

When ready to cook, coat a large skillet or sauté pan with cooking spray. Place the pan over medium heat. While waiting for the pan to heat, remove the pork from the refrigerator; drain and discard the marinade. Place the cutlets in the hot pan and cook for 5 minutes, or until nicely browned on the bottom. Using tongs, flip the cutlets and cook another 4 to 6 minutes, or until browned and opaque throughout.

Divide the pork among individual plates, and garnish each portion with some of the scallions, if desired.

Each serving contains approximately:
CAL: 350 PRO: 37g NET CARB: 3g FAT: 20g CHOL: 109mg SOD: 674mg

SERVES 5

# DIJON PORK
# WITH ONIONS

This mixture of sautéed pork cutlets, bacon, and onions is accented with a creamy sauce flavored with Dijon mustard (a French, white wine–based prepared mustard). It's quick to prepare, and is delicious served with Apple and Almond Salad with Pomegranate Seeds (page 86).

## SAUCE

- 1/4 cup heavy cream
- 2 tablespoons Dijon mustard

<br>

- 1 tablespoon olive oil
- 2 medium onions, thinly sliced (about 2 cups)
- 1/4 teaspoon kosher salt
- 1/4 teaspoon ground black pepper
- 1 1/2 pounds pork cutlets, trimmed of excess fat
- 1 slice bacon, cooked crisp and crumbled (about 2 tablespoons)
- 2 tablespoons finely chopped flat-leaf parsley for garnish (optional)

To make the sauce: In a small mixing bowl, whisk together the cream and mustard until blended; set aside.

In a large skillet or sauté pan over medium heat, warm the olive oil. Add the onions, salt, and pepper. Cook, stirring frequently, for 3 to 5 minutes, or until the onions soften. Using a spatula, push the onions to the outer edge of the pan and place the pork cutlets in the center of the pan.

Cook the cutlets for 5 minutes, or until nicely browned on the bottoms. Using tongs, flip the cutlets and cook for another 4 to 6 minutes, or until opaque throughout and browned on the second side. Add the sauce to the pan along with the bacon and bring the mixture to a simmer. Using a wooden spoon, carefully mix the onions into the sauce and coat the cutlets with the sauce.

Divide the pork, onions, and sauce among individual plates, and garnish each portion with parsley, if desired.

Each serving contains approximately:
CAL: 453 PRO: 39g NET CARB: 3g FAT: 30g CHOL: 136mg SOD: 357mg

SERVES 4

# TOASTED PECAN PORK CUTLETS WITH BOURBON SAUCE

Buttery toasted pecans and a lush bourbon sauce give these cutlets a Southern accent. Try serving them with Spiced Acorn Squash Rings (page 290).

## SPICE MIX

- 1 tablespoon light brown sugar
- 1 teaspoon dry mustard
- 1/2 teaspoon chili powder
- 1/2 teaspoon kosher salt
- 1/4 teaspoon ground black pepper

- 1 1/2 pounds pork cutlets, trimmed of excess fat
- 3 tablespoons butter, divided
- 1/2 cup pecans, chopped
- 1 tablespoon vegetable oil
- 3 tablespoons bourbon
- 1/4 teaspoon Tabasco sauce

**To make the spice mix:** In a medium mixing bowl, stir together the spice mix ingredients. Using clean hands, coat the pork cutlets with the mixture and set aside.

In a small skillet or sauté pan, over medium-low heat, melt 2 tablespoons of the butter. Add the pecans and cook, stirring constantly, for 2 to 3 minutes, or until the nuts are toasted and fragrant; set aside.

In a large skillet or sauté pan over medium heat, melt the remaining 1 tablespoon of butter with the oil. Add the spice-coated cutlets and cook for 4 to 5 minutes, until golden brown on the bottoms. Using tongs, flip the cutlets and cook for another 2 minutes, until browned on the second side.

Add the bourbon to the pan (be careful if cooking with gas, as the bourbon could flare up). Raise the heat to high and cook for 2 to 3 minutes more, until opaque throughout. Transfer the cutlets to individual plates. Add the Tabasco to the pan and let the bourbon sauce continue to cook over high heat until slightly reduced.

To serve, sprinkle the pecans over the cutlets. Pour the sauce over each portion and serve immediately.

Each serving contains approximately:
CAL: 524 PRO: 40g NET CARB: 4.5g FAT: 35g CHOL: 138mg SOD: 259mg

SERVES 4

# SKILLET PORK CHOPS WITH MUSHROOMS AND CAPERS

These delectable chops are fancy enough to serve guests, but easy enough to make on a weeknight. Pair them with the Easy Spinach Bake (page 289) for a nice color and flavor contrast.

1 tablespoon butter

2 tablespoons olive oil, divided

One 10-ounce package button mushrooms, washed and thinly sliced

$1/2$ teaspoon kosher salt

$1/4$ teaspoon ground black pepper

$1/2$ teaspoon dry mustard

4 thick, center-cut pork loin chops (about 2 pounds), trimmed of excess fat

3 tablespoons dry white wine

2 tablespoons capers, drained

2 tablespoons finely minced flat-leaf parsley for garnish (optional)

In a large skillet or sauté pan over medium heat, melt the butter with 1 tablespoon of the olive oil. Add the mushrooms, salt, pepper, and mustard. Cook, stirring constantly, for 4 to 5 minutes, or until the mushrooms have given off some of their liquid. Using a slotted spoon, transfer the mushrooms to a platter and set aside.

Add the remaining 1 tablespoon olive oil to the pan. When hot, add the pork chops; cover and cook for 6 to 7 minutes, until nicely browned on the bottoms. Using tongs, flip the chops and cook for another 2 minutes. Add the wine and capers and bring to a simmer.

Return the mushrooms to the pan, spooning them between the pork chops. Cover and cook for 4 to 6 minutes, until the pork chops are cooked but still slightly pink in the center (test by cutting into one chop).

Using tongs, transfer the chops to individual plates, then raise the heat to high. Simmer the mushroom mixture another 30 to 45 seconds to thicken the sauce slightly. Using a spoon, divide the mushroom sauce between the plates; garnish each portion with a sprinkle of parsley, if desired.

Each serving contains approximately:
CAL: 459 PRO: 50g NET CARB: 2.5g FAT: 26g CHOL: 142mg SOD: 335mg

SERVES 4

CHAPTER

# 12

## BEEF ENTRÉES

## BEEF, AN ENTERTAINING FAVORITE, IS ALSO A WEEKNIGHT STAPLE IN MANY LOW-CARB HOUSEHOLDS.

This chapter features a diverse collection of beef recipes featuring a variety of cuts (brisket, ground beef, short ribs, pot roast, beef tips, flank steak, sirloin steak, rib-eye steaks, etc). Stock up on beef when it goes on sale (and also look for marked-down packaged meat—it's fine if you eat it or freeze it by the date on the package) and with this chapter, you'll always have a way to use it.

While our grilling recipes and "company's coming" recipes for beef are found in other chapters, here we've provided you with some family favorites (American Chop Suey, Saturday Night Pot Roast) and some fresh beef ideas (Sirloin Puttanesca and Stir-Fried Beef with Edamame and Mushrooms). Many of these recipes, such as the Boneless Rib-eye Steaks with Boursin Cheese and Steak au Poivre, can be served to guests with complete confidence, not to mention ease.

Given the range of recipes here, you're sure to find something to please yourself—and all the others who'll come drifting into the kitchen once they smell what you're cooking!

# STEAK AU POIVRE

These pepper-encrusted strip steaks are finished with a brandy cream sauce—an intense combination that tastes "restaurant fancy." Serve the steaks with Creamy Cauliflower Purée (page 286) and a green salad. Substituting tuna steaks for the beef would also be delicious.

2 teaspoons ground black pepper

1/2 teaspoon kosher salt

Two 8-ounce strip steaks

1 tablespoon olive oil

3 tablespoons brandy

1/3 cup heavy cream

1 tablespoon finely chopped flat-leaf parsley for garnish (optional)

In a small bowl, stir together the pepper and salt. Pat the mixture onto both sides of each steak. In a large skillet or sauté pan over medium heat, warm the olive oil. When hot, add the steaks; cook for 3 to 4 minutes, or until nicely browned on the bottom. Using tongs, flip the steaks and cook for another 3 minutes, or until desired doneness (see the Doneness Chart on page 25). Transfer the steaks to a platter and cover with aluminum foil.

Add the brandy to the pan and step back, as it may ignite (especially if using a gas stove). If it does ignite, the flame should only last about 10 seconds. Bring the brandy to a simmer and stir in the cream using a wooden spoon. Bring the mixture to a simmer and cook for 30 to 45 seconds, or until reduced and slightly thickened. Turn off the heat.

Return the steaks to the pan. Using clean tongs, flip the steaks to coat with the sauce. Transfer the steaks to individual plates and pour the remaining sauce over the top. Garnish with a sprinkle of parsley, if desired.

Each serving contains approximately:
CAL: 589 PRO: 50g NET CARB: 2g FAT: 36g CHOL: 178mg SOD: 250mg

SERVES 2

# BONELESS RIB-EYE STEAKS WITH BOURSIN CHEESE

Creamy garlic-and-herb Boursin cheese, softened by the heat of the seasoned, panfried steaks, gives this weeknight-easy dinner a sophisticated feel. Top it off with Caramelized Vidalia Onion Relish (page 301) for yet another layer of flavor.

**SPICE MIX**

- $1/2$ teaspoon ground black pepper
- $1/4$ teaspoon kosher salt
- $1/4$ teaspoon chili powder

- Two 8-ounce boneless rib-eye steaks, at room temperature
- 1 tablespoon olive oil
- 3 tablespoons Garlic-and-Herb Boursin cheese, at room temperature, divided

**To make the spice mix:** In a small bowl, stir together the pepper, salt, and chili powder. Season one side of each steak with the seasoning mixture; set aside.

In a large, heavy skillet or sauté pan over medium-high heat, warm the olive oil. Place the steaks in the pan, unseasoned side down, and cook for 5 minutes. Using tongs, flip the steaks and cook on the second side for 3 to 4 minutes, or until they reach desired doneness (see the Doneness Chart on page 25).

Transfer the cooked steaks to individual plates, seasoned side up. Top each steak with half of the Boursin cheese. Let rest for 5 minutes before serving.

**Note**

If you'd like a more peppery steak, use the Pepper Boursin cheese.

Each serving contains approximately:
CAL: 528 PRO: 49g NET CARB: 0g FAT: 36g CHOL: 163mg SOD: 316mg

SERVES 2

# STIR-FRIED BEEF WITH EDAMAME AND MUSHROOMS

Shelled edamame (fresh soybeans), widely available frozen, is an unusual twist in this garlicky vegetable-beef stir-fry. For people who don't like tofu, edamame is an easy way to include soy in their diet.

$1^1/_2$ pounds London broil or sirloin, trimmed of excess fat

3 tablespoons soy sauce

12 cloves garlic, minced (about 2 tablespoons)

$1^1/_2$ cups frozen, shelled edamame, cooked according to package directions and drained

$^1/_2$ medium onion, thinly sliced, cut into 1-inch-long pieces (about $^1/_2$ cup)

One 8-ounce package sliced button mushrooms, washed

$^1/_2$ cup matchstick-cut carrots

**SAUCE**

3 tablespoons soy sauce

$^3/_4$ cup beef broth

1 teaspoon toasted sesame oil

1 teaspoon sugar

1 teaspoon low-carb thickener (such as Expert Foods' ThickenThin not/Starch)

2 tablespoons vegetable oil

Cut the beef into strips about 3 inches long and $^1/_4$ inch wide; put them in a medium mixing bowl. Top the beef with the soy sauce and garlic. Mix well with clean hands or a wooden spoon; set aside.

In a medium mixing bowl, combine the cooked edamame, onion, mushrooms, and carrots; set aside.

**To make the sauce:** In a small mixing bowl, working quickly, whisk together all the sauce ingredients (the sauce will thicken quickly); set aside.

In a large skillet with high sides or a wok over high heat, warm the oil. When hot, add the beef. Cook, stirring, for 2 minutes, or until the beef is partially cooked but still shows some red in the center of the pieces. Transfer the beef to a plate and set aside.

Add the vegetables to the pan and cook, stirring, for 3 to 5 minutes, or until the mushrooms have given off some of their liquid and the onions have softened slightly. Return the beef to the pan and add the sauce. Cook and stir for 2 to 4 minutes, or until the beef is completely cooked and the sauce is heated through.

Each serving contains approximately:
CAL: 395 PRO: 43g NET CARB: 11g FAT: 18g CHOL: 101mg SOD: 1,490mg

SERVES 5

# AMERICAN CHOP SUEY

The name "American Chop Suey" was completely foreign (no pun intended) to Kitty when she moved to the East Coast from the Midwest. Upon hearing the list of its ingredients from a Massachusetts-raised old-timer, she realized that she'd grown up calling the dish "goulash." Whatever you want to call it, the combination of ground beef, tomatoes, macaroni, and Italian spices is as economical as it is tasty.

2 tablespoons olive oil

1 medium onion, chopped (about 1 cup)

3 cloves garlic, minced (about 1 tablespoon)

1 1/2 teaspoons dried oregano

1/2 teaspoon kosher salt

1/4 teaspoon ground black pepper

1 pound lean ground beef

2 tablespoons tomato paste

One 14 1/2-ounce can Italian-style diced tomatoes

1/2 teaspoon Tabasco sauce

1 cup low-carb elbow macaroni, cooked according to package directions and drained

1/4 cup grated Parmesan cheese

In a large skillet or sauté pan with high sides, over medium heat, warm the olive oil. Add the onion, garlic, oregano, salt, pepper, and beef. Cook, stirring frequently, for 4 to 6 minutes, or until the beef is cooked through.

Stir in the tomato paste, tomatoes, Tabasco, and macaroni. Cook and stir for another 2 to 4 minutes, or until the mixture is heated through.

Divide the mixture among individual bowls and sprinkle each portion with 1 tablespoon of the Parmesan.

Each serving contains approximately:
CAL: 484 PRO: 41g NET CARB: 14g FAT: 27g CHOL: 91mg SOD: 862mg

SERVES 4

# SIRLOIN PUTTANESCA

Puttanesca is a distinctive tomato sauce flavored with capers, anchovies, and olives. We love it served over a thick sirloin steak, but it would be equally delicious with boneless chicken breasts or swordfish. If you like, you can prepare the sauce a day ahead and keep it refrigerated. Asparagus with Parmesan (page 277) is a nice accompaniment.

1 tablespoon olive oil

$1/2$ teaspoon kosher salt

$1/2$ teaspoon ground black pepper

2 pounds boneless sirloin steak, trimmed of excess fat

**PUTTANESCA SAUCE**

1 tablespoon olive oil

2 cloves garlic, minced (about 1 teaspoon)

One $14 1/2$-ounce can diced tomatoes

$1/2$ cup pitted Kalamata olives, chopped

1 tablespoon capers, drained

2 teaspoons anchovy paste or finely minced anchovies

$1/4$ teaspoon ground black pepper

$1/4$ teaspoon dried oregano

$1/8$ teaspoon crushed red pepper flakes

$1/8$ teaspoon onion powder

1 tablespoon butter, softened

In a small bowl, stir together the olive oil, salt, and pepper. Using clean hands, rub the mixture onto both sides of the steak. Let the steak sit at room temperature while preparing the sauce.

**To make the sauce:** In a large skillet or sauté pan over medium heat, warm the olive oil. Add the garlic and cook, stirring, for 1 minute, until fragrant. Add the remaining sauce ingredients except for the butter and bring the mixture to a simmer. Cook, stirring frequently, for 5 minutes, or until heated through and well combined. Turn off the heat and stir in the butter until melted. Set the sauce aside while cooking the steak.

Heat a large skillet or sauté pan over medium heat until hot. Add the steak, cover, and cook for 5 to 8 minutes, or until the steak is nicely browned on the bottom. Using tongs, flip the steak, then cover the pan again and cook for another 5 to 8 minutes, or until the steak reaches desired doneness (see Doneness Chart on page 25). Transfer the steak to a plate and let rest for 5 minutes before serving.

To serve, cut the sirloin into thin slices. Divide the slices among individual plates, and spoon the sauce over and around each portion of steak.

Each serving contains approximately:
CAL: 520 PRO: 62g NET CARB: 4g FAT: 27g CHOL: 185mg SOD: 543mg

SERVES 4

# FAJITA FLANK STEAK

Fajitas are a great dish to serve a buffet crowd—everyone can make his fajita the way he likes and no one feels like they're getting "diet food." Offer low-carb tortillas along with regular flour tortillas, but other than that you needn't make any special arrangements for low-carbers like yourself. Typical fajita ingredients—spicy beef or chicken, panfried onions and peppers, cheese, tomatoes, sour cream—are all fine on a low-carb diet. This recipe results in a tender, moist flank steak that has a medium amount of seasoning; no one will think it's too spicy, and those that want more spice can add the condiment of their choice.

Two 1$\frac{1}{4}$- to 1$\frac{1}{2}$-pound flank steaks, about $\frac{1}{2}$ inch thick, trimmed of excess fat

2 tablespoons vegetable oil

3 cloves garlic, minced (about 1 tablespoon)

3 tablespoons Mexican seasoning (such as McCormick)

1 teaspoon kosher salt

2 tablespoons Worcestershire sauce

Cooking spray

Working on a clean surface, with clean hands, rub both sides of the steak with the oil and garlic. Rub on the Mexican seasoning and the salt, covering both sides evenly. Transfer the steak to a gallon-sized, zip-top plastic bag or to a baking sheet. Add the Worcestershire sauce to the pan or the bag and, using tongs, flip the meat so both sides are coated. Seal the bag or cover the baking sheet with plastic wrap and refrigerate for at least 6 hours, or up to 12 hours.

When ready to cook, preheat the boiler and coat a large broiling pan with cooking spray. Broil the steaks for 8 to 15 minutes, or until they reach desired doneness (see Doneness Chart on page 25).

Let the steaks rest for 5 minutes on a clean cutting board. Slice the meat on the diagonal, against the grain, into $\frac{1}{8}$- to $\frac{1}{4}$-inch-thick slices.

Each serving (enough steak for two average fajitas) contains approximately:
CAL: 385 PRO: 42g NET CARB: 5g FAT: 20g CHOL: 105mg SOD: 677mg

SERVES 6

# TIP STEAKS WITH WILD MUSHROOM SAUCE

Kim serves sirloin tip steaks frequently because they're tender, flavorful, and cook quickly; Kitty just discovered them, and regrets she's been missing out for so long. Here, the browned steaks are smothered in a creamy sauce featuring wild mushrooms, onion, and garlic. Don't skip the cheese garnish; it adds an extra layer of savory flavor to the dish.

2 tablespoons vegetable oil

3 cloves garlic, minced (about 1 tablespoon)

2 pounds sirloin tip steaks

10 ounces wild mushrooms, such as cremini, oyster, or shiitake, coarsely chopped

$1/2$ large onion, thinly sliced (about $3/4$ cup)

$1/4$ teaspoon kosher salt

$1/4$ teaspoon ground black pepper

One $14 1/2$-ounce can beef broth

1 teaspoon low-carb thickener (such as Expert Foods' ThickenThin not/Starch)

1 cube beef bouillon

2 tablespoons heavy cream

$1/3$ cup shredded Parmesan or Asiago cheese for garnish

In a large, deep skillet or sauté pan over medium heat, warm the oil. Add the garlic and stir until fragrant, about 1 minute. Add the steaks and cook for 3 minutes, or until browned on the bottom. Using tongs, flip the steaks and cook another 5 to 7 minutes, until browned on the second sides; the centers will still be red when cut into with a sharp knife. Transfer the steaks to a plate and set aside.

In the same skillet, stir together the mushrooms, onion, salt, and pepper. Cook and stir for 5 minutes, or until the onions soften. Whisk together the beef broth and thickener; add to the skillet, along with the bouillon cube. Cook, stirring, for 3 minutes, or until the bouillon is dissolved and the sauce has thickened slightly.

Return the steaks to the pan and cook, without stirring, for 5 minutes, or until the mixture comes to a simmer and the steaks are cooked through (they should still be slightly pink inside). Using tongs, transfer the steaks to a serving platter or individual plates.

To finish the dish, stir the cream into the sauce and cook for 1 minute, or until heated through. Spoon some of the sauce over each portion and garnish with a sprinkle of the Parmesan or Asiago.

Each serving contains approximately:
CAL: 354 PRO: 43g NET CARB: 4g FAT: 17g CHOL: 118mg SOD: 638mg

SERVES 6

# SPICY BEEF TIPS WITH ONIONS AND JALAPEÑOS

This spicy dish, seasoned with cayenne, chili powder, paprika, cumin, and jalapeños, is easily prepared and wonderfully complemented by a basic green salad with Lime Vinaigrette (page 95). Serve a few low-carb tortilla chips alongside, if you like.

### SPICE MIX

- 2 teaspoons dried oregano
- $3/4$ teaspoon paprika
- $1/2$ teaspoon kosher salt
- $1/2$ teaspoon cayenne pepper
- $1/2$ teaspoon chili powder
- $1/4$ teaspoon ground cumin

- $1 1/2$ pounds sirloin tip steaks, cut into 1-inch pieces
- 3 tablespoons low-carb beer
- 1 tablespoon tomato paste
- 1 tablespoon vegetable oil
- 6 cloves garlic, minced (about 1 tablespoon)
- $2/3$ cup canned jalapeño slices, drained
- 2 medium onions, halved and thinly sliced (about 2 cups)
- 1 tablespoon plus 1 teaspoon fresh lime juice

Sour cream for garnish (optional)

Finely chopped cilantro for garnish (optional)

**To make the spice mix:** In a large mixing bowl, stir together the spice mix ingredients.

Add the beef to the bowl. Using clean hands, toss the beef with the spices to coat; set aside. In a small bowl, combine the beer and tomato paste; set aside.

In a large skillet or sauté pan over medium-high heat, warm the oil. Add the garlic, jalapeño slices, onions, and spice-coated beef. Cook, stirring frequently, for 5 minutes, or until the onions soften and the beef begins to brown. Stir in the beer and tomato paste mixture and bring to a simmer. Simmer until the beef reaches desired doneness (see Doneness Chart on page 25).

Divide the mixture among individual bowls. Top each serving with 1 teaspoon of fresh lime juice, and offer sour cream and cilantro as additional garnishes, if desired.

Each serving contains approximately:
CAL: 338 PRO: 43g NET CARB: 7g FAT: 14g CHOL: 115mg SOD: 519mg

SERVES 4

# RED WINE-MARINATED
# SIRLOIN STEAK

Kitty is a fan of simple steak preparations, so she came up with this quick and easy treatment. It's heavy on the wine, which results in a steak with lots of red wine flavor. If you'd rather a more traditional marinade, cut the amount of red wine in half—you'll still have enough marinade to cover the meat.

**MARINADE**

- 1/2 cup dry red wine
- 1 tablespoon tamari or soy sauce
- 1 tablespoon olive oil
- 2 cloves garlic, minced (about 1 teaspoon)

1- to 1 1/4-pound boneless sirloin steak, trimmed of excess fat

**To make the marinade:** In a shallow casserole dish large enough to hold the steak, stir together the marinade ingredients.

Add the steak to the dish, then, using tongs, flip the steak to coat both sides. Cover the dish with plastic wrap and refrigerate for 2 hours. Flip the steak again, cover, and marinate for 2 hours more.

When ready to cook, preheat the broiler. Place the steak on the broiling pan (discard the marinade) and broil for 8 to 12 minutes, or until the steak reaches desired doneness (see Doneness Chart on page 25). Let rest for 5 minutes on a cutting board before serving.

Each serving contains approximately:
CAL: 424 PRO: 56g NET CARB: 2g FAT: 18g CHOL: 162mg SOD: 324mg

SERVES 2

# KIM'S
# BRISKET
Kim's brisket is not the dry, flavorless brisket you may have had in the past. This version infuses flavor into the meat first via a marinade and then with a beefy cooking liquid loaded with herbs and spices. Cooked slowly and finished with a sauce fashioned from the cooking juices, this brisket may just change your notion of how brisket is supposed to taste.

## MARINADE

**One 12-ounce bottle low-carb beer**

**1 packet dry Italian dressing mix (such as Kraft Good Seasons)**

**1 tablespoon cider vinegar**

**$2^1/_2$- to 3-pound flat cut beef brisket, trimmed of excess fat**

## COOKING LIQUID

**One $14^1/_2$-ounce can beef broth**

**$1/_3$ cup low-carb ketchup**

**2 tablespoons minced dried onions**

**6 cloves garlic, minced (about 1 tablespoon)**

**1 tablespoon tomato paste**

**1 cube beef bouillon**

**$1/_2$ teaspoon ground black pepper**

**$1/_2$ teaspoon dried rosemary**

**$1/_4$ teaspoon dried thyme**

**$1/_4$ teaspoon paprika**

**1 bay leaf**

**1 tablespoon cornstarch**

**To make the marinade:** In a medium mixing bowl, stir together the beer, dressing mix, and vinegar. Place the brisket into a shallow casserole dish large enough so it lays flat; pour the marinade over the meat. Cover the dish with plastic wrap and refrigerate for 24 hours, flipping the meat once about halfway through.

When ready to cook, preheat the oven to 300°F.

**To make the cooking liquid:** In a medium mixing bowl, stir together all the cooking liquid ingredients until blended. Remove the brisket from the marinade (discard the marinade), and place it in a 13-by-9-inch baking dish; pour the liquid over the meat. Cover tightly with aluminum foil.

Bake for 4 hours. Carefully transfer the brisket to a platter (reserve the cooking juices) and let rest, uncovered, for 10 minutes. Meanwhile, in a small saucepan, whisk together the cornstarch and 2 cups of the cooking juices. Bring the mixture to a simmer over medium-high heat, whisking constantly, until the sauce thickens, about 5 minutes.

Trim any remaining fat from the brisket. Using a long, sharp knife, cut the meat against the muscle grain into $1/_2$-inch slices. Divide the meat among individual plates and top each portion with about $1/_4$ cup of the sauce.

Each serving contains approximately:
CAL: 342 PRO: 41g NET CARB: 7.5g FAT: 15g CHOL: 96mg SOD: 1,679mg

SERVES 4

# SATURDAY NIGHT
# POT ROAST

Both of us have found, in talking with friends, that many cooks of our generation haven't the slightest idea of how to cook a pot roast. It's too bad, because it's a perfect weekend evening meal—everything cooks in one pot, and it makes your house smell great all afternoon! (If you'd like, prepare the roast one day ahead—the flavors will be more developed, and you can scrape off any unwanted fat from the congealed cooking juices before reheating.) With supermarkets taking the guesswork out of choosing the right meat cuts (beef labels frequently indicate "for pot roast" or "for grilling" and the like), all that's needed is a good, classic recipe. This is it.

- 1 tablespoon olive oil
- One 2- to 3-pound chuck pot roast, trimmed of excess fat
- 6 cloves garlic, minced (about 1 tablespoon)
- 1 cup dry red wine
- One 14 1/2-ounce can beef broth
- 2 cubes beef bouillon
- 1 teaspoon ground black pepper
- 1 teaspoon dried oregano
- 1 teaspoon dried thyme
- 1 tablespoon Dijon mustard
- 1 1/2 cups peeled and chopped carrots
- 3 stalks celery, finely chopped
- 8 ounces frozen small white onions, thawed
- 8 ounces button mushrooms, washed and halved (or quartered, if large)

Preheat the oven to 325°F. In a large Dutch oven over medium heat, warm the olive oil. Add the pot roast and cook for 4 to 5 minutes, until nicely browned on the bottom. Flip the meat over and cook for another 4 minutes, until browned on all sides. Transfer the roast to a large plate and set aside.

Reduce the heat to low; add the garlic and cook for 1 minute, until fragrant. Add the wine, then raise the heat to medium. Bring to a simmer while stirring and scraping the bottom of the pan. Stir in the broth, bouillon cubes, pepper, oregano, thyme, and mustard. Return to a simmer again, then turn off the heat.

Return the meat to the Dutch oven, cover, and bake for 1 1/2 hours. Add the carrots, celery, and onions to the pot, scattering them around the roast; sprinkle the mushrooms over the top of the roast. Re-cover and cook for 1 hour more, then test the vegetables for tenderness. If not done, cook for 10 minutes more, then retest.

When done, carefully remove the meat from the Dutch oven and place it on a platter. Let rest for 10 minutes. Cut the meat into 4 portions, removing any obvious gristle. Divide the meat among individual bowls and ladle the vegetables over the top of each portion.

Each serving contains approximately:
CAL: 480 PRO: 59g NET CARB: 11g FAT: 18g CHOL: 165mg SOD: 1,119mg

SERVES 4

# SLOW-COOKED SHORT RIBS WITH TOMATOES AND RED WINE

This was a favorite food of Kim's grandfather, and the more we eat them, the more we like them, too. There are many different ways to prepare short ribs, but regardless of the recipe, when they're properly cooked, short ribs are fork-tender and intensely flavored. The portion size here is quite large; experience has shown us that people typically eat hearty portions of short ribs.

3 pounds boneless beef short ribs

$1/2$ teaspoon kosher salt

2 teaspoons ground black pepper

$1 1/2$ tablespoons olive oil

**COOKING LIQUID**

2 tablespoons olive oil

18 cloves garlic, minced (about 3 tablespoons)

1 medium onion, finely chopped (about 1 cup)

2 teaspoons dried rosemary, crushed between your fingers

$3/4$ teaspoon celery salt

1 cube beef bouillon

1 cup dry red wine

1 bay leaf

1 cup canned crushed tomatoes

1 cup of water (more if needed to thin gravy)

Preheat the oven to 300°F. Sprinkle the ribs with the salt and pepper.

In a large Dutch oven over medium heat, warm the $1 1/2$ tablespoons olive oil. Add the ribs and brown on all sides (about 2 minutes per side), then transfer to a platter using tongs.

**To make the cooking liquid:** In the same Dutch oven over medium heat, warm the 2 tablespoons olive oil. Add the garlic, onion, rosemary, celery salt, and bouillon cube. Cook, stirring frequently, for 5 minutes, or until the onion softens. Add the wine and bay leaf and continue to cook, stirring occasionally, until the mixture reaches a simmer. Stir in the tomatoes and water; bring to a simmer again, then turn off the heat. Using tongs, add the ribs to the liquid in the pot and turn to coat them with the cooking liquid.

Cover the Dutch oven, then bake the ribs for 3 hours, stirring after each hour of cooking, and adding additional water if the sauce becomes extremely thick. After 3 hours, remove the ribs from the oven and let them rest, covered, for 15 minutes before serving. Discard the bay leaf. To serve, remove the ribs from the Dutch oven using tongs, then spoon the sauce over them.

Each serving contains approximately:
CAL: 665 PRO: 57g NET CARB: 5.5g FAT: 43g CHOL: 169mg SOD: 514mg

SERVES 5

# MOZZARELLA-STUFFED MEATLOAF

A generous amount of mozzarella cheese hidden inside Italian-seasoned beef gives this meatloaf an unexpected twist. Low-carb ketchup, used both in the meat mixture and as a topping, is no longer difficult to find, and any brand will work just fine.

One 6-ounce chunk part-skim mozzarella cheese

3 slices Atkins white bread, crusts trimmed

2 pounds lean ground beef

1 medium onion, finely chopped (about 1 cup)

2 eggs

$1/4$ cup plus 1 tablespoon low-carb ketchup, divided

1 tablespoon Worcestershire sauce

6 cloves garlic, minced (about 1 tablespoon)

2 teaspoons Italian seasoning

1 teaspoon kosher salt

$3/4$ teaspoon ground black pepper

Preheat the oven to 350°F. Cut the mozzarella into sticks about $1/2$ inch wide and 4 inches long; set aside.

Cut the trimmed bread into $1/4$-inch cubes. In a medium mixing bowl, using a wooden spoon or clean hands, combine the bread cubes with the beef and onion; mix well. In a small bowl, stir together the eggs with the 1 tablespoon of ketchup, the Worcestershire, garlic, Italian seasoning, salt, and pepper. Add the mixture to the beef and stir or mix with clean hands until well combined.

In a broiling pan, shape half of the beef mixture into a loaf about 8 inches long and 5 inches wide. Arrange the mozzarella sticks in the center of the loaf, leaving a $1/2$-inch rim around the edges to help prevent the cheese from leaking out during baking, and stacking the cheese sticks as necessary. Use the rest of the beef mixture to form the top half of the loaf, covering the cheese sticks on all sides and forming an even loaf shape.

Bake the meatloaf for 45 minutes. Remove the loaf from the oven and spoon the $1/4$ cup ketchup over the top. Return to the oven and bake for another 30 minutes. Let cool 5 to 10 minutes before serving.

---

Each serving contains approximately:
CAL: 519 PRO: 51g NET CARB: 5g FAT: 31g CHOL: 220mg SOD: 610mg

SERVES 6

CHAPTER

# 13

## HOT OFF THE GRILL

# GRILLING IS AN AMERICAN PASTIME THAT PRACTICALLY EVERYONE ENJOYS.

If you're not the one cooking the food, you probably relish eating it! There's something about grilling or "cooking out" that spells p-a-r-t-y for most people—it's just downright fun to cook over a fire.

Pretty much anyone can cook a burger on the grill (or "burn some meat," as Kitty's father calls it); it's not too difficult, provided you can get the charcoal to the right level of heat (or not run out of propane). Our Salsa Cheeseburgers will satisfy your burger craving, but don't limit yourself to just burgers. In this chapter we've included recipes for shrimp, chicken, pork, lamb, and beef. None of the recipes are complicated, which would take away some of the fun of the whole process, in our opinion.

If you're rarin' to grill and it's been a while, check out our Doneness Chart (page 25) and tips on meat thermometers in the Basics chapter before you light the fire. If you don't own a meat thermometer, it's time to invest in one. It won't set you back too much, and will give you more confidence in the kitchen.

# CHILI-RUBBED SHRIMP SKEWERS

Many people save grilled shrimp for when they're dining at a restaurant, thinking it's too difficult to do at home. Frankly, it's not hard at all, as you will see in this recipe. Because good shrimp are pricey, you don't want to ruin them by over-cooking, so plant yourself at the grill for just a few minutes (that's all the time they take) and you'll be rewarded with succulent, juicy shrimp that can serve as an appetizer or main dish. For an accompaniment, try Seasoned Black Soybeans (page 285).

**SPICE MIX**

- 2 tablespoons vegetable oil
- 1 tablespoon fresh lime juice
- 2 teaspoons lime zest (see page 33)
- 1 teaspoon chili powder
- 1 teaspoon kosher salt
- 1/2 teaspoon ground cumin
- 1/2 teaspoon garlic powder
- 1/4 teaspoon ground black pepper
- 1/8 teaspoon cayenne pepper

- 2 pounds raw large shrimp (21 to 30 per pound), peeled, deveined, tails removed

**Water-soaked wooden skewers**

- 1 tablespoon fresh lime juice

**To make the spice mixture:** In a medium mixing bowl, stir together all the spice mixture ingredients until combined.

Add the shrimp to the bowl; using clean hands or a wooden spoon, toss the shrimp to coat. (At this point, you can refrigerate the shrimp for up to 6 hours, if desired.)

Preheat the grill to medium-high heat. Thread 4 to 5 shrimp on each skewer. Grill the shrimp for 4 minutes. Using tongs, flip the skewers and cook for 3 to 4 minutes more, until the shrimp are opaque throughout. (The shrimp should not be blackened or appear dried-out.)

Transfer the skewers to a platter, drizzle the lime juice over them, and serve.

Each serving contains approximately:
CAL: 208 PRO: 30g NET CARB: 1g FAT: 9g CHOL: 276mg SOD: 445mg

SERVES 4

# GARLICKY GRILLED CHICKEN LEG QUARTERS

Marinating chicken in yogurt delivers an extremely juicy, tender piece of meat. We added plenty of garlic and a sprinkling of spices to the yogurt for an even better result. The key to nicely grilled chicken legs is a medium heat. Grilled chicken takes a bit of time, but it's worth the wait.

**MARINADE**

- **2 cups plain low-fat yogurt**
- **18 cloves garlic, minced (about 3 tablespoons)**
- **1 tablespoon paprika**
- **2 teaspoons Tabasco sauce**
- **1½ teaspoons kosher salt**
- **1½ teaspoons dry mustard**
- **1½ teaspoons chili powder**
- **1 teaspoon ground black pepper**
- **¾ teaspoon ground cumin**
- **½ teaspoon cayenne**

- **4 large chicken leg quarters (about 3½ pounds), skin on, excess fat trimmed**

**Cooking spray**

**To make the marinade:** In a 4-cup liquid measuring cup or medium mixing bowl, whisk together all the marinade ingredients until combined and smooth.

Place the chicken legs in a gallon-sized, zip-top plastic bag; pour the marinade into the bag and seal. Alternatively, place the legs in a large mixing bowl, pour the marinade over, and cover with plastic wrap. Refrigerate for at least 24 hours.

Preheat the grill to medium heat. Meanwhile, remove the chicken legs from the marinade and, using clean hands, wipe off and discard as much marinade as possible from the legs. Coat the plump, meaty side of the legs with cooking spray and place them on the grill, plump side down. Close the grill and cook for 20 minutes.

Using tongs, carefully flip the legs over. Close the grill and cook for 20 minutes more, or until cooked through (see Doneness Chart on page 25).

---

Each serving contains approximately:
CAL: 306 PRO: 40g NET CARB: 1.5g FAT: 14g CHOL: 133mg SOD: 296mg

SERVES 4

# PORK SOUVLAKI SKEWERS

Souvlaki is a classic Greek preparation for either lamb or pork. The meat is marinated in a lemon, garlic, and olive oil mixture, then charcoal grilled. A fresh Greek salad is always an appropriate accompaniment to souvlaki.

## MARINADE/BASTING SAUCE

- $2/3$ cup fresh lemon juice
- $1/2$ cup olive oil
- 12 cloves garlic, minced (about 2 tablespoons)
- 1 tablespoon dried oregano
- 1 teaspoon kosher salt
- $3/4$ teaspoon ground black pepper

- $1\frac{1}{2}$ pounds boneless pork chops, trimmed of excess fat, cut into 2-inch cubes

To make the marinade: In a small mixing bowl, whisk together all the marinade ingredients until combined. Remove 3 tablespoons of the marinade and refrigerate it, covered, until ready to cook. Pour the remaining marinade into a gallon-sized, zip-top plastic bag.

Add the pork cubes to the plastic bag, seal it, and shake gently to coat the pork. Refrigerate the pork for at least 4 hours, or as long as overnight.

When ready to cook, preheat the grill to medium heat. Drain and discard the marinade. Thread the pork cubes onto 4 metal skewers.

Grill the pork for 4 minutes, then baste with the reserved marinade, using a pastry or barbecue brush. Turn the skewers, baste again, and continue to cook for 4 minutes more, or until the pork is cooked yet slightly pink in the middle (see Doneness Chart on page 25). Do not overcook or the pork will be dry.

---

Each serving contains approximately:
CAL: 316 PRO: 28g NET CARB: 3g FAT: 21g CHOL: 76mg SOD: 116mg

SERVES 4

# LAMB BURGERS WITH GARLIC, LEMON, AND CUMIN

Kim's husband calls these "gyros on the grill," which is a pretty good description. You may be tempted to cook these on the stove top—resist the temptation, they just taste so much better grilled. The burgers pair perfectly with a salad of chopped cucumbers and tomatoes, topped with Minted Yogurt Dressing (page 104). Try using any extra cooked burgers in low-carb wrap sandwiches the next day. If you'd prefer, substitute ground turkey for the lamb.

2 pounds ground lamb

5 cloves garlic, minced (about 2$\frac{1}{2}$ teaspoons)

1 teaspoon dried oregano

$\frac{3}{4}$ teaspoon kosher salt

$\frac{1}{2}$ teaspoon ground black pepper

$\frac{1}{2}$ teaspoon ground cumin

1 teaspoon lemon zest (see page 33)

Preheat the grill to medium-high heat. In a large mixing bowl, combine all the ingredients and mix well with clean hands or a wooden spoon. Divide the mixture into 5 equal portions. Roll each portion into a compact ball, then gently press the balls between your palms, making $\frac{1}{2}$-inch-thick burgers.

Grill the burgers until cooked through, about 4 to 5 minutes per side (see Doneness Chart on page 25). Transfer the burgers to a plate to rest for 5 minutes before serving.

**Each serving contains approximately:**
CAL: 358 PRO: 31g NET CARB: 1g FAT: 25g CHOL: 121mg SOD: 174mg

SERVES 5

# SALSA CHEESEBURGERS

Kim's friend Mary Jo Chapman invented these great-tasting, very juicy burgers. The beef is mixed with zesty salsa, and the burgers are topped with Cheddar. We like these served with lettuce leaves, sliced red onion, and tomatoes. Use the lettuce leaves instead of a bun, if you like, or choose one of the lower-carb burger buns.

$1\frac{1}{4}$ pounds 90% lean ground beef

$\frac{1}{2}$ cup bottled salsa

$\frac{1}{2}$ teaspoon ground black pepper

$\frac{1}{2}$ teaspoon kosher salt

Four 1-ounce slices Cheddar cheese

Lettuce leaves for serving (optional)

Sliced red onion for serving (optional)

Tomato slices for serving (optional)

Preheat the grill to high heat. In a medium mixing bowl, using clean hands or a wooden spoon, combine the beef, salsa, pepper, and salt. Divide the meat mixture into 4 equal portions. Roll each portion into a compact ball, then gently press the balls between your palms, making $3/4$-inch-thick burgers.

Grill the burgers until cooked through, about 4 to 5 minutes per side (see Doneness Chart on page 25). Top each burger with a slice of the cheese and transfer to a plate to rest for 5 minutes before serving. If desired, serve the burgers garnished with the lettuce, onion, or tomato slices.

### Note

You may be tempted to try this recipe indoors on the stovetop—don't! Because these burgers are so juicy, frying just doesn't work well.

Each serving contains approximately:
CAL: 425 PRO: 40g NET CARB: 1.5g FAT: 27g CHOL: 142mg SOD: 649mg

SERVES 4

# BBQ TIP STEAKS

When you're in the mood for BBQ, but don't have the time or energy to do it all from scratch, this is your recipe. The tip steaks are tender and the bottled sauce delivers good BBQ flavor without any fuss or time-consuming prep work.

2 tablespoons olive oil

1/2 teaspoon kosher salt

1/4 teaspoon ground black pepper

1 1/2 pounds sirloin tip steaks

1/2 cup low-carb barbecue sauce (such as Carb Options)

Preheat the grill to medium heat. In a medium mixing bowl, stir together the olive oil, salt, and pepper until mixed. Add the steaks and toss, using clean hands or a spoon, to coat the steaks.

Grill the steaks for 8 to 10 minutes, or until nearly cooked through. Using a pastry or barbecue brush, coat the top surface of each steak with the barbecue sauce. Grill for another minute, then, using tongs, flip and coat the other side with sauce; use all the sauce. Continue to cook for another 2 minutes, or until the steaks reach the desired doneness (see Doneness Chart on page 25). Serve immediately.

Each serving contains approximately:
CAL: 436 PRO: 55g NET CARB: 3g FAT: 21g CHOL: 162mg SOD: 500mg

SERVES 4

# TERIYAKI FLANK STEAK

If you've never picked up a flank steak because you did not know what to do with it, fear no more. The secrets to outstanding flank steak are a good marinade and a sharp knife to cut thin slices of meat. Kim's colleague, Chef Wilfred Beriau, was kind enough to give us his favorite recipe for teriyaki marinade. According to him, fresh ginger is an extremely powerful meat tenderizer, which helps with a cut like flank steak. For an easy appetizer, cut the meat into strips before cooking, thread onto water-soaked wooden skewers, and grill.

**MARINADE**

$3/4$ cup canned pineapple juice

$1/3$ cup soy sauce

1 tablespoon plus 1 teaspoon brown sugar

1 tablespoon sake or dry sherry

1 teaspoon peeled and minced fresh ginger

2 cloves garlic, minced (about 1 teaspoon)

$1/2$ teaspoon dry mustard

Pinch of ground black pepper

$1^1/2$ pounds flank steak, trimmed of excess fat

**To make the marinade:** In a 4-cup liquid measuring cup or medium mixing bowl, whisk together all the marinade ingredients until combined.

Place the flank steak in a gallon-sized, zip-top plastic bag; pour the marinade into the bag and seal. Refrigerate the flank steak for at least 12 hours, or as long as overnight.

Preheat the grill to medium-high heat. Remove the flank steak from the marinade (discard the marinade) and place it on the grill. Cook for 7 minutes, or until about halfway cooked through. Using tongs, flip the steak and cook for 7 minutes more or until the steak is cooked to the desired doneness (see Doneness Chart on page 25).

Transfer the steak to a cutting board and let rest for 3 minutes before slicing. Using a long, sharp knife, cut the meat on the diagonal, against the muscle grain, into 1/2-inch slices. Transfer to a platter and serve immediately.

**Each serving contains approximately:**
CAL: 263 PRO: 33g NET CARB: 3g FAT: 12g CHOL: 81mg SOD: 357mg

SERVES 4

CHAPTER

# 14

## FOOD FOR ENTERTAINING

## COOKING SPECIAL FOOD FOR SPECIAL PEOPLE IS ONE OF LIFE'S GREAT PLEASURES.

Both of us entertain often, yet even we are constantly searching for appropriate recipes to serve our guests. What makes a recipe "appropriate" for company? To us, it's a recipe that is obviously not everyday fare—the ingredients, preparation, and/or presentation are out of the ordinary, and of course, the results must be delicious. None of this means, however, that the recipe must be difficult to make. After all, who among us hasn't spent an entire day preparing food for guests that was entirely too fussy and complicated, only to have it turn out less-than-wonderfully, and leave us feeling less-than-enthusiastic about the whole process of entertaining? There's no need for this scenario ever to happen again!

This chapter includes recipes for various meals (a brunch, luncheon, or dinner), as well as appetizers and desserts that we think are especially suited to entertaining. While you wouldn't want to concoct your entire meal from this chapter, choosing one or two recipes can help you build a spectacular menu that you'll be proud of—and you won't be too tired to enjoy it all in the end!

Our basic entertaining menu formula is this: choose a stunning appetizer, such as Prosciutto and Pesto Phyllo Cups or Savory Ricotta Pie, and then an impressive, yet easy, roast for the main course (we've supplied you with five such roast recipes), along with a salad. Pull out all the stops with a do-ahead dessert, of course, to really finish on a high note . . . check out the selections in the Sweet Finales chapter.

# CHAMPAGNE FRUIT SALAD

Champagne-soaked berries and melon balls, accented with lemon, lime, and mint, make for a light, refreshing brunch dish that's stunning when served in tall Champagne glasses. For the best flavor and color, choose the most perfectly ripe fruit you can find, and splurge on a decent champagne or sparkling wine, as your guests are likely to sip the leftover liquid when they are done eating the fruit.

- 3 cups good-quality, chilled dry Champagne or sparkling wine, divided
- 1 cup Splenda Granular sweetener
- 1/2 teaspoon lemon zest (see page 33)
- 1/2 teaspoon lime zest (see page 33)
- 2 tablespoons finely chopped fresh mint leaves
- 3 cups cantaloupe or honeydew melon balls
- 1/2 pint fresh raspberries (about 1 cup)
- 1/2 pint fresh blueberries (about 1 cup)
- 1 cup fresh strawberry pieces, quartered or cut into small chunks

In a nonreactive medium mixing bowl, combine 1 cup of the Champagne, the Splenda, lemon and lime zest, and mint; stir to combine. Add the fruit to this mixture and stir gently with a wooden spoon to combine.

Cover the bowl with plastic wrap and refrigerate for at least 30 minutes to allow the fruit to soak up some of the Champagne mixture.

Divide the fruit and liquid among 8 champagne glasses and refrigerate until serving time. When ready to serve, pour the remaining Champagne over each portion.

### Note

This recipe is easily adjusted to take advantage of whichever fruits are in season. Instead of a blend of berries, you could use just one type of berry, or one type of melon. Honeydew and blueberries is a nice combination.

Each serving contains approximately:
CAL: 112 PRO: 1g NET CARB: 11g FAT: 0g CHOL: 0mg SOD: 12mg

SERVES 8

# SWEET RICOTTA CRÊPES WITH WILD BLUEBERRY SAUCE

**This is a special brunch dish that doesn't take a lot of time, but is sure to win you rave reviews. Make the filling and sauce the night before to save time the next morning.**

## FILLING

One 15-ounce container part-skim ricotta cheese

3/4 teaspoon vanilla extract

1 tablespoon Splenda Granular sweetener

1 teaspoon grated lemon zest (see page 33)

Six 9-inch packaged crêpes, at room temperature (such as Melissa's)

Wild Blueberry Sauce (page 315), at room temperature, for serving

6 sprigs fresh mint for garnish (optional)

**To make the filling:** In a small mixing bowl, stir together all the filling ingredients. Cover and refrigerate, if not using right away.

Microwave the ricotta filling for 1 to 2 minutes on medium power, stirring and taste-testing to ensure that it's heated through (it should be warm, but not piping hot). Place one crêpe on a plate. Using a 1/3-cup measuring cup, scoop out the filling and place it on the crêpe, to the right side. Fold over the left side of the crêpe to make a half-moon shape. Using clean hands, lightly press down on the crêpe to spread the filling and flatten it a little. Fold the half-moon in half again, to form a quarter-moon shape.

To serve, top the folded crêpe with 3 tablespoons of the Wild Blueberry Sauce (you'll have leftover sauce for another use) and serve immediately, garnished with fresh mint, if desired. If you prefer to serve the crêpes family style, simply assemble them all on a serving platter and pass the sauce separately.

### Note

Premade crêpes can generally be found in the produce section of the supermarket, close to the berries. They are handy for a variety of low-carb dishes, both sweet and savory.

---

Each serving contains approximately:
CAL: 159 PRO: 9g NET CARB: 14g FAT: 7g CHOL: 27mg SOD: 150mg

SERVES 6

# SOUR CREAM AND CHIVE DEVILED EGGS

A slight variation on a traditional mayonnaise-based recipe, our version combines sour cream and fresh chives to give deviled eggs a fresh face. The fact that they look so pretty when sprinkled with the chives is an added bonus.

12 hard-boiled eggs, peeled

1/2 cup finely chopped fresh chives, divided

1/2 cup sour cream

2 teaspoons Dijon mustard

1/2 teaspoon cider vinegar

1/4 teaspoon kosher salt

1/8 teaspoon ground black pepper

Cut the eggs in half, lengthwise; remove the yolks and put them in a small mixing bowl. Arrange the empty egg halves on a serving platter.

Using the back of a fork, mash the egg yolks. Add 1/4 cup of the chives and all the remaining ingredients to the mixing bowl; mix well with a spoon to combine.

Using a teaspoon or a pastry bag fitted with a star tip, fill the egg halves with the yolk mixture, mounding it slightly to create a nicely filled egg. Sprinkle the eggs with the remaining chives.

Each serving (2 egg halves) contains approximately:
CAL: 100 PRO: 7g NET CARB: 1g FAT: 7g CHOL: 216mg SOD: 98mg

SERVES 12

# SHIRRED EGGS WITH CANADIAN BACON

Easy and fun to make, these eggs are cooked and served in individual cups—a nice presentation for guests. Feel free to customize your shirred eggs with additional ingredients, or by substituting ingredients for the Canadian bacon. Some ideas include: cooked and crumbled bacon, blanched broccoli or asparagus, chives and smoked salmon, or artichoke hearts and prosciutto. Serve with low-carb toast.

Cooking spray

12 eggs

One 6-ounce package Canadian bacon slices, cut into strips $1/4$ inch wide and 1 inch long

$3/4$ cup heavy cream

$1/2$ teaspoon kosher salt

$1/4$ teaspoon ground black pepper

$1/4$ teaspoon paprika

Preheat the oven to 350°F. Coat six 6-ounce custard cups or ramekins with cooking spray and place them on a baking sheet. Crack two eggs into each ramekin. Divide the bacon strips among the ramekins, laying the strips on top of the eggs. Top each portion with 2 tablespoons of the cream, then sprinkle each with some of the kosher salt, pepper, and paprika.

Bake the eggs for 15 minutes, then check for doneness. The yolks should still be soft and bright yellow; the whites should jiggle only slightly. If not done, bake for another 4 minutes, then recheck.

When done, remove the eggs from the oven and let rest 5 minutes before serving. The ramekins will be extremely hot, so use an oven mitt to move the ramekins to the table or tray for serving.

### Note

Cooking time for the eggs will vary greatly depending on what type of custard cups or ramekins you use, and the temperature of the eggs when you begin cooking.

Each serving contains approximately:
CAL: 296 PRO: 19g NET CARB: 2.5g FAT: 23g CHOL: 481mg SOD: 556mg

SERVES 6

# CAULIFLOWER PANCAKES WITH SOUR CREAM AND APPLESAUCE

Like traditional potato latkes, these pancakes are a labor of love. The recipe requires a lot of grating (or a food processor) and frying, but the end result is totally worth it. These make a lovely brunch dish, and can be used as a base for poached eggs—sans applesauce and sour cream—if you're looking for an alternative way to serve them.

1 large head (3 pounds) cauliflower, leaves removed, trimmed

1 medium onion

4 eggs, lightly beaten

1/4 cup Atkins Bake Mix

2 tablespoons all-purpose flour

1/2 teaspoon baking powder

1/2 teaspoon kosher salt

1/2 teaspoon ground black pepper

About 1/2 cup plus 2 tablespoons vegetable oil, divided

Sour cream for garnish (optional)

Unsweetened applesauce for serving (optional)

Using a handheld grater or food processor, grate both the cauliflower and onion. Transfer the grated vegetables to a large mixing bowl.

Add the eggs, Bake Mix, flour, baking powder, salt, and pepper to the bowl and stir to combine. Working over a sink, transfer the cauliflower mix to a colander or large sieve; place the colander back over the mixing bowl to allow liquid to strain from the mixture. Put the bowl and sieve next to the stove; it will continue to drain while you cook the pancakes.

In a large skillet or sauté pan over medium heat, warm 2 tablespoons of the oil. Using a 1/3-cup measuring cup, scoop up the batter and drop it onto the skillet. Use the bottom of the measuring cup or a spoon to shape the batter into circles. Fry 3 pancakes at a time, cooking them for 3 to 4 minutes per side, until lightly browned. Transfer the cooked pancakes to a baking sheet lined with paper towels. If you like, keep the pancakes warm in a 200°F oven until all the pancakes are cooked.

Add more oil to the skillet and continue until you've made 16 pancakes. (Frying times may decrease slightly as the pan stays heated and the batter warms up.)

To serve, pass the sour cream and applesauce with a platter of pancakes, or serve individually and top with a dollop of applesauce and sour cream, if desired.

Each 2-pancake serving contains approximately:
CAL: 333 PRO: 10g NET CARB: 14g FAT: 26g CHOL: 119mg SOD: 185mg

SERVES 8

# SLICED TOMATO SALAD

This is one of Kim's favorite recipes for using up the abundance of tomatoes her father grows each summer.

- 8 medium (about 2$\frac{1}{4}$ pounds) vine-ripened tomatoes, cored
- $\frac{3}{4}$ cup Orange Mayonnaise (page 308)
- $\frac{1}{2}$ medium red onion, thinly sliced, cut into 1-inch-long pieces (about $\frac{3}{4}$ cup)
- $\frac{1}{4}$ cup chopped fresh flat-leaf parsley
- Kosher salt and ground black pepper (optional)

Using a serrated knife, cut each tomato into four thick slices. Spread a thin layer of the orange mayonnaise onto each slice, then arrange the slices in a decorative circular pattern on a platter.

Sprinkle the onion pieces and parsley over the tomatoes, then season with salt and pepper, if desired.

Note

If you prefer, use regular mayonnaise instead of the Orange Mayonnaise in this salad. Doing so will change the nutritional content of each serving to:

CAL: 117 PRO: 1g NET CARB: 3.5g FAT: 11g CHOL: 8mg SOD: 86mg

Each serving contains approximately:
CAL: 85 PRO: 1g NET CARB: 4g FAT: 8g CHOL: 5mg SOD: 72mg

SERVES 12

# SAVORY RICOTTA PIE

This is a sophisticated combination of ingredients: The crust is made with almonds and Parmesan cheese; the filling is a creamy mixture of ricotta, mozzarella, and olives; and the topping is a colorful mixture of roasted red peppers, ground black pepper, and more Parmesan. The recipe looks lengthy, but don't let that fool you—it's actually easy to prepare. You can serve the pie warm or at room temperature, so you needn't worry about timing it perfectly for your guests.

## CRUST

Cooking spray

2 tablespoons butter

1 1/2 cups almonds, finely chopped

1/3 cup grated Parmesan cheese

## FILLING

10 ounces cream cheese, at room temperature

1 cup part-skim ricotta cheese, at room temperature

2 eggs

2/3 cup (about 3 ounces) shredded part-skim mozzarella cheese

1/3 cup prepared tapenade (see Note)

2 tablespoons heavy cream

1/2 teaspoon minced dried onions

1/8 teaspoon ground black pepper

## TOPPING

3/4 cup prepared roasted red peppers, drained and patted dry

1/4 cup (1 ounce) shredded Parmesan cheese

1/2 teaspoon dried oregano

1/8 teaspoon ground black pepper

**To make the crust:** Coat the bottom and sides of a 9-inch springform pan with the cooking spray; set aside. In a medium skillet or sauté pan over medium-low heat, melt the butter. Add the almonds and cook, stirring, for 5 to 8 minutes, or until the nuts are slightly toasted and fragrant. Transfer the hot almonds to the prepared pan and let cool. When cool, add the Parmesan to the pan and stir to combine. Using clean hands, gently press the mixture onto the bottom of the pan (the mixture will be loose, not compact).

Preheat the oven to 300°F. Place a cake pan filled with 1 cup of water on the lowest rack of the oven. Position a second rack in the middle of the oven.

**To make the filling:** In a large mixing bowl, using an electric mixer, beat the cream cheese on medium speed for 5 minutes, or until light and fluffy. Mix in the ricotta and then the eggs, one at a time. Reduce the speed to low and add all the remaining filling ingredients, mixing until combined. Pour the mixture over the crust and smooth the top with a spatula.

**To make the topping:** Cut the peppers into thin strips about 1/4 inch wide. Lay the strips over the top of the filling in a random pattern. Sprinkle the top of the pie with the Parmesan, oregano, and pepper.

Put the pie on the middle rack in the oven and bake for 1 hour, then check for doneness; a knife inserted 2 inches from the edge should come out clean and the pie will appear set. If not done, bake an additional 10 minutes and then check again. If the top of the pie is browning too quickly at the edges, cover with aluminum foil. When done, let the pie cool for at least 15 minutes before serving.

To serve, run a knife around the inside edge of the pan and release the sides. Using a serrated knife, cut the pie into 12 wedges, being sure to wipe the knife between slices in order to get a clean cut. Lift out the pieces with a pie server.

### Note

If you can't find prepared tapenade in your store, feel free to substitute prepared pesto, or coarsely purée about 1/2 cup of pimiento-stuffed olives in a food processor or blender.

Each serving contains approximately:
CAL: 281 PRO: 12g NET CARB: 4.5g FAT: 24g CHOL: 286mg SOD: 427mg

SERVES 12

# PROSCIUTTO AND PESTO PHYLLO CUPS

When Kim's husband tasted these little appetizers he immediately proclaimed that they would be served at their next party. We think you'll like them just as well. Filled with a pesto, ricotta, and mozzarella mixture, and topped with prosciutto and a sprinkle of Parmesan, these tidbits are party perfect. We've allowed a generous three appetizers per person, but if you're serving other appetizers, you can easily provide just one or two cups each. If you're expecting vegetarians, skip the prosciutto and opt for roasted red peppers or Kalamata olive halves for the topping.

**FILLING**

- 1/2 cup part-skim ricotta cheese
- 1/3 cup shredded (about 3 ounces) part-skim mozzarella cheese
- 2 tablespoons prepared pesto

Pinch of ground black pepper

Pinch of kosher salt

- 1 box (15 pieces, 2.1 ounces) frozen mini phyllo cups, thawed at room temperature for 10 minutes

Two 1-ounce slices prosciutto, chopped

- 1 tablespoon grated Parmesan cheese

Preheat the oven to 350°F.

**To make the filling:** In a small mixing bowl, stir together the filling ingredients.

Place the phyllo cups into an 8-by-8-inch baking pan or on a rimmed baking sheet. Using a teaspoon, scoop the filling into the cups. Top each cup with a little of the chopped prosciutto, then sprinkle with some of the Parmesan.

Bake the cups for 10 to 12 minutes, until heated through and lightly browned. Serve hot.

Each 3-piece serving contains approximately:
CAL: 178 PRO: 9g NET CARB: 9g FAT: 11g CHOL: 20mg SOD: 203mg

SERVES 5

# WILD MUSHROOM CRÊPES

Wild mushrooms aren't everyday fare for most of us—both for cost and availability reasons. However, they're just the thing for a special dinner party, or when you really want to impress. These crêpes feature a mélange of wild mushrooms seasoned with shallot and thyme. Crème fraîche and toasted almonds top the crêpes, lending them extra texture and style. Look for packaged crêpes in the produce section of the grocery store, near the berries.

## FILLING

- 2 tablespoons butter
- 1 shallot, finely minced
- 12 ounces assorted wild mushrooms, thinly sliced
- $1/2$ teaspoon kosher salt
- $1/4$ teaspoon dried thyme
- $1/4$ teaspoon ground black pepper
- 2 tablespoons dry white wine
- $1/3$ cup light cream
- $1/4$ teaspoon Tabasco sauce
- 1 tablespoon grated Romano cheese

Four 9-inch packaged crêpes, at room temperature (such as Melissa's)

- $1/2$ cup Chive Crème Fraîche, at room temperature (page 310)
- $1/2$ cup almonds, toasted and chopped

**To make the filling:** In a large skillet or sauté pan over medium heat, melt the butter. Add the shallot, mushrooms, salt, thyme, and pepper. Cook, stirring frequently, for 3 to 5 minutes, or until the mushrooms soften. Stir in the wine and bring the mixture to a simmer. Stir in the cream and Tabasco and return to a simmer. Simmer for 1 minute, then remove from the heat and stir in the cheese; set aside.

Lay the crêpes down on a clean work surface. Working in assembly-line fashion, using a $1/4$-cup measuring cup, scoop up the mushroom mixture and place it at the bottom of each crêpe. Roll the crêpes upward into a tube shape. Using a serrated knife, cut each crêpe in half crosswise. Place both halves of a crêpe on each of 4 appetizer plates, criss-crossing the two halves. Place 2 tablespoons of the crème fraîche on each plate, in the center of the crêpe halves. Sprinkle each plate with 2 tablespoons of the toasted almonds, and serve.

### Note

No time to make crème fraîche? Substitute sour cream and sprinkle each dish with 1 teaspoon chopped fresh chives.

Each 1-crepe serving (1 crepe) contains approximately:
CAL: 364 PRO: 8g NET CARB: 15g FAT: 31g CHOL: 61mg SOD: 212mg

**SERVES 4**

# PAN-seared SCALLOPS on BABY GREENS with WARM VINAIGRETTE

Classic flavor combinations (greens, bacon, apples, and scallops) and a stunning plate presentation make this one of our favorite starters for entertaining. And, since it combines the salad and appetizer course, the cook benefits, too—more time for wine and conversation!

**VINAIGRETTE**

- $1/2$ small Granny Smith apple (not peeled), cored and grated (about $1/3$ cup)
- $1/3$ cup vegetable oil
- 2 tablespoons fresh lemon juice
- 2 tablespoons cider vinegar
- $1/4$ teaspoon kosher salt
- $1/8$ teaspoon ground black pepper

Pinch of cayenne pepper

- 3 cups baby greens (spinach, arugula, or mesclun mix)

**Cooking spray**

- 1 pound dry sea scallops (see Note page 182), side muscles removed
- 2 slices bacon, cooked and crumbled (about $1/4$ cup)

**To make the vinaigrette:** In a small mixing bowl, whisk together all the vinaigrette ingredients; set aside. Divide the baby greens between four salad plates; set aside.

Coat a large skillet or sauté pan with the cooking spray; warm over medium-high heat. When hot, add the scallops to the pan and cook, without flipping or stirring, for 4 to 6 minutes, or until a golden brown crust develops on the bottoms. Using tongs, flip each scallop over and cook for another 2 to 3 minutes, or until just opaque throughout. Pour the vinaigrette over the scallops and heat through, about 1 minute.

Using tongs, transfer the scallops to the individual plates, setting them on top of the greens. Divide the vinaigrette between each portion, pouring it over the scallops and greens. Garnish each portion with the bacon and serve immediately.

Each serving contains approximately:
CAL: 301 PRO: 21g NET CARB: 5g FAT: 22g CHOL: 39mg SOD: 577mg

SERVES 4

# CIOPPINO

Beautiful and impressive, our version of this San Francisco classic seafood stew has something to please everyone. Toss together a salad to go with this dish and you'll be ready to receive your "Most Fabulous Dinner Host" award!

1/4 cup extra-virgin olive oil

2 teaspoons anchovy paste

5 cloves garlic, minced (about 2 1/2 teaspoons)

1/2 teaspoon crushed red pepper flakes

2 bay leaves

1/2 medium onion, chopped (about 1/2 cup)

1 medium (about 8 ounces) fennel bulb, ends trimmed, thinly sliced

1/2 cup dry white wine

One 14-ounce can chicken broth

One 8-ounce bottle clam juice

One 28-ounce can crushed tomatoes

1/2 cup chopped fresh flat-leaf parsley

1/2 teaspoon kosher salt

1/2 teaspoon dried oregano

1/2 teaspoon dried thyme

1/4 teaspoon ground black pepper

1 1/2 pounds haddock or cod, cut into 2-inch chunks

18 large (21 to 30 per pound) raw shrimp, peeled and deveined

12 littleneck clams, rinsed

8 ounces raw calamari rings (no tentacles)

In a large stockpot over medium-low heat, warm the olive oil. Stir in the anchovy paste, garlic, red pepper flakes, and bay leaves. Cook for 1 to 2 minutes, stirring constantly, or until the anchovy paste dissolves and the garlic becomes fragrant. Add the onion and fennel and cook, stirring frequently, for 5 minutes, or until the vegetables soften. Stir in the wine and let it cook down for 2 minutes.

Raise the heat to medium-high. Stir in the chicken broth, clam juice, tomatoes, parsley, and spices. Cook, stirring occasionally, until the broth comes to a simmer, then add the fish. Return the mixture to a simmer and cook for 5 minutes. Add the shrimp, clams, and calamari; cover the pot and cook for 10 to 12 minutes, or until the clams open up. Do not overcook the dish or the seafood will become tough and chewy.

Turn off the heat and discard the bay leaves and any clams that failed to open. Carefully ladle the stew into bowls, making sure each bowl gets 3 shrimp, 2 clams, some fish, and some calamari.

Each serving contains approximately:
CAL: 310 PRO: 32g NET CARB: 10g FAT: 13g CHOL: 175mg SOD: 919mg

SERVES 6

# SESAME-ENCRUSTED TUNA CARPACCIO WITH TWO SAUCES

Inspired by a favorite appetizer of Kim's from her days as manager at Turner Fisheries in Boston, this impressive appetizer combines lots of Asian flavors and ingredients including sesame seeds, ginger, orange, and wasabi. Served over a bed of greens, the dish is drizzled with the sauces for a beautiful presentation.

**WASABI VINAIGRETTE**

- 1 tablespoon plus 1 teaspoon wasabi powder
- 2 teaspoons rice vinegar
- 1 tablespoon plus 2 teaspoons water
- $1/4$ cup vegetable oil

**ORANGE SESAME SAUCE**

- $1/4$ cup soy sauce
- 1 teaspoon toasted sesame oil
- 1 teaspoon rice vinegar
- $1/2$ teaspoon peeled and minced fresh ginger
- $1/2$ teaspoon orange zest (see page 33)
- $1/4$ teaspoon sugar

- 2 tablespoons sesame seeds
- 1 pound sushi-grade Ahi tuna steak

Cooking spray

- $1^1/2$ cups baby Asian greens, mizuna greens, or mesclun mix
- 3 scallions, green part only, chopped (about $1/3$ cup pieces)

**To make the Wasabi Vinaigrette:** In a small bowl, whisk together the wasabi powder, vinegar, and water until thoroughly blended. Slowly whisk in the oil; set aside. (This can be made 1 day ahead; simply cover and refrigerate until needed.)

**To make the Orange Sesame Sauce:** In a small bowl, whisk together all the sauce ingredients until blended; set aside. (This can be made 1 day ahead; simply cover and refrigerate until needed. Let this sauce come to room temperature before serving.)

Press the sesame seeds into both sides of the tuna steak; set aside. Coat a large skillet or sauté pan with cooking spray; warm the pan over medium heat. Place the tuna steak in the pan and cook for $1\frac{1}{2}$ minutes; the tuna will sear and the sesame seeds will begin to toast. Using tongs, flip the steak and cook for another $1\frac{1}{2}$ minutes on the second side. Using tongs, transfer the tuna to a plate and refrigerate for at least 1 hour to firm up the fish for easier cutting. Using a very sharp knife, cut the chilled tuna into $1/4$-inch-thick slices.

Place the greens in a row down the center of an oval serving platter. Divide the tuna slices in half; lay the pieces in two rows, one on each side of the greens. Using a teaspoon, mix the vinaigrette very well and drizzle it over one row of the tuna. Mix the orange sauce well and drizzle it over the other row of tuna. Sprinkle the entire serving platter with scallion pieces before serving.

**Note**

If you can find black sesame seeds, use them as well, along with some white seeds; just mix the two together before encrusting the tuna.

Each serving contains approximately:
CAL: 168 PRO: 14g NET CARB: 1.5g FAT: 11g CHOL: 22mg SOD: 537mg

SERVES 8

# CHICKEN BREASTS STUFFED WITH PROSCIUTTO AND FRESH MOZZARELLA

The beauty of serving this versatile dish to guests is that nearly all the work is done ahead of time, and it can be plated individually or served in slices for a buffet. The chicken itself is packed with Italian flavors from the prosciutto, mozzarella, basil, Parmesan, and tomato sauce.

$1/4$ cup (1 ounce) grated Parmesan cheese

$1/4$ cup Low-Carb Buttered Bread Crumbs (page 294)

Pinch of ground black pepper

1 cup prepared low-carb pasta sauce

4 skinless, boneless chicken breast halves (about 2 pounds), trimmed of excess fat

Two 1-ounce slices prosciutto, cut in half crosswise

4 large, fresh basil leaves

12 bite-sized pieces fresh mozzarella (about $1/4$ pound)

$1/4$ cup butter, melted

Fresh basil sprigs for garnish (optional)

Preheat the oven to 350°F. In a shallow bowl, using a wooden spoon, stir together the Parmesan, bread crumbs, and pepper; set aside.

Using a wooden spoon or rubber spatula, spread the pasta sauce over the bottom of a 9-by-9-inch baking dish; set aside.

Put 2 of the chicken breast pieces into a gallon-sized, zip-top plastic bag; seal the bag and pound the chicken with a rolling pin or the flat side of a meat mallet to a $1/4$-inch thickness. Remove the chicken and repeat with the remaining chicken.

Lay the pounded chicken pieces on a clean work surface. Working in assembly-line fashion, place a piece of prosciutto on each piece of chicken, then a basil leaf, then top with 3 pieces of the mozzarella. Tightly roll the chicken to enclose the fillings and seal each with 1 or 2 toothpicks. Brush each chicken roll with melted butter, then carefully roll the chicken in the bread-crumb mixture to coat. Place each chicken roll, toothpick side down, into the baking dish, atop the sauce.

Bake for 45 minutes, then check for doneness by slicing into the bottom of one of the chicken rolls (in order not to spoil the nicely browned top of the chicken). If not done, bake for another 5 to 10 minutes and check again. Let rest for 5 minutes before serving. To serve, remove the toothpicks from the chicken and transfer, using tongs, to individual plates. Stir the sauce that's left in the dish and spoon a little of it around each portion. Garnish with sprigs of basil, if desired.

Each serving contains approximately:
CAL: 605 PRO: 68g NET CARB: 4g FAT: 32g CHOL: 214mg SOD: 1,034mg

SERVES 4

# APRICOT-GLAZED HAM

Nothing says "holiday" like a big baked ham. Not only is this an easy entrée for the cook, but unless you have a big crowd, you'll have plenty of leftovers to use in sandwiches, frittatas, or soups. We call for Bell's Seasoning, which is an old-fashioned seasoning blend that's traditionally used for poultry—there's even a picture of a turkey on the box. We find its mixture of rosemary, thyme, oregano, sage, ginger, marjoram, and pepper is perfect for this ham, too.

One 10- to 13-pound fully cooked, bone-in ham

2 teaspoons all-purpose flour

1 large oven bag

**GLAZE**

2/3 cup sugar-free apricot preserves (such as Smucker's Light)

2 tablespoons butter

1/4 teaspoon Tabasco sauce

1/8 teaspoon Bell's Seasoning

Preheat the oven to 275°F. Rinse the ham and pat it dry. Add the flour to the oven bag, hold the bag closed, and shake to coat the inside of the bag; shake out any excess flour. Place the ham in the oven bag and seal according to the bag manufacturer's instructions. Cut 6 slits in the top of the bag and place it in a large roasting pan. Bake the ham for 15 minutes per pound, or about 2 1/2 to 3 1/2 hours.

**To make the glaze:** Near the end of the ham's cooking time, in a small saucepan over medium heat, stir together all the glaze ingredients until melted and combined. Remove from the heat.

When the ham is done, carefully remove it from the bag and return it back to the roasting pan. Raise the oven temperature to 325°F. Using a pastry brush, apply the glaze to the surface of the ham. Bake for an additional 10 to 15 minutes, or until the glaze bubbles and starts to brown. Let rest for at least 15 minutes before serving.

**Note**

In testing three different brands of ham, we decided that Morell E-Z Cut was the best-tasting; it had great flavor and wasn't overly salty. If you can't find that brand, just choose your favorite.

Each serving contains approximately:
CAL: 394 PRO: 60g NET CARB: 2.5g FAT: 14g CHOL: 135mg SOD: 3,201mg

SERVES 20

# ROSEMARY-GARLIC PORK ROAST

This bone-in pork roast looks great and actually has flavor (unlike many pork roasts that seem to turn out on the bland side). The strong flavors of rosemary and garlic mellow a little during the roasting process, yielding a well-seasoned roast that's perfect for family or guests.

**SPICE RUB**

- 2 tablespoons dried rosemary, crushed between your fingers
- 2 tablespoons olive oil
- 12 cloves garlic, minced (about 2 tablespoons)
- 2 teaspoons minced dried onions
- 1 teaspoon ground black pepper
- $1/2$ teaspoon celery salt
- $1/2$ teaspoon kosher salt

- One 3-pound center cut pork rib roast, pierced with a knife 6 to 8 times on the meat side
- 2 cups dry white wine

Preheat the oven to 325°F.

**To make the spice rub:** In a small bowl, stir together all the rub ingredients. Using clean hands, rub the mixture all over the roast and into the slits.

Place the roast onto a rack in a roasting pan, bone side down (or to the side). Add the wine to the roasting pan.

Roast the meat about $1 3/4$ hours or until it reaches desired doneness (see the Doneness Chart on page 25). Cover with aluminum foil and let rest at least 15 minutes before serving.

**Note**

The length of cooking time will vary depending on the temperature of the roast when you start cooking. A roast taken directly from the refrigerator will take longer to cook than one that has been allowed to come up to room temperature before roasting.

Each serving contains approximately:
CAL: 407 PRO: 45g NET CARB: 2g FAT: 23g CHOL: 111mg SOD: 294mg

SERVES 5

# ROASTED LEG OF LAMB

Lamb is one of the most popular meats ordered in restaurants today, so serving it at home should help establish your position on the "in" list! Most leg of lamb is sold semi-boneless. Ask your butcher to completely debone the lamb, trim it, and tie it. Butchers have super sharp knives and great knife skills that they're usually happy to show off; save yourself the time and trouble!

## MARINADE

- 2 tablespoons fresh lemon juice
- 1/2 teaspoon lemon zest (see page 33)
- 1 tablespoon dried oregano
- 6 cloves garlic, minced (about 1 tablespoon)
- 1 tablespoon minced dried onions
- 2 tablespoons olive oil
- 1 tablespoon honey
- 1 teaspoon ground cumin
- 1/4 teaspoon kosher salt
- 1/2 teaspoon ground black pepper
- 6 ounces plain low-fat yogurt

- 1 deboned and tied leg of lamb (about 5 pounds)
- 2 tablespoons olive oil
- 1/2 cup water
- 1 cup dry white wine

**To make the marinade:** In a small mixing bowl, whisk together all the marinade ingredients until combined and smooth. Using clean hands, rub the marinade mixture all over the lamb roast. Wrap the roast in plastic wrap and refrigerate for at least 6 hours, or preferably overnight.

When ready to cook, preheat the oven to 300°F. Remove the lamb from the refrigerator and scrape off any excess marinade. Using clean hands, rub the lamb with the olive oil and place the roast on a rack in a roasting pan. Add the water and wine to the pan.

Roast the lamb for about 2 3/4 hours, or until it reaches desired doneness (see the Doneness Chart on page 25). Cover with aluminum foil and let rest at least 15 minutes before serving. If desired, pour the pan drippings through a sieve to make a quick gravy to serve with the roast.

Each serving contains approximately:
CAL: 426 PRO: 57g NET CARB: 4g FAT: 19g CHOL: 175mg SOD: 161mg

SERVES 8

# OVEN-ROASTED VEAL AND VEGETABLES

Oven roasted dinners make dinner-time entertaining very easy. In this dish, rosemary, garlic, and orange complement the tender veal, and the vegetables give the dish great color. Ask your butcher to tie the roast for you.

268

### SPICE RUB

- 1 tablespoon fresh orange juice
- 1 tablespoon olive oil
- 1 teaspoon ground black pepper
- 1 tablespoon dried rosemary, crushed between your fingers
- 6 cloves garlic, minced (about 1 tablespoon)
- $1/2$ teaspoon orange zest (see page 33)
- $1/4$ teaspoon kosher salt

<br>

- One $2^1/_2$- to 3-pound veal roast (also called shoulder roast), tied
- 1 cup baby carrots, quartered lengthwise
- $1/2$ cup dry white wine
- $1/2$ cup fresh orange juice
- $1/4$ large red onion, thinly sliced (about $1/2$ cup)
- 1 pound asparagus, trimmed, cut into 2-inch lengths
- 2 tablespoons olive oil
- $1/2$ teaspoon kosher salt
- $1/8$ teaspoon ground black pepper

**To make the spice rub:** In a small bowl, stir together all the ingredients for the rub. Cut several small slits into the veal roast. With clean hands, spread the rub all over the veal and into the slits. Wrap the roast in plastic wrap and refrigerate for at least 6 hours and up to 24 hours.

When ready to cook, preheat the oven to 350°F. Put the roast in a roasting pan large enough to hold both the meat and vegetables. Spread the carrots around the roast. Add the white wine and orange juice to the pan. Using a pastry brush, brush the roast with some of the wine and juice mixture.

Bake, uncovered, for 1 hour and 15 minutes. While the roast is cooking, toss the onion and asparagus with the olive oil, salt, and pepper in a medium bowl. Remove the roast from the oven and baste it with the cooking juices. Add the onion-asparagus mixture to the pan and return the pan to the oven for another 30 minutes, or until it reaches desired doneness (see the Doneness Chart on page 25).

Cover with aluminum foil and let rest for at least 10 minutes before serving. Serve the meat with the roasted vegetables, using the pan drippings as a quick gravy, if desired.

---

Each serving contains approximately:
CAL: 549 PRO: 66g NET CARB: 11g FAT: 22g CHOL: 240mg SOD: 296mg

SERVES 4

# RIB-EYE ROAST
## WITH HORSERADISH AND CARAWAY CRUST

Kitty serves this no-fuss roast on Christmas day as the centerpiece of her holiday meal. The crunchy horseradish, salt, and caraway coating gives the beef texture as well as flavor. Don't let the amount of horseradish scare you—it mellows significantly during the roasting process. In fact, if you're a horseradish fan, you may want to serve the roast with our Easy Horseradish Cream (page 309) for extra flavor.

2 tablespoons prepared horseradish

$1/4$ cup olive oil

2 tablespoons kosher salt

$1^1/_2$ teaspoons caraway seeds, crushed between your fingers

One 4- to 6-pound beef rib-eye roast, tied

Preheat the oven to 350°F. In a small bowl, stir together the horseradish, olive oil, salt, and caraway seeds. Rub the mixture over the entire surface of the beef roast.

Place the roast in a medium roasting or broiling pan. Roast the beef for approximately $1^1/_2$ to $2^1/_2$ hours, or until it reaches desired doneness (see the Doneness Chart on page 25).

Cover with aluminum foil and let rest for at least 10 minutes before serving.

Each serving contains approximately:
CAL: 445 PRO: 48g NET CARB: 0g FAT: 27g CHOL: 136mg SOD: 481mg

SERVES 8

CHAPTER

15

ON THE SIDE

# HAVE YOU TIRED OF THE MEAT-AND-SALAD ROUTINE YET?

If so, this chapter's for you. A tasty side dish not only complements the flavors of an entrée, it also rounds out the meal nutritionally and, well, makes it a *meal.* Take the time to prepare a side dish and you won't be sorry (plus the leftovers are frequently good the next day, making your low-carb leftover lunch that much better)!

You'll notice this chapter is bursting with recipes. We love side dishes, and vegetables are our side dish of choice in most cases. Not only do most low-carbers need to incorporate more veggies into their eating plans, but many of us don't eat a wide enough variety of vegetables, and therefore miss out on nutrients *and* new tastes! If you seek a selection of vegetable dishes, we've included cubanelle peppers, asparagus, green beans, broccoli, cauliflower, Brussels sprouts, cabbage, escarole, bok choy, black soybeans, celery root, carrots, fennel, tomatoes, spinach, acorn squash, and mushrooms—basically, something to suit everyone.

And, since not all entrées demand a veggie (entrée salads, for example), we created a hip cheese-cracker side (Asiago-Parmesan Tuiles), a focaccia that utilizes a packaged low-carb pizza crust mix, and a corn bread. Let's face it, some main courses practically cry out for a bit of bread on the side, so it's nice to have some lower-carb options.

# ASIAGO-PARMESAN TUILES

We've taken some liberty with the term *tuile,* which traditionally is a crisp French almond cookie that's made into a curved shape by draping it over a rolling pin while warm. While we've used the same technique to make these cheesy tidbits curved, our tuiles function more like substantial garnishes. When served alongside a salad (the way we've noticed high-end restaurants are doing these days), these tuiles provide an incredible textural and flavorful contrast.

$1/4$ cup finely grated, good-quality Parmesan cheese

2 teaspoons shredded Asiago cheese

Preheat the oven to 325°F. Using a tablespoon measure, divide the Parmesan into 4 mounds, spaced about 4 inches apart on an ungreased baking sheet. Using clean fingers, gently flatten each mound of Parmesan into an oval about 2 inches in length and about $1\frac{1}{2}$ inches wide. Using a $1/2$ teaspoon measure, divide the Asiago and carefully sprinkle over each portion, staying within the borders of the Parmesan.

Bake for about 8 minutes, or until the tuiles are golden brown (they'll be slightly darker on the edges). Let the tuiles cool on the sheet for about 1 minute so that they firm up a bit.

Using a metal spatula, carefully transfer the tuiles to a rolling pin or narrow bottle, draping them over so that they form a curved shape as they cool. Let cool completely, about 20 minutes, then remove them from the rolling pin and serve.

Each serving contains approximately:
CAL: 38 PRO: 3g NET CARB: 0g FAT: 2g CHOL: 6mg SOD: 119mg

SERVES 4

# SOUTHWESTERN CORN BREAD

This corn bread has just a hint of spice. It makes a great accompaniment to entrées that have some kick to them, such as Texas Chili (page 125). Plus, it's quick and easy to prepare, since it uses a muffin mix as its base. Stir it up while the chili is cooking and you'll have a complete meal in a snap.

Cooking spray

One 8 1/2-ounce package Atkins Quick Quisine Corn Muffin Mix

One 4 1/2-ounce can diced green chiles, drained

1/4 teaspoon ground cumin

1/4 teaspoon chili powder (or ground cayenne pepper, if you want it really spicy)

2 eggs

1/4 cup vegetable oil

3/4 cup plus 3 tablespoons cold water

Preheat the oven to 425°F. Coat an 8-by-8-inch baking pan with cooking spray; set aside.

In a small mixing bowl, using a wooden spoon, stir together the corn muffin mix and the drained chiles. Add the remaining ingredients and stir briefly to blend (the batter may not be completely smooth). Transfer the batter to the prepared pan and smooth the top using the spoon.

Bake for 20 minutes, or until the top of the corn bread is lightly browned. Remove from the oven and let cool for 15 minutes before cutting into squares.

Each serving contains approximately:
CAL: 128 PRO: 9g NET CARB: 8g FAT: 6g CHOL: 36mg SOD: 192mg

SERVES 12

# FOCACCIA WITH CARAMELIZED ONIONS AND MOZZARELLA

When you're dying for some chewy bread to go alongside an entrée or you need a nice and easy appetizer for a crowd, this focaccia fits the bill. Be sure to use the CarbSense brand of pizza mix, as it has the herbs added and others may not.

## DOUGH

**One 12-ounce box CarbSense garlic and herb pizza crust mix**

**6 tablespoons olive oil, divided**

**1 cup hot water**

**Cooking spray**

## TOPPING

**1/2 medium onion, thinly sliced (about 1/2 cup)**

**1/2 teaspoon kosher salt**

**1/2 cup shredded part-skim mozzarella cheese**

**1 tablespoon grated Parmesan cheese**

**To make the dough:** Prepare the pizza crust mix using the focaccia directions listed on the package (using the included yeast, as well as 3 tablespoons of the olive oil and the hot water). Mix it very well, adding additional water if needed, to get the dough to hold together in a ball. Put the dough ball in a clean medium mixing bowl and cover with a clean kitchen towel. Set the bowl in a warm place for 20 minutes to let the dough rise.

Coat a baking sheet lightly with cooking spray; set aside.

**Prepare the topping while the dough is rising:** In a medium skillet or sauté pan, over medium-low heat, stir together the onion and 1 tablespoon of the olive oil. Cook, stirring occasionally, for 10 to 15 minutes, or until the onions become limp and are nicely browned. Turn off the heat and set the onions aside.

When the dough has risen, turn out onto a clean cutting board or counter; sprinkle any extra loose crumbs from the dough mixture onto the cutting board to keep the dough from sticking. Using a rolling pin, roll the dough into a rectangle about 1/4 to 1/2 inch thick. (It doesn't matter if it's a perfect rectangle; the thickness is the important part.) Brush the dough with the remaining 2 tablespoons olive oil and let rest for 5 minutes.

Top the dough with the cooked onions, then sprinkle the surface evenly with the salt and cheeses.

Bake for 15 to 20 minutes, or until cooked through and the cheese is just beginning to brown. Let the focaccia rest for 2 minutes before cutting it with a pizza-cutting wheel. Serve warm or at room temperature.

Each serving contains approximately:
CAL: 182 PRO: 20g NET CARB: 4g FAT: 9g CHOL: 3mg SOD: 223mg

SERVES 12

# CUBANELLE PEPPERS WITH GARLIC AND BUTTERED BREAD CRUMBS

Kim fell in love with these peppers while working on this book, and we think you'll like them, too. If you haven't seen them before, look for the bright green, long, narrow peppers (sometimes called Italian peppers). They're not too spicy or overpowering, which makes them a great side-dish ingredient.

1 tablespoon plus 1 teaspoon olive oil

4 cubanelle peppers, halved, seeded, and cut into thin, 3-inch strips

2 garlic cloves, minced (about 1 teaspoon)

1/2 teaspoon kosher salt

3 tablespoons Low-Carb Buttered Bread Crumbs (page 294)

In a medium skillet, over medium heat, warm the oil. When hot, add the peppers, garlic, and salt. Immediately reduce the heat to medium-low and cook, stirring, for 5 to 8 minutes, or until the peppers are soft and beginning to brown.

Remove from the heat and stir in the bread crumbs. Serve hot or at room temperature.

Each serving contains approximately:
CAL: 62 PRO: 2g NET CARB: 3.5g FAT: 5g CHOL: 2.5mg SOD: 74mg

SERVES 6

# COLORFUL
# PEPPERS
## AND ONIONS

Peppers and onions are a classic combination that's tailor-made for sausages and other grilled foods. Serve this hot or at room temperature.

2 tablespoons vegetable oil

1 medium onion, halved and thinly sliced (about 1 cup)

½ teaspoon kosher salt

½ teaspoon ground black pepper

1 medium (about 8 ounces) green bell pepper, halved, seeded, and thinly sliced

1 medium (about 8 ounces) red bell pepper, halved, seeded, and thinly sliced

1 medium (about 8 ounces) yellow bell pepper, halved, seeded, and thinly sliced

In a large skillet over medium heat, warm the oil. Add the onions, salt, and pepper. Cook, stirring frequently, for 2 minutes, or until the onions are fragrant. Add the peppers; cook and stir another 5 minutes, or until the peppers are tender but not mushy.

Each serving contains approximately:
CAL: 61 PRO: 1g NET CARB: 3.5g FAT: 5g CHOL: 0mg SOD: 42mg

SERVES 6

# ASPARAGUS WITH PARMESAN

The color and big flavor of this side dish makes it a perfect match for roasted meats and simple seafood, like Panfried Scallops (page 182).

- 1 tablespoon butter
- 1 tablespoon olive oil
- 1 bunch asparagus (about 1$\frac{1}{4}$ pounds), ends trimmed, cut into 2-inch pieces
- $\frac{1}{8}$ teaspoon kosher salt
- $\frac{1}{4}$ teaspoon ground black pepper
- $\frac{1}{4}$ cup finely shredded Parmesan cheese

In a medium skillet, melt the butter with the olive oil. Add the asparagus, salt, and pepper. Cook, stirring occasionally, for 6 to 10 minutes, or until the asparagus is crisp-tender.

Remove from the heat, add the Parmesan, and toss. Serve hot or at room temperature.

Each serving contains approximately:
CAL: 111 PRO: 6g NET CARB: 3g FAT: 8g CHOL: 13mg SOD: 175mg

SERVES 4

# GREEN BEANS WITH ALMONDS, ONIONS, AND BACON

This recipe pulls together lots of super flavors and textures. It's great for summertime entertaining, as it's delicious served at room temperature (you can make it ahead of time). If you prefer broccoli to the beans, substitute a 16-ounce bag of frozen broccoli florets, thawed.

3 tablespoons olive oil

1/2 medium onion, thinly sliced (about 1/2 cup)

1/2 cup slivered almonds

1/4 teaspoon kosher salt

1/2 teaspoon ground black pepper

One 16-ounce bag frozen green beans

3 slices bacon, cooked crisp and crumbled (about 1/3 cup)

1 tablespoon balsamic vinegar

In a medium skillet over medium heat, warm the olive oil. Add the onions, almonds, salt, and pepper. Cook, stirring occasionally, for 2 to 3 minutes, or until the onions soften. Add the green beans and cook, stirring occasionally, for 8 to 10 minutes, until the beans are crisp-tender.

Remove the pan from the heat, add the bacon and balsamic vinegar, and toss well. Serve hot or at room temperature.

Each serving contains approximately:
CAL: 263 PRO: 7g NET CARB: 8g FAT: 21g CHOL: 4mg SOD: 116mg

SERVES 4

# BROCCOLI WITH PINE NUTS AND LEMON

Toasted pine nuts tossed with tender-crisp broccoli and lemon zest gives this dish a lot of zing. Try it with the Apricot Chicken (page 197).

1 medium head broccoli (about 1$^1/_2$ pounds)

3 tablespoons olive oil, divided

$^1/_3$ cup pine nuts

$^1/_2$ teaspoon kosher salt

$^1/_8$ teaspoon ground black pepper

$^1/_4$ cup warm water

1 tablespoon fresh lemon juice

2 teaspoons lemon zest (see page 33)

Cut the broccoli into florets and discard the stems (you should have about 5 cups florets).

In a large skillet or sauté pan over medium heat, warm 1 tablespoon of the olive oil. Add the pine nuts and cook, stirring, until the nuts start to brown, about 1 minute. Add the broccoli and sprinkle with the salt and pepper. Cook and stir for another 2 minutes, until the broccoli becomes bright green.

Add the water and bring to a simmer. Stir well, then cover and cook for 4 to 6 minutes, or until the broccoli becomes tender, but not soft or limp. (Most of the water will cook off.) Turn off the heat. Drizzle the remaining oil and the lemon juice over the broccoli; sprinkle with the lemon zest, stir well, and serve.

Each serving contains approximately:
CAL: 191 PRO: 8g NET CARB: 5g FAT: 16g CHOL: 0mg SOD: 105mg

SERVES 4

# CAULIFLOWER "COUSCOUS"

In her book *Living Low Carb,* Fran McCullough suggests grating cauliflower and substituting it for rice. We thought this was a brilliant idea, so we played with it a while and came up with this seasoned cauliflower "couscous," which is a suitable accompaniment to various saucy meat dishes, stews, and Asian-style recipes. For extra flavor, add a little grated Parmesan cheese to your "couscous."

1 medium head (about 2 pounds) cauliflower, cored, trimmed, and cut into florets

$\frac{1}{4}$ cup butter

$\frac{3}{4}$ teaspoon kosher salt

$\frac{1}{4}$ teaspoon ground black pepper

Using the large holes on a hand-held grater or a food processor with a grater attachment, grate the cauliflower.

In a large skillet or sauté pan over medium heat, melt the butter. Add the cauliflower, salt, and pepper. Cook, stirring frequently, until the "couscous" is softened and cooked through, about 5 minutes.

Each serving (about 3/4 cup) contains approximately:
CAL: 106 PRO: 3g NET CARB: 5g FAT: 8g CHOL: 21mg SOD: 184mg

SERVES 6

# MAPLE-BACON BRUSSELS SPROUTS

**While some of us like Brussels sprouts just as they are—strongly flavored and slightly bitter—many people avoid them because of these characteristics. We created this recipe for non-sprout lovers. Here the sprouts are sliced, tossed with bits of bacon, and coated with a slightly sweet, maple-flavored sauce.**

1/4 cup sugar-free maple syrup

2 tablespoons real maple syrup

1 teaspoon Dijon mustard

6 slices bacon, chopped

1 1/4 pounds fresh Brussels sprouts, trimmed and thinly sliced

1/2 cup water

1/2 teaspoon kosher salt

1/4 teaspoon ground black pepper

In a 1-cup liquid measuring cup or a small bowl, stir together the maple syrups and the mustard; set aside.

In a large skillet or sauté pan over medium heat, cook the chopped bacon, stirring constantly, until just crisp, about 4 minutes. Remove the pan from the heat; using a slotted spoon, transfer the bacon to paper towels to drain. Pour off all but about 3 teaspoons of the bacon fat; return the pan to the heat.

Add the sprouts and water to the skillet. Cook, stirring frequently, for 4 to 5 minutes, or until the sprouts have turned bright green and softened slightly, but aren't limp. Add the syrup mixture, salt, and pepper and stir to coat the sprouts. Cook for another minute to heat through, then return the bacon pieces to the skillet and stir to combine. Serve hot.

Each serving contains approximately:
CAL: 85 PRO: 5g NET CARB: 6g FAT: 3g CHOL: 5mg SOD: 204mg

SERVES 6

# DIJON CABBAGE WITH TOASTED PECANS

Preshredded cabbage is now a stock item in the produce section of most supermarkets. We love the convenience of it, and it's extremely versatile. In this recipe, we've braised the cabbage in a Dijon-seasoned broth, then finished it with butter-toasted pecans. This is a great accompaniment for Red Wine–Marinated Sirloin Steak (page 232).

2 tablespoons butter

1 cup pecans, chopped

1/2 cup chicken broth

1/2 teaspoon Tabasco sauce

3 tablespoons Dijon mustard

1 tablespoon light brown sugar

1/4 cup dry white wine

1 tablespoon vegetable oil

1/3 medium onion, finely chopped (about 1/3 cup)

1/4 teaspoon kosher salt

1/4 teaspoon ground black pepper

One 16-ounce bag preshredded cabbage (about 3 1/2 cups)

In a small skillet or sauté pan over medium heat, melt the butter. Add the pecans and cook, stirring, for about 3 minutes, or until the pecans become fragrant. Remove from the heat and set aside.

In a small mixing bowl, using a fork or whisk, combine the chicken broth, Tabasco, Dijon mustard, brown sugar, and wine; set aside.

In a large skillet or sauté pan over medium heat, warm the oil. Add the onion, salt, and pepper. Cook, stirring, until the onions are softened and fragrant, about 5 minutes. Add the cabbage to the pan and stir to combine. Add the broth mixture and reduce the heat to medium-low. Stir to coat the cabbage with the broth mixture. Cover and cook for 5 to 7 minutes, stirring occasionally; the cabbage should be cooked through but still somewhat crisp. Stir again; divide the cabbage among individual plates and sprinkle with the toasted pecans.

Each serving contains approximately:
CAL: 232 PRO: 3g NET CARB: 7g FAT: 20g CHOL: 11mg SOD: 340mg

SERVES 6

# WILTED ESCAROLE
## WITH ALMONDS

Eat your way out of your salad rut with this unusual dish. If you've never tried escarole before, you'll be pleasantly surprised at how the slight bitterness of the greens is softened by cooking and complemented by the almonds. And don't worry if it seems like there's too much escarole in the pan—it cooks down a lot.

2 tablespoons butter

$1/2$ cup almonds, chopped

1 medium head escarole, well washed and chopped (about 7 cups)

$1/2$ teaspoon kosher salt

$1/4$ teaspoon ground black pepper

$1/2$ teaspoon sherry vinegar

In a large skillet or sauté pan over medium heat, melt the butter. Add the almonds and cook, stirring constantly, for about 3 minutes, or until the almonds become fragrant.

Add the escarole, salt, and pepper. Using two spoons, toss the escarole with the almonds while cooking, until the greens are softened and wilted, about 3 minutes. Remove from the heat, add the vinegar, and toss again. Serve hot or at room temperature.

Each serving contains approximately:
CAL: 162 PRO: 4g NET CARB: 3g FAT: 14g CHOL: 15mg SOD: 110mg

SERVES 4

# BOK CHOY STIR-FRY

Who needs rice or potatoes when you've got a full-flavored veggie dish like this on your plate? Perfect with grilled meats or broiled fish, this stir-fry is also a good complement to Sesame Fried Tempeh (page 167). Be sure to have all ingredients prepped and ready to go before you start cooking.

**SAUCE**

$1/4$ cup chicken broth

$3/4$ teaspoon cornstarch

3 tablespoons soy sauce

1 teaspoon Splenda Granular sweetener

1 tablespoon sake

1 teaspoon toasted sesame oil

1 to 2 teaspoons crushed red pepper flakes (optional)

1 tablespoon peanut oil

$1/2$ medium onion, thinly sliced (about $1/2$ cup)

6 cloves garlic, minced (about 1 tablespoon)

1 tablespoon peeled and grated fresh ginger

1 large head (about 1 pound) bok choy, ends trimmed, cut into thin strips (about 8 cups)

1 medium (about 8 ounces) red bell pepper, seeded, thinly sliced, and cut into 1-inch pieces

**To make the sauce:** In a small bowl, whisk together all the sauce ingredients; set aside.

In a large skillet with high sides or a wok over medium-high heat, warm the oil. When very hot, add the onion, garlic, and ginger. Cook, stirring constantly, for 1 to 2 minutes, or until the onion begins to soften. Add the bok choy and red pepper. Cook, stirring occasionally, for another 4 minutes, or until the bok choy wilts.

Pour the sauce into the skillet and stir, coating the vegetables with the sauce. Bring the sauce to a simmer, stirring occasionally, and cook for another 2 minutes to thicken. Serve immediately.

Each serving contains approximately:
CAL: 58 PRO: 2g NET CARB: 4g FAT: 3g CHOL: 0mg SOD: 617mg

SERVES 6

# SEASONED BLACK SOYBEANS

Seasoned in a Southwest style with jalapeños, Adobo seasoning, and the bright kick of fresh lime juice, these beans can be served alongside simple grilled meats or seafood. They're also a good filling for low-carb tortillas—just add some shredded cheese and sour cream and you've got a nice burrito! Look for adobo seasoning in the ethnic section of the supermarket (we use the Goya brand).

2 tablespoons butter

$1/_2$ medium onion, finely chopped (about $1/_2$ cup)

2 celery stalks, finely chopped

$1/_2$ large carrot, finely chopped (about $1/_2$ cup)

2 tablespoons chopped, canned jalapeños, drained, or more to taste

$1^1/_4$ teaspoons adobo seasoning

$1/_4$ teaspoon ground black pepper

Two 15-ounce cans black soybeans, one can drained and rinsed, one can undrained

1 lime, cut into 8 wedges

1 tablespoon finely chopped cilantro for garnish (optional)

Sour cream for garnish (optional)

In a medium skillet or sauté pan over medium heat, melt the butter. Add the onion, celery, carrot, jalapeños, adobo, and black pepper. Cook, stirring frequently, for 3 to 5 minutes, or until the onions and carrot begin to soften.

Reduce the heat to medium-low and stir in the beans. Cook for another 8 to 10 minutes, stirring frequently, until the beans are heated through and the vegetables are completely cooked.

Serve the beans with the lime wedges, and garnish with the cilantro and sour cream, if desired.

Each serving contains approximately:
CAL: 111 PRO: 7g NET CARB: 2g FAT: 7g CHOL: 8mg SOD: 310mg

SERVES 4

# CREAMY CAULIFLOWER PURÉE

Kim doesn't pull out her food processor for many recipes, but this is one that definitely benefits from a good "processing." To make it worth all the cleaning time that a food processor requires, prepare a double recipe and freeze some. To reheat the frozen purée, just let it thaw in the refrigerator during the day, then bake it in an ovenproof dish at 350°F for 20 to 25 minutes, or until heated through.

1 medium head (about 2 pounds) cauliflower, trimmed and cut into florets (stems discarded)

$1/2$ cup light cream, warmed

2 tablespoons butter

$1/2$ teaspoon Tabasco sauce

$1/2$ teaspoon kosher salt

$1/8$ teaspoon ground white pepper

$1/4$ cup (1 ounce) shredded Swiss cheese

2 tablespoons grated Parmesan cheese

In a large saucepan, cook the cauliflower in boiling water to cover for 10 to 12 minutes, or until tender.

Drain the cauliflower and place it in the bowl of a food processor. Add all the remaining ingredients except the cheeses. Pulse the processor a few times, then process until the mixture is smooth.

Add the cheeses to the mixture and process again until smooth and blended. Serve immediately.

Each serving contains approximately:
CAL: 177 PRO: 6g NET CARB: 4.5g FAT: 15g CHOL: 44mg SOD: 229mg

SERVES 4

# CELERY ROOT AND CARROT PURÉE

Celery root (also called celeriac) is the gnarly-looking root of celery. When puréed with a few baby carrots, it produces a smooth, mildly flavored dish that's a nice low-carb substitute for potatoes. It's suitable for guests and makes a unique addition to a holiday table.

2 celery roots (about $1\frac{1}{4}$ pounds), peeled, ends trimmed

1 cup baby carrots

1 tablespoon kosher salt

5 tablespoons butter

$\frac{1}{3}$ cup heavy cream, warmed

$\frac{1}{2}$ teaspoon ground black pepper

Cut the peeled celery root into chunks. Put the pieces in a medium saucepan; add the carrots, salt, and water to cover. Bring to a boil over high heat; reduce the heat and simmer for 15 to 20 minutes, or until the carrots are soft. Drain off the water.

Combine the cooked vegetables, butter, warmed cream, and pepper in the bowl of a food processor. Pulse the food processor a few times, then process the vegetables for 1 to 2 minutes, until the mixture is smooth.

Note

Put away your peelers; we've found that using a sharp paring knife to peel the celery root yields the best results.

Each serving contains approximately:
CAL: 162 PRO: 2g NET CARB: 5g FAT: 14g CHOL: 42mg SOD: 417mg

SERVES 6

# BAKED FENNEL
## WITH TOMATOES

This dish is a nice complement to a simple main course such as Swordfish with Olive Oil and Lemon (page 189). Be sure to keep the fennel slices thin, as thicker slices will require a longer baking time. If you're unsure of your knife skills, try slicing the fennel with a food processor.

2 tablespoons butter

1 tablespoon olive oil

2 large fennel bulbs (about 20 ounces), ends trimmed, cut into 1/4-inch-thick slices

1/2 medium onion, thinly sliced (about 1/2 cup)

1/2 teaspoon kosher salt

1/2 teaspoon ground black pepper

1 clove garlic, minced (about 1/2 teaspoon)

2 tablespoons dry red wine

1 cup canned crushed tomatoes

1/4 cup grated Romano cheese

Cooking spray

1/3 cup Low-Carb Buttered Bread Crumbs (page 294)

In a large skillet or sauté pan over medium heat melt the butter with the olive oil. Add the fennel, onions, salt, pepper, and garlic. Cook, stirring frequently, for 10 minutes, or until the fennel softens and shrinks a bit and the onions are soft. Add the red wine and tomatoes and continue to cook, stirring, until the mixture simmers. Remove from the heat and stir in the cheese.

Preheat the oven to 350°F. Coat a 9-inch glass pie plate or 2-quart casserole dish with cooking spray; transfer the fennel mixture to the prepared dish and sprinkle the top with the bread crumbs.

Bake for 35 to 50 minutes, or until the fennel is soft and the mixture bubbles. Let cool for 5 minutes before serving.

Each serving contains approximately:
CAL: 146 PRO: 5g NET CARB: 6g FAT: 10g CHOL: 19mg SOD: 286mg

SERVES 6

# EASY SPINACH BAKE

This recipe is a tasty way to get your family to eat more spinach. It uses frozen spinach; keep some on hand and you can prepare this side dish with ingredients you probably have on hand.

1 cup heavy cream

2 egg yolks

2 tablespoons grated Parmesan cheese

$1/2$ teaspoon kosher salt

$1/2$ teaspoon ground black pepper

$1/2$ teaspoon Tabasco sauce

2 tablespoons minced dried onions

Two 10-ounce packages frozen chopped spinach, thawed, water squeezed out

$1/3$ cup Low-Carb Buttered Bread Crumbs (page 294)

Preheat the oven to 350°F. In a medium mixing bowl, stir together the cream, egg yolks, Parmesan, salt, pepper, Tabasco, and onions. Add the spinach and mix with a fork until well combined.

Transfer the spinach mixture to a $1 1/2$-quart casserole dish and sprinkle the top with the bread crumbs. Bake for 30 to 35 minutes, or until heated through. Let cool for 5 minutes before serving.

Each serving contains approximately:
CAL: 229 PRO: 7g NET CARB: 6g FAT: 20g CHOL: 131mg SOD: 232mg

SERVES 6

# SPICED ACORN SQUASH RINGS

Here is an easy and elegant way to fix this nutritious vegetable. The ring presentation (as opposed to halving or quartering the squash) builds in automatic portion control. If you've never used cardamom (a Middle Eastern herb in the ginger family), you'll find that it's frequently paired with sweet seasonings, as it is here.

- 1 tablespoon SugarTwin brown-sugar substitute
- 1/4 teaspoon ground cardamom
- 1/4 teaspoon ground cinnamon
- 1/4 teaspoon kosher salt
- 1/4 teaspoon ground black pepper
- Cooking spray
- 1 medium acorn squash (1 1/2 to 2 pounds), ends trimmed, cut into 6 slices, seeds removed
- 2 tablespoons butter, melted

Preheat the oven to 350°F. In a small bowl, combine the Sugar-Twin, cardamom, cinnamon, salt, and pepper; set aside.

Coat a baking sheet with cooking spray; place the squash rings on the baking sheet. Using a pastry brush, coat the top of each squash ring with the melted butter. Sprinkle the spice mixture evenly over the squash rings.

Bake for 30 minutes, or until fork tender; serve immediately.

Note

Cutting winter squash is one of the most dangerous kitchen jobs. You'll need good, sharp knives and some elbow grease, as it can be difficult to get through the tough outer skin of a hard squash. Be careful!

Each serving contains approximately:
CAL: 78 PRO: 1g NET CARB: 8g FAT: 4g CHOL: 10mg SOD: 63mg

SERVES 6

# SPINACH-STUFFED
## MUSHROOM CAPS

We love stuffed mushrooms—both as an appetizer for serving company and as an unusual side dish for a family meal. The filling—a rich combination of spinach, onion, Parmesan cheese, black olives, and mozzarella—nicely stuffs 8 larger mushrooms, but feel free to substitute about 12 regular-sized button mushrooms if you prefer. Either way, consider assembling them early, to save on last-minute preparations.

Cooking spray

8 large "stuffing" mushrooms

2 tablespoons butter

1/4 medium onion, finely chopped (about 1/4 cup)

One 10-ounce package frozen chopped spinach, thawed, water squeezed out

1/4 cup grated Parmesan cheese

One 2 1/4-ounce can sliced black olives, drained

2 eggs, slightly beaten

1/2 teaspoon kosher salt

1/4 teaspoon ground black pepper

1/2 cup (2 ounces) shredded part-skim mozzarella cheese

Preheat the oven to 375°F. Spray a 9-by-9-inch baking pan with cooking spray; set aside.

Wash the mushrooms and remove the stems (reserve the stems for the filling). Place the mushroom caps in the baking pan, tops down. Trim off the discolored ends of the reserved mushroom stems, and chop the stems.

In a medium skillet or sauté pan over medium heat, melt the butter. Add the onion and chopped mushroom stems. Cook, stirring frequently, for about 5 minutes, or until the onion softens; remove from the heat and set aside.

In a small mixing bowl, using a fork, stir together the spinach, Parmesan, black olives, eggs, salt, and pepper. Add the cooked onion and mushroom mixture; stir well to combine all ingredients.

Using a teaspoon, divide the filling between the mushrooms, mounding it in the center of each mushroom cap. Bake the stuffed caps for 20 minutes, or until the mushrooms are cooked and the filling is cooked through. Remove the mushrooms from the oven and top each with a little of the shredded mozzarella. Return the pan to the oven for another 2 minutes, to melt the cheese. Serve immediately.

Each serving contains approximately:
CAL: 208 PRO: 14g NET CARB: 7g FAT: 14g CHOL: 134mg SOD: 489mg

SERVES 4

# 16

## SAUCES, RELISHES, RUBS, AND TOPPINGS

THIS IS THE CHAPTER WHERE YOU CAN FIND RECIPES FOR ALL THOSE LITTLE THINGS THAT MAKE FOOD TASTE BETTER—crumb coatings for meat and fish; spicy, sweet, and savory sauces; and tangy relishes, for example. We've divided the chapter into savory and sweet sections to make it easier to find what you're seeking.

Our picks for recipes you absolutely should not miss: Olive and Caper Sauce, Spicy Sesame Sauce, Crème Fraîche, and Jam Butter (any flavor). With just these few easy recipes, you'll improve your low-carb cooking immeasurably—try them!

# LOW-CARB BUTTERED BREAD CRUMBS

Seasoned, buttered bread crumbs are an essential pantry item for any kitchen. Of course, our version uses low-carb bread, which makes these bread crumbs a guilt-free addition to any recipe. Use them to thicken a sauce, as a crispy topping on a vegetable dish, or to coat a piece of meat before cooking. If you'd prefer seasoned crumbs, add your favorite dried herb to the bread crumbs (parsley or Italian seasoning is nice).

6 slices very stale low-carb bread (if your bread isn't stale, let it sit out overnight, uncovered)

3 tablespoons butter

$1/2$ teaspoon kosher salt

$1/2$ teaspoon ground black pepper

In a food processor, process the bread into fine crumbs.

In a medium skillet or sauté pan over medium heat, melt the butter and heat until it's foamy. Add the bread crumbs, salt, and pepper. Cook, stirring, until the crumbs are golden brown, 3 to 5 minutes. Remove from heat and let cool completely.

Store the bread crumbs in an airtight container in the refrigerator or freezer.

Each 1-tablespoon serving contains approximately:
CAL: 26 PRO: 2g NET CARB: 0.5g FAT: 2g CHOL: 3mg SOD: 47mg

MAKES ABOUT 1 $3/4$ CUPS;
SERVES 28

# BASIC CRUMB COATING FOR MEAT AND POULTRY

This is an easy, low-carb coating to have on hand for when you want to quickly panfry a pork chop or chicken breast. It adds flavor and a little texture, but virtually no carbs. Keep in mind that the meat needs to be dipped into beaten egg white or milk prior to coating, or the mixture won't stick. Note that the nutritional information is for the entire recipe; the rub's carb contribution to each serving is negligible.

$1/4$ cup Low-Carb Buttered Bread Crumbs (facing page)

$1/2$ teaspoon kosher salt

$1/2$ teaspoon garlic powder

Pinch of paprika (optional)

Stir together all the ingredients in a small bowl. Store in an airtight container.

Entire recipe contains approximately:
CAL: 91 PRO: 12g NET CARB: 0.5g FAT: 4g
CHOL: 114mg SOD: 197mg

MAKES ABOUT $1/4$ CUP, OR ENOUGH TO COAT 1 POUND OF MEAT OR POULTRY

# PEPPERY SPICE RUB FOR POULTRY

This rub really perks up roast poultry, and is great on grilled poultry, too (rub it on before grilling). Note that the nutritional information is for the entire recipe, not per serving. On a per-serving basis, the rub's carb contribution is minimal.

1 tablespoon chili powder

1 tablespoon ground black pepper

1 tablespoon dried thyme

1 tablespoon celery salt

Stir together all the ingredients in a small bowl. Store in an airtight container.

### Variation

For added flavor interest, combine 1 tablespoon of the spice rub with 1 tablespoon olive oil and 1 tablespoon fresh orange juice; rub all over and inside the chicken before roasting.

Entire recipe contains approximately:
CAL: 52 PRO: 2g NET CARB: 6g FAT: 2g
CHOL: 0mg SOD: 6,476mg

MAKES $\frac{1}{4}$ CUP, OR ENOUGH TO SEASON 1 AVERAGE TURKEY OR 2 LARGE ROASTING CHICKENS

# AFGHAN-INSPIRED POULTRY RUB

When Kitty and her husband lived in New York city, they frequently visited Afghan restaurants, where they enjoyed the kebabs—either lamb or chicken. Now that they live in Maine, Afghan restaurants are hard to come by. So, together they came up with this rub, which comes pretty close to tasting like the restaurant version. Note that the nutritional information is for the entire recipe; the rub's carb contribution to each serving is minimal.

1 tablespoon ground turmeric

1 tablespoon ground coriander

1 tablespoon ground cumin

1 tablespoon garlic powder

1 teaspoon chili powder

1 teaspoon kosher salt

3/4 teaspoon ground cardamom

1/2 teaspoon ground ginger

Stir together all the ingredients in a small bowl. Store in an airtight container.

Entire recipe contains approximately:
CAL: 105 PRO: 4g NET CARB: 14g FAT: 3g
CHOL: 0mg SOD: 522mg

MAKES ABOUT 3/4 CUP, OR ENOUGH TO SEASON 8 POUNDS OF MEAT

## DAN'S
# RIB RUB

Kitty's husband, Dan, is famous (in their neighborhood, at least) for his smoked, boneless, country-style pork ribs. Although his combination of spices has been a highly guarded secret for years, Kitty was able to break down his defenses and obtain the recipe. Dan prefers a rub over a wet sauce for smoking and grilling meat—it makes for tidier eating, doesn't burn on the meat, and is just as tangy and flavorful as any sauce around. Note that the nutritional information is for the entire recipe; the rub's carb contribution to each serving is negligible.

¼ cup paprika

¼ cup kosher salt

2 tablespoons cayenne pepper or other ground, dried chile peppers

1 tablespoon garlic powder

1 tablespoon onion powder

1 tablespoon ground black pepper

2 teaspoons Splenda Granular sweetener

2 teaspoons sugar

1 teaspoon ground sage

1 teaspoon dry mustard

1 teaspoon ground cardamom (optional)

Stir together all the ingredients in a small bowl. Store in an airtight container.

Entire rub recipe contains approximately:
CAL: 19 PRO: 1g NET CARB: 4g FAT: 1g
CHOL: 0mg SOD: 482mg

MAKES ABOUT 1 CUP, OR ENOUGH TO SEASON 10 POUNDS BONELESS, COUNTRY-STYLE PORK RIBS

# SPICE RUB FOR STEAKS

We love the simplicity of a good spice rub. Sprinkle this rub onto steaks in the morning and refrigerate. When you get home at night, you'll only need to fire up the grill or get out your frying pan. Look for the adobo seasoning in the ethnic section of the grocery store, near the Hispanic foods. Note that the nutritional information is for the entire recipe, not per serving. On a per-serving basis, the rub's carb contribution is about 0.5g net carbs per ½-pound serving of meat.

2 tablespoons adobo seasoning

1 tablespoon onion powder

2 teaspoons paprika

½ teaspoon dry mustard

½ teaspoon ground black pepper

Stir together all the ingredients in a small bowl. Store in an airtight container.

Entire recipe contains approximately:
CAL: 47 PRO: 2g NET CARB: 7g FAT: 1g
CHOL: 0mg SOD: 8,406mg

MAKES ¼ CUP, OR ENOUGH TO SEASON
ABOUT 8 POUNDS OF STEAK

# CUCUMBER-ONION RELISH

In this relish, the delicate flavor of the cucumber is heightened by the onion and vinegar. Hot dogs have never had it so good!

- 2 medium cucumbers, peeled, seeded, and grated
- 1/2 medium onion, grated (about 1/2 cup)
- 3 tablespoons cider vinegar
- 1 teaspoon Splenda Granular sweetener
- 1 teaspoon sugar
- 1 teaspoon kosher salt
- 1/4 teaspoon Tabasco sauce

Pinch of ground black pepper

Place the grated cucumber and onion in a fine-mesh sieve and press the water out. Transfer the cucumber and onion to a medium mixing bowl and stir in the remaining ingredients until well mixed.

Refrigerate the relish for at least 4 hours or as long as overnight.

Each 2-tablespoon serving contains approximately:
CAL: 10 PRO: 0g NET CARB: 2g FAT: 0g CHOL: 0mg SOD: 42mg

MAKES ABOUT 1 3/4 CUPS;
SERVES 12

# CARAMELIZED
# VIDALIA
# ONION RELISH

**At Kim's house, this relish is a table condiment whenever she serves beef or pork. If Vidalia onions are not available, choose another sweet onion.**

2 tablespoons vegetable oil

4 medium Vidalia onions, thinly sliced, cut into 1-inch-long pieces (about 5 cups)

1/2 teaspoon kosher salt

1/2 teaspoon ground black pepper

1/4 teaspoon sugar

2 tablespoons balsamic vinegar

1 tablespoon butter

1/2 teaspoon Worcestershire sauce

In a large skillet or sauté pan over medium heat, warm the oil. When hot, add the onions, salt, pepper, and sugar. Reduce heat to medium-low and cook, stirring occasionally, for 20 to 30 minutes, or until the onions become very soft and brown (caramelized).

Remove from the heat and stir in the balsamic vinegar, butter, and Worcestershire sauce.

### Note

Our recipe-testers thought this relish would make a flavorful addition to steamed vegetables—a great idea!

---

**Each 2-tablespoon serving contains approximately:**
**CAL: 26 PRO: 0g NET CARB: 2g FAT: 2g CHOL: 2mg SOD: 20mg**

**MAKES ABOUT 2 1/2 CUPS;**
**SERVES 20**

# OLIVE AND CAPER SAUCE

Kim's friend Barbara Gulino inspired this recipe when she told Kim that "olives and capers are old friends that love to be together." This sauce is delicious over swordfish, and pairs equally well with panfried or grilled boneless chicken breasts.

1/2 cup Kalamata olives, pitted and chopped

2 tablespoons capers, drained and chopped

1/4 teaspoon dried thyme

1/4 cup extra-virgin olive oil

1/2 teaspoon ground black pepper

1/8 teaspoon crushed red pepper flakes, or more to taste

1/4 teaspoon finely chopped anchovy or 1/4 teaspoon anchovy paste

1/4 cup fresh orange juice

In a small bowl, stir together all the ingredients. Store the sauce in the refrigerator until ready to use. Bring to room temperature before serving.

**Note**

Capers are small and can be difficult to chop. For this recipe, you may find they chop more easily if you place them on top of the olives on your cutting surface, then chop them together.

Each 2-tablespoon serving contains approximately:
CAL: 74 PRO: 0g NET CARB: 1g FAT: 8g CHOL: 0mg SOD: 146mg

MAKES ABOUT 1 CUP;
SERVES 8

# SPICY SESAME SAUCE

This sauce was inspired by a seafood dish that Kim regularly enjoys at her favorite Thai restaurant. The waitress told her to use three flavors—salty, sweet, and spicy—to create her own approximation of the sauce at home. It's great over panfried or grilled seafood. For even more flavor and a dash of color, garnish your finished dish with chopped scallions.

1/3 cup bottled Thai fish sauce

2 tablespoons fresh orange juice

1 tablespoon sugar

1 tablespoon Splenda Granular sweetener

3 tablespoons rice vinegar

2 tablespoons water

2 teaspoons toasted sesame oil

2 teaspoons crushed red pepper flakes

Combine all the ingredients in a jar and shake well. Refrigerate for at least 4 hours or up to overnight to allow the flavors to blend. Shake well before using.

Each 2-tablespoon serving contains approximately:
CAL: 42 PRO: 2g NET CARB: 4g FAT: 2g CHOL: 8mg SOD: 1,088mg

MAKES ABOUT 3/4 CUP;
SERVES 6

# CLASSIC
# CRANBERRY SAUCE

We have offered two cranberry sauce recipes in this book because we realize that some people are purists, and don't want to see orange juice in their cranberry sauce! In this version, the combination of regular sugar plus Splenda makes for a better-tasting sauce than using just Splenda alone.

**1 pound fresh cranberries**

**1 cup water**

**$1/3$ cup sugar**

**$1 1/3$ cups Splenda Granular sweetener**

**Pinch of kosher salt**

In a medium saucepan over medium heat, stir together all ingredients. Bring the mixture to a boil, stirring frequently. When the cranberries begin to pop, reduce the heat to medium-low and let the sauce simmer for 6 to 8 minutes, or until the berries are tender.

Let the sauce cool for at least 30 minutes before serving (it tastes best at room temperature). Store any unused sauce in the refrigerator.

Each $1/4$-cup serving contains approximately:
CAL: 23 PRO: 0g NET CARB: 5g FAT: 0g CHOL: 0mg SOD: 3mg

MAKES ABOUT 5 CUPS;
SERVES 20

# CRANBERRY-ORANGE

## SAUCE
Cranberry sauce typically contains quite a lot of sugar. Using orange juice and Splenda Granular sweetener, we've created a cranberry sauce that is just as delicious as its traditional counterpart, with no added sugar at all. This sauce is perfect at holiday time, but is also great over grilled chicken breasts or pork chops for a regular weeknight dinner.

1 pound fresh cranberries

3/4 cup fresh orange juice

1/4 cup water

1 1/2 cups Splenda Granular sweetener

Pinch of kosher salt

In a medium saucepan over medium heat, stir together all ingredients. Bring the mixture to a boil, stirring frequently. When the cranberries begin to pop, reduce the heat to medium-low and let the sauce simmer for 6 to 8 minutes, or until the berries are tender.

Let the sauce cool for at least 30 minutes before serving (it tastes best at room temperature). Store the unused sauce in the refrigerator.

Each 1/4-cup serving contains approximately:
CAL: 17 PRO: 0g NET CARB: 3g FAT: 0g CHOL: 0mg SOD: 16mg

MAKES ABOUT 5 CUPS;
SERVES 20

# BASIC WHITE SAUCE

This versatile sauce can be used as a starter sauce for many other sauces. Using this basic recipe, you can create a divine cheese sauce or an herbed cream sauce, for example (see the variations). We've also used it in Turkey and Cauliflower Gratin with Toasted Hazelnuts (page 159). This recipe is easily doubled, and the sauce stores well in the refrigerator and reheats nicely, too. Save yourself some time and prepare it a day before you need it.

2 tablespoons butter

1 tablespoon whole-wheat pastry flour

2 tablespoons all-purpose white flour

$\frac{1}{4}$ teaspoon kosher salt

$1\frac{1}{4}$ cups chicken broth, at room temperature

1 cup light cream

$\frac{1}{8}$ teaspoon Tabasco sauce

In a medium saucepan over medium heat, melt the butter. Remove from the heat and whisk in both flours and the salt until combined. Return to the heat and cook until the mixture bubbles, about 1 minute.

Remove from the heat and add the broth, whisking vigorously to prevent lumps. Whisk in the cream and the Tabasco.

Return the mixture to medium heat and bring to a simmer, whisking constantly as it thickens. Use immediately or refrigerate for later use.

EACH $\frac{1}{4}$-CUP SERVING CONTAINS APPROXIMATELY:
CAL: 100 PRO: 1g NET CARB: 3g FAT: 9g CHOL: 29mg SOD: 265mg

MAKES 2 CUPS;
SERVES 8

# CREAMY HERB SAUCE

¹/₃ cup finely chopped fresh herbs (parsley, basil, oregano, chives)

3 tablespoons dry white wine

¹/₄ teaspoon ground black pepper

Prepare the Basic White Sauce through whisking in the cream and Tabasco. Stir in the herbs, wine, and pepper. Proceed with the recipe as directed.

EACH ¹/₄-CUP SERVING CONTAINS APPROXIMATELY:
CAL: 70 PRO: 1g NET CARB: 2g FAT: 6g CHOL: 19mg SOD: 178mg

MAKES ABOUT 2 CUPS;
SERVES 8

# CLASSIC CHEESE SAUCE

²/₃ cup (about 4 ounces) shredded Swiss cheese, at room temperature

¹/₃ cup chicken broth, warmed

¹/₄ cup grated Parmesan cheese

¹/₂ teaspoon ground black pepper

¹/₂ teaspoon paprika

Prepare the Basic White Sauce according to the main recipe. Remove from the heat and whisk in the Swiss cheese, broth, Parmesan, pepper, and paprika.

EACH ¹/₄-CUP SERVING CONTAINS APPROXIMATELY:
CAL: 100 PRO: 4g NET CARB: 2g FAT: 9g CHOL: 26mg SOD: 256mg

MAKES ABOUT 3 CUPS;
SERVES 12

# SPICY LEMON MAYONNAISE

This lemony mayonnaise definitely packs a cayenne punch. Try it with the Crab Cakes (page 181).

1 cup mayonnaise

3/4 teaspoon cayenne pepper

3/4 teaspoon Tabasco sauce

2 teaspoons fresh lemon juice

1 teaspoon lemon zest (see page 33)

Pinch of kosher salt

In a small mixing bowl, whisk together all the ingredients until blended. Refrigerate overnight before serving, if possible, to allow the flavors to blend.

Each 1-tablespoon serving contains approximately:
CAL: 99 PRO: 0g NET CARB: 1g FAT: 11g CHOL: 8mg SOD: 85mg

MAKES ABOUT 1 CUP;
SERVES 16

# ORANGE MAYONNAISE

This is one of those condiments where you can easily think of myriad ways to use it. We use it in Sliced Tomato Salad (page 255), and it's just as good on a simple turkey sandwich.

1/2 cup mayonnaise

1 tablespoon orange zest (see page 33)

1 tablespoon fresh orange juice

Pinch of kosher salt

Pinch of ground black pepper

1/8 teaspoon Tabasco sauce

1/4 teaspoon soy sauce

In a small bowl, stir together all the ingredients until well combined. Refrigerate overnight before serving, if possible, to allow all the flavors to blend.

Each 1-tablespoon serving contains approximately:
CAL: 67 PRO: 0g NET CARB: 1g FAT: 7g CHOL: 5mg SOD: 64mg

MAKES ABOUT 3/4 CUP;
SERVES 12

# EASY **HORSERADISH CREAM**

This tasty sauce is easy to whip up, and is a great accent to beef in any form. Try it with a roast beef sandwich, grilled steak, burgers, or our Rib-eye Roast with Horseradish and Caraway Crust (page 269).

1 cup sour cream

$1/4$ cup prepared horseradish

$1/2$ teaspoon Worcestershire sauce

$1/2$ teaspoon Tabasco sauce

Pinch of kosher salt

Pinch of ground black pepper

In a small bowl, whisk together all the ingredients until well blended. Refrigerate the cream overnight before serving, if possible, to allow the flavors to blend.

---

Each 2-tablespoon serving contains approximately:
CAL: 52 PRO: 1g NET CARB: 1.5g FAT:5g CHOL: 10mg SOD: 31mg

MAKES ABOUT 1 $1/4$ CUPS;
SERVES 10

# CRÈME FRAÎCHE

Crème fraîche is a versatile sauce, topping, and recipe ingredient. We think one of the benefits of living low-carb is being able to enjoy crème fraîche without any guilt! Be sure to try the variations listed below; they make excellent dips for fresh vegetables. Also try the Crème Fraîche Dressing (page 105).

$1/2$ cup sour cream (not "light" or reduced fat)

$1/2$ cup heavy cream

In a small bowl, whisk together both creams until blended. Cover with plastic wrap and let the crème fraîche rest at room temperature for 5 to 6 hours.

When the cream is done resting, add any additional ingredients desired (see variations below). Use immediately, or cover and refrigerate for future use. If a thinner crème fraîche is desired, thin the finished recipe with additional heavy cream.

Variations

## CHIVE CRÈME FRAÎCHE

Add $1/4$ cup finely chopped fresh chives, a pinch of kosher salt, and a pinch of ground black pepper to the rested cream mixture.

Each 2-tablespoon serving contains approximately:
CAL: 82 PRO: 1g NET CARB: 1g FAT: 9g CHOL: 27mg SOD: 19mg

## DILL CRÈME FRAÎCHE

Add 2 tablespoons finely chopped fresh dill, a pinch of kosher salt, and a pinch of black pepper to the rested cream mixture.

Each serving contains approximately:
CAL: 82 PRO: 1g NET CARB: 1g FAT: 9g CHOL: 27mg SOD: 19mg

Each 2-tablespoon serving contains approximately:
CAL: 82 PRO: 1g NET CARB: 1g FAT: 9g CHOL: 27mg SOD: 13mg

MAKES ABOUT 1 CUP;
SERVES 8

# JAM BUTTER

Jam butter is a nice alternative to plain jam or plain butter. Experiment with different preserves to come up with your own favorite combination. We like 2 tablespoons of sugar-free strawberry preserves mixed with 2 tablespoons sugar-free apricot preserves—delicious! Be sure to let the butter come up to room temperature before serving, or warm it briefly in the microwave on low power.

2 sticks (1 cup) butter, at room temperature

1/4 cup sugar-free preserves (such as Smucker's Light), any flavor or combination, at room temperature

In a medium mixing bowl using an electric mixer, whip the butter on high speed for 3 to 5 minutes, until light and fluffy.

Add the preserves and mix on low speed. Increase the speed to high and whip for another 3 minutes, until blended and smooth, scraping the sides of the bowl occasionally with a rubber spatula. (The mixture may look separated initially, but keep whipping, it will come together.) Store unused butter in the refrigerator.

Each 1-tablespoon serving contains approximately:
CAL: 60 PRO: 0g NET CARB: 0g FAT: 7g CHOL: 18mg SOD: 67mg

MAKES ABOUT 1 3/4 CUPS;
SERVES 28

# MAPLE BUTTER

This is the ultimate topper for Ricotta Pancakes (page 44); it's also great on low-carb toast. Be sure to let the butter come up to room temperature before serving, or warm it briefly in the microwave on LOW power.

2 sticks (1 cup) butter, at room temperature, divided

1/4 teaspoon vanilla extract

1/8 teaspoon maple extract

1 tablespoon Splenda Granular sweetener

1/4 cup sugar-free maple syrup

2 teaspoons real maple syrup

In a microwavable dish, heat 2 tablespoons of the butter on low power until melted. Stir in the vanilla, maple extract, Splenda, and the syrups; set aside.

In a medium mixing bowl, using an electric mixer, whip the remaining butter on high speed for 3 to 5 minutes, until light and fluffy. Reduce the mixer speed to medium, and add the melted butter mixture to the whipped butter. Raise the speed to high again and whip for another 2 to 3 minutes, scraping the bowl occasionally with a rubber spatula. Store the unused butter in the refrigerator.

Each 1-tablespoon serving contains approximately:
CAL: 60 PRO: 0g NET CARB: 0g FAT: 7g CHOL: 18mg SOD: 71mg

MAKES ABOUT 1 3/4 CUPS;
SERVES 28

# SWEET VANILLA-CINNAMON BUTTER

This sweetened butter is made more flavorful by the addition of cinnamon and vanilla extract. It's a perfect breakfast spread for low-carb toast or bagels. If you'd like a cinnamon-almond butter, try the variation, below.

2 sticks (1 cup) butter, at room temperature, divided

1 tablespoon ground cinnamon

1 tablespoon vanilla extract

$1/4$ cup Splenda Granular sweetener

In a microwavable dish, heat 2 tablespoons of the butter on low power until melted. Stir in the cinnamon and vanilla; set aside.

In a medium mixing bowl, using an electric mixer, whip the remaining butter on high speed for 3 to 5 minutes, until light and fluffy. Reduce the mixer speed to medium, and add the melted butter mixture to the whipped butter. Raise the speed to high again and whip for another 2 to 3 minutes, until blended, scraping the bowl occasionally with a rubber spatula. Store the unused butter in the refrigerator.

### Variation

For Cinnamon-Almond Butter, reduce the vanilla extract to 1 teaspoon and add $1/2$ teaspoon almond extract. Combine both extracts with the melted butter in step 1, then proceed with the recipe. This change does not affect the nutritional content.

---

Each 1-tablespoon serving contains approximately:
CAL: 52 PRO: 0g NET CARB: 0g FAT: 6g CHOL: 16mg SOD: 59mg

MAKES ABOUT 2 CUPS;
SERVES 32

# LEMON CURD

**If you've never tried lemon curd before, you might be surprised at how it tastes tart and sweet at the same time. Lemon curd is very versatile; try it as a spread on low-carb toast or low-carb bagels, as a topping for plain cheesecake or fresh berries, or even mixed with cottage cheese for a quick breakfast. We've also included it as an ingredient in the Berry and Lemon-Cream Parfaits (page 333).**

1 cup Splenda Granular sweetener

1 teaspoon cornstarch

3/4 cup fresh lemon juice

4 tablespoons butter

1 egg, lightly beaten

2 egg yolks, lightly beaten

In a heavy, small saucepan, whisk together the Splenda, cornstarch, and lemon juice until well combined. Add the butter and turn the heat to low. Whisk the mixture until the butter melts.

Raise the heat to medium and whisk constantly until the mixture thickens, about 5 minutes. Quickly whisk in the whole egg and egg yolks; cook, whisking constantly, for 1 minute, or until the mixture thickens.

Pour the lemon curd into a bowl; do not scrape the bottom of the saucepan (some egg white lumps may be clinging to the bottom). Place a piece of plastic wrap directly on the surface of the curd to prevent a skin from forming, and refrigerate for at least 3 hours before serving.

### Note

If you happen to notice a few egg white lumps in your lemon curd after it has chilled, blend it briefly in your blender, or use an immersion blender.

Each 1-tablespoon serving contains approximately:
CAL: 41 PRO: 1g NET CARB: 1g FAT: 4g CHOL: 48mg SOD: 34mg

MAKES ABOUT 1 CUP;
SERVES 16

# WILD
# BLUEBERRY SAUCE

Wild blueberries (available nationally in canned or frozen forms) have a more intense blueberry flavor than highbush blueberries, and therefore are frequently used in desserts and baked goods. If you can't find wild blueberries, feel free to substitute regular blueberries. The small amount of regular sugar in this recipe really makes a flavor difference and adds only minimal carbs—don't skip it. Serve this sauce over low-carb French toast or with Sweet Ricotta Crêpes (page 251).

1 tablespoon sugar

$^{1}/_{2}$ cup Splenda Granular sweetener

1 tablespoon cornstarch

$^{1}/_{2}$ cup cold water

2 cups wild blueberries (fresh; canned and drained; or frozen, no need to thaw first)

$^{1}/_{2}$ teaspoon fresh lemon juice

1 teaspoon lemon zest (see page 33)

1 teaspoon vanilla extract

Pinch of ground cinnamon (optional)

In a medium saucepan, whisk together the sugar, Splenda, cornstarch, and cold water until the cornstarch and sugar are completely dissolved.

Over medium-high heat, add the blueberries and bring the mixture to a boil. Reduce the heat to a simmer and cook for 5 minutes, or until the mixture is thickened and clear. Remove from the heat and stir in the remaining ingredients. Serve warm or at room temperature.

Each 3-tablespoon serving contains approximately:
CAL: 25 PRO: 0g NET CARB: 5g FAT: 0g CHOL: 0mg SOD: 2mg

MAKES ABOUT 2 CUPS;
SERVES 10

CHAPTER

17

BEVERAGES: HOT AND COLD

# THERE IS LIFE BEYOND WATER AND DIET SODA! QUENCH YOUR DESIRE FOR FLAVORFUL, REFRESHING, LOW-CARB DRINKS BY PLUNGING INTO THIS CHAPTER.

Included here are beverages for any season, any reason. Cool off on a steamy afternoon with a frosty glass of tart Lemonade, or if you've got limes to excess, a Lime Rickey would be just as welcome. Start a garden party or cookout with Strawberry Agua Fresca or a pitcher of Anytime Bloody Marys. Soothe yourself with a tall Iced Mocha (best served with a straw and drunk while reclining peacefully in a lawn chair). Warm yourself with a mug of Homemade Hot Cocoa by the fire, or get your morning off to a quick and nutritious start with our Vanilla Soy Chiller.

Whatever your pleasure, do expand your low-carb cooking horizons to include beverages: they're quick, easy, and less expensive than buying protein drinks or special low-carb packaged beverages.

# HOMEMADE
# HOT COCOA

If cocoa from a mix doesn't live up to your memories of "real" cocoa, try this recipe. While it does take a few minutes longer than mixing up a store-bought version, you'll be delighted at how much better the result is. To make a "grown-up" cocoa, add a little liqueur to your mug before pouring in the cocoa. Try Bailey's, amaretto, Frangelico, crème de menthe or your favorite. Of course, this will increase the carb content, so save it for a special treat!

1 cup hot water

¹/₃ cup Splenda Granular sweetener

3 tablespoons plus 2 teaspoons unsweetened cocoa powder

1 tablespoon sugar

Pinch of kosher salt

3 cups light cream

1 cup low-carb whole milk

³/₄ teaspoon vanilla extract

1 cup Real Whipped Cream (page 332) for garnish (optional)

In a medium saucepan over medium heat, whisk together the water, Splenda, cocoa powder, sugar, and salt. Bring the mixture to a boil, whisking frequently.

Add the cream and milk; whisk constantly until the mixture comes to a simmer, about 5 minutes. Remove from the heat and whisk in the vanilla.

Serve in mugs, topped with Real Whipped Cream, if desired.

Each serving contains approximately:
CAL: 290 PRO: 7g NET CARB: 9g FAT: 26g CHOL: 89mg SOD: 198mg

SERVES 4

# LEMONADE

Our lemonade is perfectly sweet and "puckery" at the same time. Squeezing the lemons by hand for fresh juice makes a huge difference in flavor, so do make the effort! If you like limes, use fresh lime juice, instead.

5 cups cold water

1 1/3 cups fresh lemon juice

1 cup Splenda Granular sweetener

Combine all the ingredients in a pitcher and stir until the Splenda is dissolved. Serve over ice.

Each serving contains approximately:
CAL: 13 PRO: 0g NET CARB: 4g FAT: 0g CHOL: 0mg SOD: 0mg

SERVES 6

# LIME RICKEY

Lime Rickeys are an East Coast fair favorite. A good Lime Rickey is ice cold, sweet, tart, and fizzy all at once. These are great to offer friends who don't drink alcohol, and this recipe is easily multiplied to serve a crowd—just set up an assembly line and grab an assistant.

4 **ice cubes**

2 **tablespoons fresh lime juice**

2 **tablespoons Splenda Granular sweetener**

1 **cup club soda**

**Lime slice for garnish (optional)**

Place the ice cubes in a 16-ounce glass. Add the lime juice, Splenda, and half of the club soda; stir. Add the remaining club soda and stir again. Garnish with a lime slice, if desired, and serve with a straw.

Each serving contains approximately:
CAL: 8 PRO: 0g NET CARB: 2.5g FAT: 0g CHOL: 0mg SOD: 50mg

SERVES 1

# ZIPPY
# GINGER
# DRINK

If you love ginger, this drink is for you. The simmering and steeping take some of the bite out of the fresh ginger, and the lemon really accents the ginger flavor. Fresh lime juice may be substituted for the lemon juice, if you prefer.

- 5 cups water, divided
- 1/4 cup peeled and grated fresh ginger
- 1/2 lemon, sliced
- 1/2 cup Splenda Granular sweetener
- 1/4 cup fresh lemon juice

In a small saucepan over medium-high heat, stir together 2 cups of the water, the ginger, and the lemon slices. Bring to a boil, then reduce the heat and gently simmer for 20 minutes, stirring occasionally. Remove from the heat and let cool for 15 minutes before refrigerating for at least 12 hours, or preferably overnight.

When ready to prepare the drink, strain the ginger mixture to remove the ginger and lemon pieces (a fine-mesh sieve works well). You should have about 1 1/4 cups of base left after straining. Pour the strained base into a pitcher and add the remaining 3 cups water, the Splenda, and the lemon juice; stir to combine. Serve over ice.

Each serving contains approximately:
CAL: 7 PRO: 0g NET CARB: 2g FAT: 0g CHOL: 0mg SOD: 1mg

SERVES 4

# MANGO-LIME AGUA FRESCA

Agua frescas are Mexican in origin, and can be made in a variety of different fruit combinations. Incredibly refreshing, they're a great way to satisfy a fruit craving with just a small amount of fruit.

1 medium (about 11 ounces) ripe mango, peeled, pitted, and chopped (about 1 cup)

3 cups cold water

$\frac{1}{3}$ cup fresh lime juice

$\frac{1}{2}$ cup Splenda Granular sweetener

Place all the ingredients in a blender; process on high for about 30 seconds, or until smooth and frothy. Serve over ice with a straw.

Note

An average-sized whole mango has about 30 net carbs. This drink gives you the taste of mango *and* lime, for one-third the net carbs!

Each serving contains approximately:
CAL: 43 PRO: 0g NET CARB: 10g FAT: 0g CHOL: 0mg SOD: 1mg

SERVES 3

# STRAWBERRY AGUA FRESCA

This recipe produces a perfectly pink drink that's bursting with a refreshing strawberry-lime flavor combination. Try it for a summertime party or barbecue.

3 cups cold water

1 cup fresh strawberries, chilled

$^2/_3$ cup Splenda Granular sweetener

2 tablespoons fresh lime juice

Place all the ingredients in a blender; process on high for about 30 seconds, or until smooth and frothy. Serve over ice with a straw.

Each serving contains approximately:
CAL: 13 PRO: 0g NET CARB: 2.5g FAT: 0g CHOL: 0mg SOD: 0mg

SERVES 4

# BERRY SPRITZER

Many juice companies have begun to produce lower carb, light versions of their juice blends. Combining these juices with club soda is an easy way to make a refreshing alternative to soda pop.

4 ice cubes

1/3 cup "light" cranberry-raspberry juice blend (such as Ocean Spray)

1 cup club soda

Lemon slice for garnish (optional)

Place the ice cubes in a 16-ounce glass. Pour in the juice, then the club soda. Garnish the glass with the lemon slice, if desired.

**Note**

Keep in mind that, although this recipe uses only a small amount of juice, not all "light" juice blends may be low enough in carbs for your particular diet. Be sure to check the Nutrition Facts on product labels.

Each serving contains approximately:
CAL: 12 PRO: 0g NET CARB: 3g FAT: 0g CHOL: 0mg SOD: 72mg

SERVES 1

# BLUEBERRY COOLER

According to recent research, blueberries are an incredibly healthful fruit, offering lots of antioxidants and beneficial phytochemicals. Plus, we'll admit that we're partial because we live in Maine, where wild blueberries (and their juice) are widely available. Look for the juice in shelf-stable cartons at your natural foods store or supermarket. Oh, and don't be afraid of the tiny bit of banana we've used—it's not a major ingredient here.

3 cups cold water

²/₃ cup wild blueberry juice (such as Wyman's)

¹/₂ cup fresh lemon juice

¹/₃ cup Splenda Granular sweetener

2 tablespoons mashed ripe banana (freeze the remaining banana for later use, if desired)

Place all the ingredients in a blender; process on high for about 30 seconds, or until smooth and frothy. Serve over ice with a straw.

Each serving contains approximately:
CAL: 36 PRO: 0g NET CARB: 9.5g FAT: 0g CHOL: 0mg SOD: 5mg

SERVES 4

# ICED MOCHA

We gave up waiting for our local coffee shop to create a low-carb version of iced mocha and decided to make our own. This recipe makes a good-sized batch of mocha base (enough for seven finished drinks) that you can keep in the refrigerator so you can whip up a cool and decadent Iced Mocha any time the mood strikes you—no waiting in line!

**MOCHA BASE**

2 cups light cream, divided

Three 1-ounce squares unsweetened baking chocolate

$1^2/_3$ cups Splenda Granular sweetener

Pinch of kosher salt

$1^1/_4$ cups low-carb whole milk

1 teaspoon vanilla extract

**ICED MOCHA (1 DRINK)**

4 ice cubes

$^1/_2$ cup prepared mocha base

1 cup strong coffee, chilled

Real Whipped Cream (page 332) for garnish (optional)

**To make the mocha base:** In a medium saucepan over medium-low heat, bring 1 cup of the cream to a simmer. Add the chocolate, one square at a time, stirring until melted and blended (the mixture will be thick). Remove from the heat and stir in the Splenda and salt. Gently stir in the remaining 1 cup cream, the milk, and the vanilla. Transfer the mixture to a 1-quart storage bottle and refrigerate until needed.

**To make an individual iced mocha:** Place the ice cubes in a 16-ounce glass. Top with $^1/_2$ cup of the mocha base, then pour in the cold coffee. Top with whipped cream, if desired, and serve with a straw.

Each serving (1 drink) contains approximately:
CAL: 225 PRO: 5g NET CARB: 5g FAT: 21g CHOL: 52mg SOD: 79mg

MAKES ENOUGH MOCHA
BASE FOR 7 DRINKS

# VANILLA SOY CHILLER

If you like the convenience of a liquid breakfast, give this recipe a try. It's tastier than those canned or powdered low-carb shakes, and only takes a minute to prepare. In fact, to save time in the morning, you can put all the ingredients (except the ice cubes) into the blender pitcher the night before, then cover and refrigerate it. The next day, add the ice cubes and whip it up! Be sure to purchase unsweetened soymilk (check the label); other varieties have too many carbs.

BEVERAGES: HOT AND COLD

1 cup plain unsweetened soymilk

1/4 cup Splenda Granular sweetener

2 tablespoons (1 ounce) silken tofu

1 tablespoon plain unsweetened soy protein powder

1/4 teaspoon plus 1/8 teaspoon vanilla extract

3 ice cubes

Place all the ingredients in a blender and process on low speed for 20 to 30 seconds to break up the ice. Raise the speed to high and process for another 15 to 20 seconds, or until frothy.

Each serving contains approximately:
CAL: 163 PRO: 19g NET CARB: 3g FAT: 7g CHOL: 0mg SOD: 74mg

SERVES 1

# STRAWBERRY PROTEIN SMOOTHIE

This thick, strawberry yogurt drink tastes "juice bar" good, but is easy to make at home (not to mention less expensive). It makes a nice breakfast or snack, too. To save time in the morning, you can put all the ingredients (except the frozen berries) into the blender pitcher the night before, then cover and refrigerate it. The next day, just add the berries and whip it up.

½ cup low-carb strawberry yogurt (such as Carb Control)

½ cup frozen unsweetened strawberries (about 4 berries)

⅓ cup water

3 tablespoons Splenda Granular sweetener

2 tablespoons light cream

2 tablespoons plain unsweetened soy protein powder

¼ teaspoon vanilla extract

Place all the ingredients in a blender and pulse on low speed several times. Raise the speed to high and process for another 15 seconds, or until smooth.

Each serving contains approximately:
CAL: 222 PRO: 16g NET CARB: 10g FAT: 13g CHOL: 43mg SOD: 175mg

SERVES 1

# ANYTIME
# BLOODY MARY

Bloody Marys may bring to mind relaxing brunches, but actually this potent tomato-based mixture can be enjoyed without the alcohol anytime you feel the need for a perky pick-me-up. You decide whether to spike it—depending on the occasion! Feel free to make up the mixture ahead of time and keep it in the refrigerator until serving time (it keeps nicely for up to 1 week).

3 cups tomato juice cocktail (such as V8)

2 cups canned tomato juice

2 tablespoons prepared horseradish

3 tablespoons fresh lime or lemon juice

2$^1/_2$ teaspoons Worcestershire sauce

1 teaspoon Tabasco sauce

$^1/_2$ teaspoon celery salt

$^1/_8$ teaspoon ground black pepper

5 ounces (slightly less than $^3/_4$ cup) good-quality vodka or gin (optional)

20 ice cubes

5 celery stalks, washed and trimmed, for garnish (optional)

In a 2-quart pitcher, whisk together all the ingredients except for the ice cubes and the celery, if using (omit the alcohol, if desired).

Place 4 ice cubes in each of five 16-ounce glasses. Pour 1 cup of the tomato-juice mixture over the ice and garnish with celery stalks, if desired.

Each serving contains approximately:
CAL: 58 PRO: 2g NET CARB: 10g FAT: 0g CHOL: 0mg SOD: 934mg

SERVES 5

# 18

## SWEET FINALES

# ANYONE WHO HAS FOLLOWED A LOW-CARB DIET

long enough to miss desserts knows that many of the manufactured sweets on the market just don't measure up to the goodness of a homemade dessert. We agree, which is why this chapter is packed with ideas to tempt your sweet tooth without blowing your carb "budget." If you're a baker, we've got you covered. If you like easy, "semi-homemade" desserts, we're with you. If you're looking for something seasonal, perhaps with a holiday feel, look no further than this chapter.

When entertaining, guests expect dessert, and these recipes will certainly not disappoint. In fact, even if your guests are not low-carbing, they're bound to enjoy these sweets. Many of our neighbors and taste-testers raved over these desserts, claiming that they'd never have known they were low-carb. To us, that's high praise, indeed.

Some desserts easily lend themselves to low-carb makeovers—ice cream, pots de crème, some fruit dishes, and cheesecakes, for example. Others take more work, such as baked items. Still others can be made quickly and easily using low-carb convenience foods and packaged mixes. Whichever recipe you choose (and we hope you'll try them all eventually), we're confident that your dessert efforts will be well received by all.

# REAL WHIPPED CREAM

A staple for topping low-carb desserts and cocoa, this whipped cream takes just a few minutes and tastes loads better than store-bought.

1 cup (¹/₂ pint) heavy cream

2 tablespoons Splenda Granular sweetener

¹/₄ teaspoon vanilla extract

In a medium mixing bowl, using an electric mixer on medium-high speed, whip the cream for 2 minutes, or until soft peaks form.

Add the Splenda and vanilla, raise the mix speed to high, and continue to whip until stiff peaks form, about 3 minutes.

### Note

If you've kept your whipped cream in the refrigerator for a while, or prepared it the day before you plan to use it, it may lose some of its "fluff." You can easily remedy this by whisking it by hand until the peaks return.

Each ¹/₄-cup serving contains approximately:
CAL: 103 PRO: 1g NET CARB: 1g FAT: 11g CHOL: 41mg SOD: 11mg

MAKES ABOUT 2 CUPS;
SERVES 8

# BERRY AND LEMON-CREAM PARFAITS

This multilayered dessert features the popular combination of lemon and berries. Feel free to use your favorite berry combination, or even just one type of berry in this sensational summer dessert.

**LEMON CREAM**

- 1 cup heavy cream
- 1/3 cup Lemon Curd (page 314)
- 1 teaspoon lemon zest (see page 33)

- 1/2 pint fresh blueberries (about 1 cup)
- 1/2 pint fresh raspberries (about 1 cup)
- 8 ounces fresh strawberries, quartered (about 2 cups)
- 6 fresh mint sprigs for garnish (optional)

To make the lemon cream: In a medium mixing bowl, using an electric mixer on medium-high speed, whip the cream until stiff peaks form. Add the lemon curd and lemon zest to the bowl and whip again on medium speed until all the ingredients are thoroughly blended.

In a medium mixing bowl, using a spoon, gently mix all of the berries together. In each of 6 standard wineglasses, place about 1 tablespoon of the lemon cream, then top with 1/3 cup of the berry mixture. Add a second layer of lemon cream, using 2 tablespoons this time, and another 1/3 cup berries. Top with a final 2 tablespoons of the lemon cream. Garnish with mint sprigs, if desired.

### Note

Fresh berries are expensive and spoil quickly. Ideally, you should purchase the best berries you can find, but not more than 1 day before you plan to serve them.

Each serving contains approximately:
CAL: 205 PRO: 2g NET CARB: 8.5g FAT: 18g CHOL: 93mg SOD: 44mg

SERVES 6

# PUMPKIN AND MAPLE TIRAMISU

This is a New England twist on a classic Italian dessert. The ladyfingers are soaked with maple syrup and the mascarpone is blended with pumpkin and vanilla pudding. It's easy to make, and very delicious; don't count on leftovers. This is a good make-ahead dessert; it holds up well in the refrigerator.

**SYRUP**

1 tablespoon real maple syrup

$1/4$ teaspoon maple extract

$1/4$ cup sugar-free maple syrup

$1/4$ cup water

**FILLING**

1 cup heavy cream

One 8-ounce tub mascarpone cheese

2 tablespoons water

$1/2$ cup canned pumpkin (not pumpkin pie filling)

$3/4$ teaspoon ground cinnamon

$1/2$ teaspoon pumpkin pie spice

$1/2$ teaspoon vanilla extract

$1/4$ cup Splenda Granular sweetener

One 1-ounce package sugar-free, fat-free, instant vanilla pudding mix

$3/4$ cup light cream

One 3-ounce package soft ladyfinger cookies (12 whole ladyfingers), split in half

Ground cinnamon for dusting

**To make the syrup:** In a small mixing bowl, stir together all the syrup ingredients; set aside.

**To make the filling:** In a medium mixing bowl, using an electric mixer on medium-high speed, beat the cream until stiff peaks form; set aside. In another mixing bowl, using an electric mixer on medium speed, beat together the mascarpone, water, pumpkin, cinnamon, pumpkin pie spice, vanilla, and Splenda for about 3 minutes, or until fluffy. Add the pudding mix and light cream; blend well for 1 minute, scraping down the bowl at least once with a rubber spatula. Gently stir in the whipped cream until well mixed.

Layer 12 ladyfinger halves on the bottom of an 8-by-8-inch baking dish; spoon half of the syrup mixture over the ladyfingers. Using a rubber spatula, carefully spread half the filling over the ladyfingers. Add another layer of ladyfingers, then pour the remaining syrup over them. Finally, top with the remaining filling. Dust the top with cinnamon. Refrigerate for at least 2 hours before serving.

**Each serving contains approximately:**
CAL: 294 PRO: 4g NET CARB: 13g FAT: 25g CHOL: 87mg SOD: 255mg

SERVES 9

# CREAMY COFFEE DREAM CUPS

A different way to serve your after-dinner coffee, this dreamy, coffee-flavored whipped cream dessert looks as good as it tastes when you present it in glass coffee mugs or dessert bowls.

**COFFEE BASE**

- ½ cup low-carb skim milk
- ½ cup light cream
- 2 tablespoons instant coffee granules
- 2 tablespoons Splenda Granular sweetener
- ½ teaspoon vanilla extract

<br>

- One 1-ounce package sugar-free, fat-free white chocolate instant pudding mix
- 2 ½ cups Real Whipped Cream (page 332), divided
- ¼ teaspoon ground cinnamon

**To make the coffee base:** In a 4-cup liquid measuring cup or small bowl, whisk together the milk, cream, coffee, Splenda, and vanilla until the coffee granules are completely dissolved.

In a medium mixing bowl, using an electric mixer on low speed, blend the coffee base with the pudding mix. Gradually raise the speed and beat until the mixture is well blended and thickened, about 3 minutes. Using a whisk, gently combine the pudding mixture with 2 cups of the whipped cream until blended and fluffy.

Spoon the mixture into glass mugs or dessert bowls. Garnish each portion with some of the remaining ½ cup whipped cream, and sprinkle with a pinch of the cinnamon. Serve immediately or refrigerate, covered, for up to 12 hours before serving.

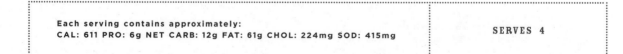

Each serving contains approximately:
CAL: 611 PRO: 6g NET CARB: 12g FAT: 61g CHOL: 224mg SOD: 415mg

SERVES 4

# PORT-POACHED PEARS WITH VANILLA RICOTTA CREAM

If you've never made them before, you'll be surprised at how easy poached pears are to make—and how elegant they are. You can even make them up to 2 days ahead of time and keep them in the refrigerator, covered and still in the poaching liquid. Tawny Port could also be used in this recipe, but it's typically more expensive than ruby port.

## POACHING LIQUID

- 2 cups water
- 2 cups ruby Port wine
- 2/3 cup Splenda Granular sweetener
- 1 teaspoon vanilla extract
- 1 teaspoon ground cinnamon

- 3 ripe, yet firm Bosc pears

## RICOTTA CREAM

- 3/4 cup part-skim ricotta cheese
- 3/4 cup heavy cream, whipped to stiff peaks
- 1 teaspoon vanilla extract
- 1/2 cup Splenda Granular sweetener

Fresh mint sprigs for garnish (optional)

**To make the poaching liquid:** Stir together all the poaching liquid ingredients in a saucepan large enough to hold the pears and liquid. Bring to a simmer over medium-high heat.

While waiting for the poaching liquid to simmer, peel the pears and slice them in half lengthwise. Using a melon baller, remove the core and seeds. Using a paring knife, remove the stem portions on the tops and bottoms of the pears.

Once the poaching liquid is simmering, add the pear halves, reduce the heat to medium, and simmer, uncovered, for 8 to 10 minutes, or until the pears have softened and can be easily pierced with a knife. Remove the pan from the heat and cool to room temperature. Refrigerate the pears in the poaching liquid until you're ready to serve.

**To make the ricotta cream:** In a small mixing bowl, stir together all the filling ingredients. Assemble the pears immediately, or cover the cream and refrigerate until ready to serve.

Divide the ricotta cream among individual dessert plates. Remove the pears from the poaching liquid (discard the liquid) and slice each pear half lengthwise into 5 or 6 pieces. Arrange the pear slices on top of the ricotta cream and garnish with mint sprigs, if desired.

Each serving contains approximately:
CAL: 203 PRO: 4g NET CARB: 12g FAT: 14g CHOL: 50mg SOD: 51mg

SERVES 6

# CHOCOLATE-MINT POTS DE CRÈME

Pots de crème is one of our all-time favorite desserts. It's like a cross between a pudding and a custard... smooth, rich, and very creamy. This peppermint version has a holiday feel, and can be made one day ahead, which makes it handy for entertaining. If you'd prefer a straight chocolate version, omit the peppermint extract and increase the vanilla extract to 1 teaspoon.

2 cups light cream

Pinch of kosher salt

2 tablespoons Splenda Granular sweetener

6 egg yolks, lightly beaten

Two 3-ounce bars sugar-free chocolate, chopped (milk, dark, or a combination)

1 ounce bittersweet chocolate, chopped (not sugar-free)

$1/_2$ teaspoon vanilla extract

$1/_2$ teaspoon peppermint extract

1 cup Real Whipped Cream (page 332)

8 sprigs fresh mint for garnish (optional)

In a medium saucepan over medium heat, stir together the cream, salt, and Splenda. Cook, stirring frequently, until the mixture simmers, then remove from the heat. Place the egg yolks in a bowl and whisk $1/_2$ cup of the hot cream mixture into the egg yolks. Return the egg yolk mixture to the saucepan with the remaining hot cream mixture and whisk to combine. Place over medium-low heat and cook, stirring constantly, for 3 to 4 minutes, or until thickened; the mixture should coat the back of a wooden spoon and your finger should leave a trail when you run it over the coated spoon. Do not let the mixture simmer!

Remove the mixture from the heat and whisk in the chocolate until blended. Add the vanilla and peppermint extracts and whisk again until smooth. Pour the mixture into 8 dessert dishes or ramekins and refrigerate for at least 4 hours, or preferably overnight.

To serve, top each serving with 2 tablespoons of Real Whipped Cream. Garnish with mint sprigs, if desired.

---

Each serving contains approximately:
CAL: 369 PRO: 6g NET CARB: 3g FAT: 35g CHOL: 240mg SOD: 47mg

SERVES 8

# CHOCOLATE HAZELNUT CREAM For when you want to really impress, nothing beats a sinful dessert like this rich chocolate cream.

**One** 3-ounce bar sugar-free dark chocolate, chopped (such as Guylian)

**One** 3-ounce bar sugar-free milk chocolate, chopped

**1/4** cup plus 2 tablespoons light cream

**3** tablespoons Atkins Hazelnut Syrup

**1/4** teaspoon vanilla extract

**Pinch of kosher salt**

**1** cup heavy cream

**3/4** cup Real Whipped Cream (page 332) for garnish

**18** whole hazelnuts, toasted, for garnish (see page 33)

In a heavy, medium saucepan over low heat, melt the dark and milk chocolate with the light cream and hazelnut syrup, whisking frequently, for 3 minutes, or until smooth. Remove from the heat, stir in the vanilla and salt, and let cool to room temperature.

While the chocolate mixture is cooling, using an electric mixer on high speed, whip the heavy cream in a medium mixing bowl until stiff peaks form. When the chocolate mixture is cool, gently whisk one-third of the whipped cream into the chocolate mixture. Then scrape the chocolate mixture into the bowl with the remaining whipped cream and whisk gently to combine.

Divide the mixture among 6 dessert bowls or cups; refrigerate for 3 hours, or until set. Before serving, garnish each portion with a dollop of whipped cream and three toasted hazelnuts.

## Variation

You can easily turn this into Chocolate Raspberry Cream by substituting Atkins raspberry syrup for the hazelnut syrup. Garnish with fresh raspberries and mint springs instead of the toasted nuts.

Each serving contains approximately:
CAL: 448 PRO: 4g NET CARB: 2g FAT: 44g CHOL: 115mg SOD: 78mg

SERVES 6

# GINGERBREAD BARS

Spicy and moist, these bars make it easy to have homemade gingerbread—without the work of rolling and cutting out cookies.

Cooking spray

$2/3$ cup vegetable oil

2 eggs

2 tablespoons heavy cream

$2/3$ cup Splenda Granular sweetener

2 tablespoons light molasses

2 tablespoons light brown sugar

$1/4$ cup plus 2 tablespoons Atkins Bake Mix

$1/4$ cup whole-wheat flour

$1/4$ cup all-purpose flour

$1/4$ teaspoon baking soda

1 teaspoon ground cinnamon

1 teaspoon ground ginger

$3/4$ cup Cream Cheese Frosting (facing page)

Preheat the oven to 350°F. Coat the bottom and sides of a 9-by-9-inch baking pan with cooking spray; set aside.

In a medium mixing bowl, using a wooden spoon, stir together the oil, eggs, cream, Splenda, molasses, and brown sugar until well combined; set aside.

In a small bowl, stir together the Bake Mix, flours, baking soda, and spices. Add the dry ingredients to the wet ingredients and mix thoroughly with a wooden spoon. Using a rubber spatula, spread the batter into the prepared pan.

Bake for 18 to 20 minutes, or until the bars spring back slightly when touched in the middle. (Do not underbake or the center will be soggy.) Let cool completely, then frost with Cream Cheese Frosting. Cut into 16 squares. Refrigerate any leftover bars.

Each serving contains approximately:
CAL: 175 PRO: 4g NET CARB: 6g FAT: 15g CHOL: 29mg SOD: 87mg

SERVES 16

# CREAM CHEESE FROSTING

**This frosting is delicious, versatile, and every bit as good as the "real thing." The recipe makes enough to frost a single cake layer or pan of bar cookies.**

4 ounces cream cheese, softened

2 tablespoons butter, softened

3 tablespoons Splenda Granular sweetener

2 tablespoons heavy cream

$1/4$ teaspoon vanilla extract

In a medium mixing bowl, using an electric mixer on medium speed, beat together all the ingredients for about 2 minutes, or until smooth.

Each serving contains approximately:
CAL: 78 PRO: 1g NET CARB: 0g FAT: 8g CHOL: 25mg SOD: 65mg

MAKES ABOUT $3/4$ CUP;
SERVES 9

# EASY BROWNIE COOKIES

**A cinch to make, these cookies are great for taming those chocolate cravings.**

One 8$\frac{1}{2}$-ounce package Atkins Quick Quisine Fudge Brownie Mix

1 egg

$\frac{1}{4}$ cup vegetable oil

$\frac{1}{4}$ cup plus 1 tablespoon Atkins Bake Mix

3 to 4 tablespoons cold water

2 tablespoons chopped sugar-free dark chocolate (about $\frac{3}{4}$ ounce)

$\frac{1}{4}$ cup walnuts, chopped

Cooking spray

In a medium mixing bowl, using a wooden spoon, combine the brownie mix, egg, oil, Bake Mix, and water and mix well (the mixture will be very thick and sticky). Add the chopped chocolate and nuts; stir to combine. Let the dough sit at room temperature for 10 minutes.

Meanwhile, preheat the oven to 350°F. Coat 2 baking sheets with cooking spray; set aside. Using a teaspoon, scoop up the dough and shape into balls with clean hands. Place the balls on the prepared baking sheets, about 2 inches apart.

Bake for 10 to 11 minutes, until puffed; do not overbake. Let cool on the baking sheets for 1 minute before transferring them with a spatula to a wire rack.

Each cookie contains approximately:
CAL: 68 PRO: 2g NET CARB: 5g FAT: 4g CHOL: 9mg SOD: 51mg

MAKES ABOUT 24 COOKIES

# MINI PEPPERMINT CHEESECAKES

These bite-sized beauties are the perfect make-ahead dessert for a holiday open house. They can be refrigerated (ungarnished) for 2 days prior to serving, or frozen (ungarnished) up to 1 week ahead of time. On the day of the party, just thaw them in the refrigerator and garnish before serving.

| | |
|---|---|
| Two | 8-ounce packages cream cheese, softened |
| 2 | eggs |
| 1/4 | cup heavy cream |
| 1/2 | cup Splenda Granular sweetener |
| 1 | teaspoon peppermint extract |
| 24 | mini foil cupcake liners |
| 24 | vanilla wafer cookies |
| 1 1/2 | cups Real Whipped Cream (page 332), for garnish |
| 12 | sugar-free peppermint candies, crushed, for garnish |

Preheat the oven to 350°F. In a medium mixing bowl, using an electric mixer on medium speed, beat together the cream cheese and eggs until blended. Add the heavy cream, Splenda, and peppermint extract and beat on medium speed until smooth, scraping down the bowl occasionally with a rubber spatula.

Place 12 cupcake liners on each of two baking sheets, evenly spaced, with at least 1 inch between them. Place a vanilla wafer cookie in the bottom of each cupcake liner. Using a tablespoon, carefully spoon some of the cream cheese mixture into each of the cupcake liners, filling them to the rim. Smooth the tops with the spoon (do not mound the mixture or it will spill over during baking).

Bake the cheesecakes for about 15 minutes, or until set but not browned. Let cool completely, then cover lightly with plastic wrap and refrigerate for at least 2 hours. Garnish the chilled cheesecakes with a tiny dollop of whipped cream and a sprinkling of crushed peppermint candy before serving.

Each serving contains approximately:
CAL: 132 PRO: 2g NET CARB: 4g FAT: 11g CHOL: 54mg SOD: 77mg

SERVES 24

# EGGNOG **CHEESECAKE** This rich dessert is a nice alternative to serving cups of carb-heavy liquid eggnog at your holiday gathering. The eggnog-flavored cake is nicely complemented by Rum-Spiked Whipped Cream.

## CRUST

Cooking spray

16 sugar-free shortbread cookies, crushed fine

2 tablespoons butter, melted

## FILLING

$\frac{1}{2}$ cup Splenda Granular sweetener

$\frac{1}{2}$ teaspoon ground nutmeg

One 8-ounce package cream cheese, softened

One 8-ounce package Neufchatel cheese, softened

2 eggs

1 cup dairy eggnog

1 cup Rum-Spiked Whipped Cream for garnish (facing page)

$\frac{1}{4}$ teaspoon nutmeg for garnish

**To make the crust:** Preheat the oven to 350°F. Coat an 8-inch springform pan with cooking spray. In a small bowl, stir together the crushed shortbread cookies with the melted butter. Using clean hands, pat the mixture into the bottom of the springform pan. Bake for 7 minutes, or until lightly browned. Remove from the oven and leave the oven on. Let the crust cool while preparing the filling.

**To make the filling:** In a small bowl, stir together the Splenda and nutmeg; set aside. In a large mixing bowl, using an electric mixer on medium speed, beat together the softened cheeses and the eggs until smooth, scraping down the bowl occasionally with a rubber spatula. Add the eggnog and beat on medium speed about 5 minutes, until very smooth and almost fluffy. Pour the mixture into the cooled crust. Cover the top of the pan with aluminum foil, tenting it slightly in the middle so the cake doesn't touch the foil when it rises during baking.

Bake for 50 minutes, or until mostly set (the cake may not be completely set in the center). Remove from the oven, lift off the aluminum foil, and run a knife around the inside edges of the pan to loosen the cake. Let cool for 1 hour, then refrigerate for at least 4 hours, or preferably overnight.

Before serving, release the sides of the pan and remove the ring. Garnish the cake by spreading the Rum-Spiked Whipped Cream over the top, filling in the depression in the middle. Sprinkle the nutmeg over the whipped cream. Serve immediately, or refrigerate again until serving time.

Each serving contains approximately:
CAL: 401 PRO: 9g NET CARB: 11g FAT: 36g CHOL: 173mg SOD: 306mg

SERVES 8

# RUM-SPIKED WHIPPED CREAM

A "grown-up" whipped cream that makes a wonderful topping for desserts or special coffee drinks.

½ cup heavy cream

1 tablespoon Splenda Granular sweetener

2 teaspoons white rum

In a medium mixing bowl, using an electric mixer on medium-high speed, whip the cream for about 2 minutes, or until soft peaks form.

Add the Splenda and rum, raise the speed to high, and continue to whip the cream until stiff peaks form, about 3 minutes.

Each ¼-cup serving contains approximately:
CAL: 108 PRO: 1g NET CARB: 1g FAT: 11g CHOL: 41mg SOD: 11mg

MAKES ABOUT 1 CUP;
SERVES 4

# STRAWBERRY SWIRL CHEESECAKE

A beautiful springtime dessert, this cheesecake uses both fresh strawberries and strawberry preserves to enrich its fruit flavor.

**CRUST**

Cooking spray

3/4 cup graham cracker crumbs (about 5 large graham cracker rectangles, crushed fine)

2 tablespoons butter, melted

**FILLING**

One 8-ounce package cream cheese, softened

One 8-ounce package Neufchatel cheese, softened

2 eggs

1/4 cup heavy cream

1/2 cup Splenda Granular sweetener

1 teaspoon vanilla extract

2 tablespoons sugar-free strawberry preserves (such as Smucker's Light)

**TOPPING**

3/4 cup sliced fresh strawberries

1 teaspoon water

1 tablespoon sugar-free strawberry preserves

**To make the crust:** Preheat the oven to 350°F. Coat an 8-inch spring-form pan with cooking spray and set aside. In a small bowl, combine the graham cracker crumbs with the melted butter. Pat the mixture into the bottom of the springform pan. Bake for 7 minutes, or until lightly browned; remove the crust from the oven and let cool. Leave the oven on.

**To make the filling:** In a large mixing bowl, using an electric mixer, beat together the softened cheeses and the eggs on medium speed until smooth, scraping the bowl occasionally with a rubber spatula. Add the cream, Splenda, vanilla, and preserves and beat for about 5 minutes on medium speed, until very smooth and almost fluffy. Pour the mixture into the cooled crust.

**To make the topping:** In a small bowl, using a mini food processor or chopper, process the topping ingredients until smooth, about 1 minute. Drop the topping by spoonfuls onto the top of the cheese-cake. Using a butter knife, gently swirl the topping decoratively, being careful not to scrape the crust of the cheesecake with the knife. Cover the top of the pan with aluminum foil, tenting it slightly in the middle so the cake doesn't touch the foil when it rises during baking.

Bake for 50 minutes or until mostly set (the cake may not be completely set in the center). Remove from the oven, lift off the aluminum foil, and run a sharp knife around the inside edges of the pan to loosen the cake. Let cool for 1 hour, then refrigerate for least 4 hours, or preferably overnight, before serving.

**Each serving contains approximately:**
CAL: 300 PRO: 8g NET CARB: 13g FAT: 25g CHOL: 124mg SOD: 313mg

SERVES 8

# SUPER-RICH FRENCH VANILLA ICE CREAM

Ultra rich, this frozen concoction will satisfy any ice cream craving. Feel free to embellish this ice cream with sugar-free chocolates or low-carb cookie pieces. If you like to see flecks of vanilla bean in your ice cream, add $1/4$ teaspoon vanilla paste (available from baking catalogs and gourmet specialty stores).

1 cup low-carb 2% milk

3 cups heavy cream

7 egg yolks

1 cup Splenda Granular sweetener

1 tablespoon sugar

Pinch of kosher salt

1 tablespoon vanilla extract

In a medium saucepan over medium heat, combine the milk and cream and bring to a simmer. Remove from the heat; set aside.

In a medium mixing bowl, whisk together the egg yolks, Splenda, sugar, and salt. Whisk $3/4$ cup of the hot cream mixture into the egg mixture. Repeat, whisking another $3/4$ cup of the hot cream into the egg mixture.

Return the saucepan with the remaining cream mixture to the stove over low heat. Slowly whisk all the egg mixture into the remaining cream mixture. Using a wooden spoon and stirring constantly, cook the mixture for 8 to 10 minutes, or until thickened; the mixture should coat the back of the spoon and your finger should leave a trail when you run it over the coated spoon. Remove from the heat and stir in the vanilla.

Transfer the mixture to a plastic storage container with a cover; refrigerate until completely cooled, at least 4 hours. Process the mixture in an ice-cream maker according to the manufacturer's instructions.

### Note

This ice cream is at its best right out of the ice-cream maker. Once it has frozen hard in the freezer, it needs to soften for at least 20 minutes for optimal scooping.

Each $1/2$-cup serving contains approximately:
CAL: 339 PRO: 5g NET CARB: 4g FAT: 34g CHOL: 277mg SOD: 82mg

MAKES ABOUT $4 1/2$ CUPS; SERVES 9

# SINFULLY RICH
# CHOCOLATE
# ICE CREAM

This ice cream requires a bit of effort and skill, but it's certainly worth it. It's best eaten immediately, right out of the ice-cream maker. If you decide to make it ahead of time and freeze it hard in the freezer, be sure to let it soften for about 20 minutes at room temperature before serving, or it will be hard to scoop.

1 cup low-carb 2% milk

3 cups heavy cream

7 egg yolks

$3/4$ cup Splenda Granular sweetener

1 tablespoon sugar

Pinch of kosher salt

Four 3-ounce bars sugar-free chocolate (dark, milk, or combination), finely chopped or grated

$1/2$ teaspoon vanilla extract

In a medium saucepan over medium heat, combine the milk and cream and bring to a simmer. Remove from the heat; set aside.

In a medium mixing bowl, whisk together the egg yolks, Splenda, sugar, and salt. Whisk $3/4$ cup of the hot cream mixture into the egg mixture. Repeat, whisking another $3/4$ cup of the hot cream into the egg mixture.

Return the saucepan with the remaining cream mixture to the stove over low heat. Slowly whisk all the egg mixture into the remaining cream mixture. Using a wooden spoon and stirring constantly, cook the combined mixture for 8 to 10 minutes, or until thickened; the mixture should coat the back of the spoon and your finger should leave a trail when you run it over the coated spoon. Remove from the heat and stir in the chopped chocolate and vanilla until smooth and blended.

Transfer the mixture to a plastic storage container with a cover; refrigerate until completely cooled, at least 4 hours. Process the mixture in an ice-cream maker according to the manufacturer's instructions.

Each $1/2$-cup serving contains approximately:
CAL: 445 PRO: 7g NET CARB: 1g FAT: 41g CHOL: 249mg SOD: 75mg

MAKES ABOUT 5 CUPS;

SERVES 10

# CHILLY CHOCOLATE PEANUT BUTTER SQUARES

This rich dessert satisfies those ice cream cravings with a good dose of peanut butter to boot—a real crowd pleaser.

## CRUST

Cooking spray

- 5 large chocolate graham cracker rectangles, crushed fine
- 2 tablespoons butter, melted

Two 16-ounce containers Atkins Endulge Chocolate Peanut Butter Swirl Ice Cream, softened

- 4 ounces non-dairy whipped topping, thawed
- 3/4 teaspoon vanilla extract
- 1 tablespoon low-carb peanut butter
- 6 low-carb peanut butter cup candies (such as Russell Stover), coarsely chopped

**To make the crust:** Coat the bottom of an 8-by-8-inch baking pan with cooking spray; set aside. In a small bowl, stir together the graham cracker crumbs and melted butter until the crumbs are moistened. Using clean hands, press the mixture into the bottom of the prepared pan and set aside.

In a medium mixing bowl, using an electric mixer on low speed, beat the softened ice cream until smooth. Using a rubber spatula, spread the ice cream over the graham cracker crust, being careful not to stir up the graham cracker crumbs. Place the pan in the freezer for 2 hours, or until the surface is firm (the mixture may not be completely frozen).

While waiting for the ice-cream layer to harden, stir together the whipped topping and vanilla in a small mixing bowl. Using a fork, stir in the peanut butter and chopped peanut butter cups. Refrigerate the peanut-butter mixture until the ice cream layer is ready.

When the ice cream layer is firm, spread the chilled peanut-butter mixture over the ice cream using a rubber spatula; smooth the top. Return the dessert to the freezer for about 3 hours, or until frozen through.

To serve, remove from the freezer and let stand at room temperature for about 5 minutes to soften slightly. Using a knife dipped in hot water and wiped dry, cut the dessert into 9 squares.

---

Each serving contains approximately:
CAL: 387 PRO: 6g NET CARB: 13g FAT: 31g CHOL: 65mg SOD: 184mg

SERVES 9

# CHOCOLATE-COCONUT ICE CREAM SANDWICHES

Making these ahead of time ensures that a cool treat is always at hand during those hot summer days. Who needs the ice-cream truck?

- **1 cup Atkins Endulge Chocolate Ice Cream, softened slightly, divided**
- **1 teaspoon coconut extract**
- **8 chocolate wafer cookies (such as Nabisco's Famous)**
- **4 teaspoons unsweetened coconut, toasted (see Note)**

In a small mixing bowl, stir together the softened ice cream and coconut extract until combined.

Working quickly, make one sandwich at a time: Using a $1/4$-cup measuring cup, scoop the ice-cream mixture onto 1 of the wafer cookies. Top with a second wafer and press them together gently to form a sandwich. Roll the edges of the sandwich in the toasted coconut, then wrap the sandwich in plastic wrap and freeze.

Repeat with the remaining ice cream, cookies, and coconut to make 4 sandwiches. Let the sandwiches freeze at least 2 hours, or until firm, before serving.

**Note**

To toast coconut, spread it on a baking sheet and bake at 350°F for 5 to 8 minutes, or until light brown in color. Keep an eye on it, as it can overbrown quite quickly.

Each serving contains approximately:
CAL: 131 PRO: 2g NET CARB: 12g FAT: 3g CHOL: 3mg SOD: 110mg

SERVES 4

# INDEX

BIG BOOK OF LOW CARB

# TABLE OF EQUIVALENTS The exact
equivalents in the following tables have been rounded for convenience.

## LIQUID/DRY MEASURES

| U.S. | Metric |
|---|---|
| ¼ teaspoon | 1.25 milliliters |
| ½ teaspoon | 2.5 milliliters |
| 1 teaspoon | 5 milliliters |
| 1 tablespoon (3 teaspoons) | 15 milliliters |
| 1 fluid ounce (2 tablespoons) | 30 milliliters |
| ¼ cup | 60 milliliters |
| ⅓ cup | 80 milliliters |
| ½ cup | 120 milliliters |
| 1 cup | 240 milliliters |
| 1 pint (2 cups) | 480 milliliters |
| 1 quart (4 cups, 32 ounces) | 960 milliliters |
| 1 gallon (4 quarts) | 3.84 liters |
| 1 ounce (by weight) | 28 grams |
| 1 pound | 454 grams |
| 2.2 pounds | 1 kilogram |

## LENGTH

| U.S. | Metric |
|---|---|
| ⅛ inch | 3 millimeters |
| ¼ inch | 6 millimeters |
| ½ inch | 12 millimeters |
| 1 inch | 2.5 centimeters |

## OVEN TEMPERATURE

| Fahrenheit | Celsius | Gas |
|---|---|---|
| 250 | 120 | ½ |
| 275 | 140 | 1 |
| 300 | 150 | 2 |
| 325 | 160 | 3 |
| 350 | 180 | 4 |
| 375 | 190 | 5 |
| 400 | 200 | 6 |
| 425 | 220 | 7 |
| 450 | 230 | 8 |
| 475 | 240 | 9 |
| 500 | 260 | 10 |